Veronica and Paul

SOUTH AFRIKA IS FANTASTIK

Janni Beldenhuys

Pretoria · 17 Aug 07

By the same author:

A General's Story – From an Era of War and Peace.

Dié wat wen – 'n Generaal se Storie uit 'n Era van Oorlog en Vrede.

Basjan & Wilhelm – Die Skewe Wonders en Ander Verhale.

Basjan & Wilhelm – Die Houtperd en Ander Verhale.

Basjan & Wilhelm – en die Manne van die Kamp.

SOUTH AFRIKA IS FANTASTIK

Everyone's Guide How Not To Be Politically Incorrect

Who Cares For Jimmy, Tarentaal And Gnu?
The Miracle Is Over.

Jannie Geldenhuys

Protea Book House
Pretoria
2007

© 2007 by Jannie Geldenhuys

First editon, first impression in 2007 by Protea Book House

PO Box 35110, Menlopark, 0102
1067 Burnett Street, Hatfield, Pretoria
8 Minni Street, Clydesdale, Pretoria
protea@intekom.co.za
www.proteaboekhuis.co.za

Editor: Karen Horn
Cover design: Jigsaw Graphic Design and Layout, Pretoria (jigdesign@telkomsa.net).
Cover image: Wim Bosman
Illustrations: Wim Bosman
Set in 11 on 13 pt Californian by Ada Radford
Printed and bound by Paarl Print

ISBN 978-1-86919-152-8

Contents

With gratitude to Miss Katie

With love from Kattys

CHAPTER 1

Foreword

From the Man in the Street to the Man in the Street

This book is not for politicians and academics – Jimmy the Reed de Umhlanga.

Please don't bite My Finger

I wrote this book for fun. And my only wish is that you will have fun reading it. It is not for *political animals*. It is not a professor's thesis for scholars. It is not a master's textbook for pupils. It is meant to entertain you. It will not win a prize and I won't mind if you doubt my credentials.

> I am an expert on nothing
> So I can write about everything.
> A guru always has to be correct.
> But I don't mind making a fool of myself
> Because it is my democratic right to do so.

I couldn't find anyone willing or courageous enough to write the Foreword for me, so I did it myself. However, this book is not for the black market; you should be able to find it in any decent bookshop.

At this early stage you may rightly ask why I call this a chapter instead of something like a Preamble. Of course, the main reason is that I would very much like you to read it; I wouldn't like you to miss out on any of the fun. My concern is that perhaps you do the same as I do: I often skip the passages under headings such as Preamble, Preface and Foreword and usually start straightaway with chapter number one.

I would like to give you some idea of the contents. This book is about common and uncommon sense – conventional wisdom can cause you a lot of problems.

It is about nature, naturalness and naturality. It is about life itself.

It is about the heat and deceit of the Cold War; it still spooks the ignoramuses. But I have written much more about the Comedy and Art of Governance, because I know much less about it than I do about the Science of War.

It is about politics, the bad and the good, about the governors of Political Correctness and about us, the Good People – Jimmy, Tarentaal and Gnu.

It is an Afrikan safari winding through a wacky world, reaching the end of the sweet years of illusions, and a new beginning in South Afrika. But I admit it is not everyone's cup of tea. It may not go down well if you are a dedicated supporter of any one of the following parties:

the Republican Party
the Democratic Party
the Conservative Party
the Labour Party
the Liberal Party
the Cocktail Party
the African National Congress
the Democratic Alliance
the National Party, by whatever name
the Pan Africanist Congress *et al*

You may be extremely embarrassed to be found with this book in your possession, more so than if you were caught with *The Rise and Fall of the British Empire* by Idi Amin and Robert Mugabe, or *The Fall and Rise of the African Empire* by Eugene TerreBlanche and Ngconde Balfour, the South African minister of sports.

Find fault with me if you wish, I don't mind, but please don't criticise me because I actually dared to write something; rather argue about *what* I wrote. Like Warren S McCulloch I plead, don't bite my finger – look where it's pointing.[1]

I wrote this book by following the hints of the inimitable late Daantjie Saayman. He was a sports cyclist of note and a passionate hiker of mountains and forests. He loved to quote Shakespeare, and was the publisher of some of the early books of the internationally acclaimed author Andre P Brink. He was also eulogised in a collection of poems dedicated to him by the equally renowned Breyten Breytenbach.

---

1 Mackay, 1977.

Daantjie told me, you don't *write* a book – you *develop* it. The most important thing is to make a start. That's exactly what I did. I made a start, jotting down notes and randomly typing bits and pieces on my favourite topics every time they came to mind – in my best Afrikaans English.

As the manuscript grew, I realised that these titbits were becoming a compilation of stories that I could generally group under the headings of Fun, Business, and People – especially females... and politicians. I also discovered that they were interrelated, and it became quite entertaining to compare different aspects from inside the political jungle with those in the outside world. I take you with me on this journey of how the book developed.

Forms of governance, such as democracy, autocracy and kleptocracy, and Functions of governance, such as education, national security and public safety, had been for too long the exclusive domain of authors like politicians, professors, psychologists, contortionists, jokers and other experts. The Man in the Street should also be heard. I voice his observations.

Over a period of decades I picked up anecdotes here and there, and I heard a multitude of stories and quotations. If you ask me where I got them from, I would in many cases not be able to recall the origin. On a few odd occasions I do come up with quotations from books; this does not mean that I have actually read them.

I picked up many sayings from the wise Man in the Street – the Gentleman of the Boulevards – and made them my own. You could say this book is *from* the Man in the Street *to* the Man in the Street.

You may agree with Ralph Waldo Emerson who said: "I hate quotations – tell me what you know", and with Winston Churchill: "it is a good thing for an uneducated man to read books of quotations".[2] But I admit to having a soft spot for so-called wise words.

I started this chapter with my finger, and now I end it with another part of my anatomy.

Pardon My Leg

You may sometimes get the impression that certain themes and concepts appear to repeat themselves in this book. In a sense this may be ascribed to the RLS – Right Leg Syndrome.

2 Mackay, 1977.

My drill every morning when I have a bath is to wash my left leg first, thereafter the right one, then the rest. But since I suffer from Alzheimer's, it happens without fail that at an uncertain stage of the cleansing proceedings I know that I have definitely already washed at least one leg, and I know which one, but I can't remember if I have washed both, so I do the right leg again.

On the other hand the repetitions may well be deliberate in order to stress matters of the utmost national and even global importance.

* * *

I now have an important announcement to make, and my dear little friend Jimmy, whom you will meet shortly, told me you always make your announcement in the next chapter. It involves a dormant international political anomaly that now awakens, causing serious political friction.

CHAPTER 2

Beginning of the End

I have great pleasure in announcing: *Modern democracy is on the verge of collapse.*

The Sunset Hour

International, continental and regional politics have become the topic of the day. Globalisation is rampant. This is happening at a time when the development of national politics, and especially that of regional and continental politics, has not yet been sorted out.

One such case is the former Soviet Union and Eastern Europe where a vast number of independent states emerged. After much conflict, with barely time to get organised, they were catapulted into the international arena. They are not the only ones.

Western democracy, as the perceived ideal universal form of government, is nearing its sunset hour. As international politics inexorably marches on, the big powers of the world are going to chicken out of global democracy – that will be the end.

One of the cornerstones of a national democracy is the principle of an unqualified "one person one vote". It would not make sense if this essential basic element of democracy did not also apply to regional, continental and, ultimately, to global democracy. Democracy is democracy.

The continental African Union (AU) should also observe the principle of one country one vote, yes? Let's consider the following hypothesis: If the United Nations (UN) is regarded as the overseeing body of a global society of continents and states, this principle should also apply there during voting, for example "one continent one vote", or "one state one vote", *n'est-ce pas?*

No. Some countries would rightfully and logically argue that every member state of any international body should have one vote for every ten million of its population. This would apply to voting at the UN, the European Union (EU) and the AU.

It is most important to realise that if we do not unconditionally subscribe to an unqualified franchise, we most definitely cannot argue that we are supporters of modern democracy in practice. It is vital that we make up our minds.

The process of political continentalisation, like the formation of the EU and the AU, is in full swing. And as globalisation gains momentum, the move that will lead to the end of democracy has already started in the developing world in general, and more specifically in Africa.

The presidents of South Africa and Nigeria, Mbeki and Obasanjo, are at the helm, and they have the authoritative support of the UN secretary general, Ghana's Kofi Annan. The UN, they say, is not a modern and fair organisation. It should be democratised. They correctly claim that at present the permanent members of the Security Council, consisting of the major powers, have veto prerogatives and rule the roost. Why? That's not right and just, is it?

No, it isn't. One could hypothetically but logically argue that all member states in the General Assembly, let's say the "world parliament", acting as an electoral body, should vote on an equal footing for who will become members of the Security Council, say the "world cabinet"; and in this "cabinet" every member should have an equal vote.

However, this absolutely politically correct system will not solve problems; rather it will raise embarrassing questions.

The major powers will never accept an unqualified one country one vote system at the UN. If they do, it will be only because they are crazy, or because they surreptitiously believe that the G6, 7, 8, 9 and all the other Gs are going to be the real future world government in disguise.

In principle, I wholeheartedly agree with our African leaders – the UN is not democratic.

As you will find out in due course I am not overly keen on the outdated modern type of democracy anyway. But even so, if democracy is a prerequisite for the UN to perform its functions, let's have a brief but serious look at the implications.

National governments are instituted by the people. Governments derive their just powers to rule from their voters. The UN, by contrast, cannot claim that it derives its power from the people. Let's put this matter under the magnifying glass.

Only 85 out of the 191 states in the UN are democratic! The people of only 85 countries enjoy political rights such as voting and civil liberties! This is far less than 50% of the member states. The rest are controlled either by dicta-tors or by one-party governments.

In 48 of the states, dictators wield an iron hand. Fifty-nine other coun-tries are controlled by one-party governments. In these countries, institu-tions like the judiciary and the press are not free from strong government in-fluence or control.

In assessing globalisation we must seriously ask ourselves whether it is acceptable that the majority, the *undemocratic* and one-party states, should be allowed to constitute a *democratic* UN? Should non-democratic countries enjoy full membership rights at the UN at all? You be the judge...

* * *

I realise I've now uncovered an itch, and it gets scratched throughout the book. However, as much as I dislike interrupting your reading, I have to put you on hold while I make a very important confession that you simply must know before we can continue. Jimmy told me you always make your confes-sion in the next chapter.

CHAPTER 3

The Blues and the Reds

I confess. I am a liberal.

Liberalism – A Dying Virtue

There are two types of liberals, the Blues and the Reds.

A blue liberal like me is an undaunted, free and independent thinker without a cause, always searching for the truth in any matter. He is indifferent to the possible reactions to his deliberations and findings.

I am a lazy, lay and true blue liberal. I sponsor myself, and I am responsible to myself. If you don't agree with my ideas, that is fine with me, as long as you enjoy them.

To be saddled with a cause is bad; it is an encumbrance to genuine freethinking. My only cause is liberalism itself, which is the sole burden that I permit to influence my thinking.

Freethinking should be void of any restraints. It should be rational, but to be a blue liberal does not mean that you may not be imaginative. You may give your mind free rein as long as you base your thinking on nature and the best knowledge available. You may also be creative as long as you apply the science of best thinking – vertical and lateral thinking, as well as logic, common and uncommon sense.

When deliberating on any aspect of life and living, one has to draw inferences from the relevant facts and information, then synthesise these, identify patterns, and arrive at conclusions. During this mental process logic is a key element.

However, no matter how entertaining logic may be, it is not always as simple a matter as one may think. Suffice it to say for now that logic is distorted by customs and traditions, emotions, sentiment, personal agendas, politics – and causes.

Blue liberals, free from fighting for causes, do not concern themselves with the popularity and outcomes of their findings. The sky is the limit.

An example of the ideal blue liberal would be a wealthy, retired, professor at his own self-financed research institute. He is not attached to any political party or non-governmental organisation (NGO) with a cause. Such individuals generally have no desire for sensation and fame.

You too may be a blue liberal. Are we of a dying breed?

Red liberals are dangerous. They are the prime source of the problems that we have with democracy today. The red liberal is a pseudo freethinker with a cause. But he is generally manageable.

A red liberal with a cause – and a sponsor – is extremely dangerous. If you don't agree with him, he becomes red with anger, aggressive and relentless. If you don't succumb to his hang-ups, he will legislate against you. With money or power behind him, he is unmanageable. There are many of them chasing and pushing causes all over the world and in South Africa.

The most dangerous of them all is when the red liberal with a cause is a mogul like multi-billionaire George Soros. You'll inevitably hear more about him soon.

Red liberals stick to their sponsor's conditions and remain focused on the set goals. They, possibly in the employ of an NGO, will coerce a government into legislation. They drive their causes to the bitter end, for the good or the bad. Red liberal NGOs, such as the anti-hunting, anti-gun lobbies, or those fighting AIDS or protecting illegal aliens, present their projects to the government as if every one of them is the foremost priority for the country, if not for the salvation of the whole planet.

The next holier-than-thou red liberal does exactly the same. His cause is also priority number one. Eventually the poor government has to go through the agony of sorting out its diverse newly acquired ad hoc projects. It may end up with a list of ten, all number one, top red liberal priority projects. It now has to decide which are the top, topper, and toppest.

By unloading all their red liberal causes converted into projects onto the government, red liberals seriously embarrass the politicians. The ministers, by their own admission, don't really know much about the subject matter and, in any case, their priorities are totally different – politics comes before charity.

Of course, we do not find red liberals operating only in the field of the do-gooders.

Many active red liberals push political causes as well. For a considerable time some of them have been quite negative; they have not so much promoted political systems as fought them. They fought monarchies and almost wiped them out. They have also taken on nationalism and theocracy with some success.

However, they have now encountered a major problem. Having destroyed most of the –isms and –cracies, they discover that all political parties and governments, including democracies are bad and they have no idea with what to replace them!

At this stage, since the frustrated Reds find themselves scratching their encumbered heads for new –isms and –cracies, they will probably have to fall back on the blue liberals who all the time have bravely been thinking positively with uncluttered, causeless minds.

There are two types of red liberals and you find them in and out of politics.

There are those with one-track minds who have a cause at the end of the tunnel and they stick to it to the bitter end, come hell or high water. They direct their vengeance at those whom they regard as obstacles in their way to achieving their noble goals. They are the real baddies.

Then there is the other type, those who also fight for causes but manage to keep an open mind of sorts. As a result they could have one cause today and another tomorrow, and these two causes may even appear to be conflicting: today's cause may be a leftish one, while tomorrow's may be rightish.

These types could be very useful Reds and sometimes can actually be called light Blue.

One such liberal was Daniel Patrick Moynihan. He was a US democrat who worked his way up from shoe shining to become a senator for New York. In the US he was described as a liberal democrat, but it was difficult to categorise him as left or right.

He backed *democrat* JF Kennedy, and was soon appointed as special assistant to the secretary of labour after Kennedy's election in 1960. Some people branded him as a *liberal* liberal. But in 1965 the *republican* president Nixon made him chairman of the Urban Affairs Council, and later appointed him ambassador to India. So other people called him a *conservative* liberal.

All this happened not because he changed his views or political affiliations, but because the different presidents regarded his different convictions as just and appropriate at the time. This type of red liberal demonstrates some objectivity in his thinking.

Both blue and red liberals can adopt positions which will induce people to classify them as right or left wing permanently or from time to time.

This phenomenon should not be confused with the trend among politicians in South Africa during the early 2000s. These politicians zoomed into causes and parties like blue bottles into dung, and from one to the other.

Most liberals have turned red, but their time may be running out. The Blues have been fading, but they may find themselves at a new dawn.

The Blues love to argue in order to find genuine solutions. The Reds forbid argument and fight to win – to hell with solutions! They pursue their causes regardless.

Are you a red liberal too? Are you part of their proliferation? I don't think so. If you were, you would have been reading something like *How to succeed by being Politically Correct.*

To solve modern mankind's current problems, starting with the voting dilemma at the UN, I suggest the Reds take their cue from the Blues. However, the Blues' efforts are seriously hampered by the persistent opposition of their biggest enemy and the main obstacle to freethinking – Political Correctness.

*   *   *

Having declared my blue persuasion, I now take great pleasure in introducing my crew.

CHAPTER 4

Who cares for Jimmy, Tarentaal and Gnu?

I confess, I am a patriot
I love my fathers' land; I love my mothers' tongue
I didn't choose to be born here, I was just lucky
I am for the people

All for One and One for All

The people – you and I, Jimmy, Ms Tarentaal and Mr Gnu – play the most important role in this entertaining drama. We can no longer dwell in the world of academic hypotheses; let's be practical, and let's be realistic.

Plants, one-celled organisms and other life forms were the first to appear on the scene. Although people came into the picture only very recently, millions of years after the plants and animals, they have a very interesting story to tell. The people's history becomes more exciting day by day.

Let's start with the story of the land of our forefathers and those who live here. However, I can't do better than the esteemed and acclaimed academic, Professor Pieter Scholtz of KwaZulu-Natal University. The first to appear on stage is Jimmy.

Long, long ago, longer ago than people can remember, the vast continent of Africa was inhabited by tiny creatures called Tokoloshes. Every stream, waterfall and pool had its tokoloshe, for they were water sprites and couldn't bear to venture very far from the tinkle and ripple of the water.

They took a particular liking to the rivers in the south, in the land called Zululand... and they gambolled and frolicked in the sparkling streams.

They loved to invent words to describe what they did and the first word they invented was "fun". Then they immediately set about giving a meaning to the word and had lots of fun.

The next word they invented was "mischief" and this was even better because it made them feel naughty (a word that they hadn't quite invented yet).

As the tokoloshes became more inventive, the human beings, whom they called "big ones", became more and more possessive. They wanted to possess the land, build towns, cities and factories, and the tokoloshes were driven further and further into the far reaches of their streams and rivers.

Some fled the land and found refuge in other countries, where they crept into the minds of poets and writers who then wrote about tokoloshes, but called them names like "Puck" and "Hobbit". Others found refuge in the company of kindred spirits called leprechauns and gnomes.

Those who remained decided it would be safer to find themselves a human shape, for at that stage they were still gleamings of energy, but they found most human shapes quite boring. Then one day they saw a troupe of monkeys and they immediately knew they had found their corporal form.

And that is how tokoloshes came to be small, hairy creatures, while retaining the power to change themselves into gleamings of energy and become invisible to human eyes.[1]

The amiable and impish Jimmy the Reed de Umhlanga is one of them. We have been friends since as far back as I can remember, and longer.

This is our country. It is the province of KwaZulu-Natal (KZN). South Africa is our land, and our people are you and me, Jimmy and others.

In order to put the case for the people, I have to leave the historical data and facts for a while to give you a little of our country's more ethereal history.

The second to grace the stage is a bird. Jimmy told me that the name KwaZulu-Natal means the place of the Zulus, but it is the home of many more than only Zulus. "There are also Indians for Africa, if you know what I mean," he said.

KZN is for live and let live, graciously accommodating Ulundi and also Little England, New Germany, Pietermaritzburg and that great Zulu warrior, Lance Klusener. It is also the home of the famous chicken of the veld.

Chicken of the veld? On the 25 December 1497, the Portuguese navigator Vasco da Gama rounded the Cape and reached the south-east coast of Africa. His mariners called this majestic garden of austral Africa, *Terra do Natal*, Land of the Birth – Christmas. They observed the little veld chicken, killed it and ate the poor thing. They called it *Galinha da Terra do Natal*.

This bird was very important to the Portuguese seafarers because they still had a long way to go to India, and scurvy was an ever-present danger

---

1 *The Citizen*, 3 September 2004.

owing to the lack of fresh food. So they recorded the *Galinha da Terra do Natal* in the ship's logbook, the official report of the journey, and talked a lot about it... *Ternatals*... *Tran'taal*... And so the veld chicken, *Numida meleagris*, got its written name of *Tarentaal*, or as some of my compatriots call it, *Trantraal*, the dark, white-spotted, feathered beauty, Lady of the Veld. Like Jimmy, she never wanders far from water.

And the third to appear on the scene is that magnificent Lord of the Highlands, the Gnu.

Some people call the gnu the wildebeest. Others call the wildebeest the gnu. South Africa is very colour conscious, so to prevent any confusion, the one got called the black wildebeest and the other one the blue wildebeest.

The black wildebeest is not black; it is rather a dark buffy-brown. This gregarious antelope has massive humped shoulders sloping to his slighter hindquarters. He has a shaggy mane, a distinct beard and an elongated patch of long hair on the chest. He probably has the noisiest tail in the world; it can be heard swishing almost a kilometre away. He is the real gnu. He is found to the west of the Drakensberg in the Free State. On the eastern side in KZN, you'll find this gnu's close cousin, as Flanders put it, "a g-nother gnu", the blue wildebeest – which is actually grey.

The more elevated Free State black wildebeest got its name from the early KhoiKhoi who called it *gnu* because of its cry when alarmed (*Connochaetes gnou*).

Talking of colour, in English they call us the rainbow nation. This of course is a mistake, because we are much more colourful than that. The rainbow is short of black, white and brown, and officially we are classified either as black – sometimes also called African; or white – sometimes affectionately called whiteys; or Asian – sometimes also called Indian; or brown – sometimes called coloured.

Be that as it may, one thing is certain, South Africa has made its mark in English culture. It scores many hits in the English dictionary. In fact, the first full word in the dictionary is *aardvark* (earth-hog, or anteater); followed by *aardwolf* (African hyena), and then soon *aasvogel* (vulture) appears, and if you page right through the dictionary, you'll find that it almost closes with the famous *Zulu*. In between you will find more gems such as *boorish, kaffir, rooinek, wildebeest* and, of course, the *gnu*.

The British royals simply loved the gnu. The entire royal family turned up one night in 1957 to sing their famous gnu song in chorus from the dress circle. This was a salon review, in the Noel Coward tradition, by the British composer Donald Swann and lyricist Michael Flanders. The Queen Mother loved it. The second verse goes like this:

22

I'm a g-nu,
A g-nother g-nu!
I wish I could g-nash my teeth at you.
I'm a g-nu,
How do you do?
You really ought to k-now w-ho's w-ho.

I'm a g-nu, spelt G-N-U,
Call me "bison" or "okapi" and I'll sue.
G-nor am I in the least,
Like that dreadful hartebeest,
Oh, g-no, g-no, g-no...
G-know, g-know, g-know, I'm a g-nu...
G-know, g-know, g-know, I'm a g-nu![2]

Our Jimmy is erratic. He can be serious but also full of fun. He is not averse to female attention to say the least. Our Ms Tarentaal can be hoity-toity, but motherly. Our Mr Gnu may appear not always to be with it, but he may surprise you! On the head or tail side of the 2004 five rand coin you'll see the highveld's nobleman in capricious style. However, they are all only human like the rest of us.

*   *   *

I queried the UN, I confessed to being a liberal, I have introduced my friends, Jimmy, Tarentaal and Gnu – the three musketeers. Let's now go back to the dilemma at the UN and get on with the job.

2 *The Best of Flanders & Swann.* Compact disc © 1994 EMI Records Ltd. UK. CD 16858.

CHAPTER 5

Global Divide

The Hallmark of Politics – Nonsensicalities

Now we resume with the principle of equality and the democratisation of the UN. In the General Assembly every nation is equal. Population giants, such as Russia, China, India, the US, Indonesia and Brazil, are every one equal to all the others – including the mountain town-republics like Andorra and San Marino, and such speck-island states as the Maldives and Mauritius.

At the UN it often happens that the puppets delegated by dictators or one-party regimes preach, postulate and demand at the expense of true democracies.

Hypothetically, if the General Assembly should operate on the principle of majority vote, such as in Sweden and other democratic countries, it means that the minority of the members comprising the major democratic countries of the world, including South Africa, would be outvoted by the many non-democratic and tiny countries.

"Such as Ťröllandia," suggests Jimmy.
"And Terra do Natal," adds Ms Tarentaal.
"And what about the Free State?" queries Gnu.

The prevailing motley arrangement has already led to the most ridiculous moves, which we accept in our stride without a challenge. During early 2003, for ulterior motives, Libya of all countries was elected to the chairmanship of the UN Human Rights Commission! So much for democracy, so much for human rights, and so much for the UN! By the way, South Africa promoted Libya for this position. Gaddafi's Libya is not a democracy and its proven disregard for human rights is well known all over the world! My farmer uncle would say it is like appointing the wolf to protect the sheep.

Probably all of us have some explanation for this trick, but is it fair to normal, decent and honest people? My question is can the people and countries that were responsible for this manoeuvre claim to be fair and honest, and deserving of our respect? The politically correct preachers, who are gutless tricksters backed by money and political power, will probably give a "that's life, that's politics" shrug.

The nonsensicalities of modern democracy are endless.

If the democratisers of the UN were really serious, I would support them; if they intended to expel the undemocratic countries from the UN, I would sympathise with them. This still doesn't mean that I believe in democracy as it is practised in modern times though.

Let us also look at the unfair treatment of countries at the UN from a different perspective. We can take the size of business (the GDP – Gross Domestic Product) as a norm for making comparisons between countries.

The size of business of the African continent roughly equals that of Texas, one of the 50 states of the US.

The business of Africa south of the Sahara compares with that of Ohio, and the business of South Africa equates to that of Maryland (comparisons based on GDP data in standard encyclopaedia).

From an African perspective, is it fair that Swaziland and Zimbabwe each have a vote equal to that of South Africa at the AU, or from a global perspective, equal to that of Australia at the UN, even if the issue on the table concerns the rights of women and freedom of the press?

The Defenders and the Demanders

If the present trend continues, the big democratic states will have to bend the knee to the multitude of undemocratic and tiny countries, and subject themselves to the will of these. This sets the stage for the following questions: Will the peoples of the democratic states be prepared to do that? Will it be fair? If not, what are they going to do about it? And if decisions at the UN are not taken on the basis of one state one vote, what then happens to one person one vote in any one country?

The democratic countries, especially the big ones, will undoubtedly defend their interests.

As we know, the democratic states are in the minority in the UN. If democracy is good, they are the good guys – the Defenders. Many of them are incidentally also those countries whose people possess the know-how required by modern society. They are the most literate, the most educated and trained (and I don't mean in political science), the freest and the wealthiest. Most of these countries are located in Europe, North America and in some parts of the East.

On the other hand, the undemocratic states, those demanding more say, are in the majority at the UN. If non-democracy is bad, they are the bad guys – the Demanders. Many of them are incidentally also those countries whose people more than others lack the know-how required by today's world. By comparison their populations are the most illiterate, uneducated and untrained (especially in science and technology); the majority are also the least free and the poorest. Most of these countries are located in South America, Africa and Asia. The ambassadors of these countries at the UN are usually extremely suave, erudite, and often rich, but their standing doesn't reflect the real status of their populations.

However, a victory of the minority, the good guys – the Defenders – over the majority, the bad guys – the Demanders – resulting in a protracted status quo will not produce a sustainable solution. Conversely, a takeover by the Demanders, by means of the democratic vote at the UN, will lead to a showdown and the unmanageable collapse of the society of states.

Therefore, we should shed antiquated concepts and create an entirely new dispensation. There is a better solution and I trust we'll reach it before the end of this book. Let me say at this stage that the main obstacle to finding a solution is the outdated, unqualified and uncontrolled concept of modern representative democracy. The Defenders should initiate a new system of international order – an honourable, fair and effective dispensation for the benefit of the people.

For a start, ponder this question: Do we need the General Assembly? Can anyone tell me what the General Assembly is actually doing for us and the world at large? Do we need a Security Council with permanent and rotating members? Why can't a body akin to, say, the International Monetary Fund, the World Bank, or the World Health Organisation perform the function of the present Security Council?

The threat of the Global Divide between the Defenders and the Demanders should be defused to avoid disaster. The miracle is over.

How did it happen that we are suddenly confronted with this imminent implosion of democracy?

Jimmy appears out of thin air, shaking his head and splashing me with water, "Sorry Uncle Joe," he says (Jimmy and friends often call me Uncle Joe), "but our whole problem is the propagators of political correctness. They bury our ostrich heads in the sand and this blinds us to realities. However, they remain a formidable force to be overcome if we want to manage the impending self-destruction of democracy."

We take a penetrating look into the nature and dynamics of Political Correctness in the next few chapters.

CHAPTER 6

Ignorance – Key to Success

Ignorance sure does cause some interesting arguments – Cy the Cynic in Frank Stewart's bridge column.[1]

The Political Commissars

The politically correct activists keep ignorance intact to prevent vitally important arguments from surfacing. That is why, during the early days of the Roman Catholic Church, they restricted access to the Holy Bible to only a few.

Political Correctness does not exist. It is a misnomer and also a contradiction in terms.

But we'll stick to the nomenclature for the time being:
Political Correctness or Politically Correct – PC
Politically Correct + Activists = Political Correctivists – PCs

In the West the governors of political correctness carefully avoided revealing the origin of modern political correctness, the doyenne of the PCs – the Soviet Political Commissar. The Western PCs skilfully remained untagged leaders in many fields: politics, pedagogy, ecclesiasticism and others.

In the East, particularly in China and the Soviet Union and its satellite states, the political commissars instructed people what not to think and how not to think about it. They played the commanding role in liberation, insurgent and terrorist movements and they were also the leading lights of political warfare and re-education. Their close red blood cousins in the West are quite similar, only they are much better camouflaged.

---

1 *The Citizen*, 30 May 2004.

Political correctness is defined by *The Reader's Digest Oxford Complete Word-finder* as "advocacy of avoidance of forms of expression and action that exclude or marginalize racial and cultural minorities"[2]. For a start, I don't think this old definition will be overwhelmingly popular in the early third millennium Zimbabwe and South Africa.

In the meantime PC has become much more complicated and comprehensive. The red liberals have lobbied politicians and used them to legislate or at the very least to promote their devious ideas. And since politicians make politics out of everything imaginable, PC has spread its tentacles to embrace almost all aspects of life.

PC prescribes what is correct about race, gender, sex and religion. It also drags along much other paraphernalia regarding humour and nomenclature. PC is not user friendly. It doesn't suggest what you may think, do and say. It aggressively orders you about what you are *not allowed* to think, do and say. It is not only a pain in the butt, it is also venomous and dangerous – a slimy pestilence of the dark.

Political correctivists are negative people, stubborn and persistent. You will seldom hear one of them tell you what *is* in fact politically correct. He will mostly tell you what *is not* politically correct. The rare bold ones with balls among them may venture to say, "The Muslims, Christians, women, or the Society against the Prevention of Fertilisation won't like it."

So what? It does not mean that whatever you and I said which was regarded as politically incorrect was not perhaps reasonable and very important. It might have contained a useful truth, vital to finding the solution to a real problem affecting society. In any event, we didn't mean any malice. Even if we were a bit cheeky, what has happened to freedom of expression?

PCs do not promote the asking of good questions. The governors of PC lay down the rules and enforce them. They not only prescribe what you are not allowed *to think and say*, but they also prescribe what questions you are not allowed *to ask*.

And then there are us, the victims – the ordinary good people.

The best people are children. "Children don't know enough not to ask important questions," says Carl Sagan, the eminent scientist from Cornell University in his introduction to Stephen Hawking's book, *A Brief History of Time*.[3] The PCs don't ask the important questions, but not only that, they also for-

2 Tulloch, 1993.
3 Hawkins, 1989.

bid you to ask and discuss them. They may be grown up and learned, but are certainly not mature.

Children are innocent and ignorant – they ask the important questions that raise eyebrows. We embarrassingly apologise for the kids and turn the issue into some sort of clever little joke, and then chuckle and wink.

Law, Life and Politics

As a result of PC over the years we have lost the ability to identify the right questions. This has happened because the red liberals have kept telling us that when we entertain these right but embarrassing questions, we are not "in", we are not "with it", "we only demonstrate our ignorance", meaning backwardness. In other words we are uncouth, social misfits.

The PCs are very fond of campaigning for peace or pretending to do so. They believe that history has taught us that the truth in response to the right but sensitive question may disturb the peace. That is why the noble governors and propagators of PC quash topics on sensitivities such as tribes and intra- and international borders, thus maintaining a false and unstable peace as we will see later on.

The PCs are not useful to mankind. They are schemers. In their title they shrewdly use the word "political" as a prefix to their brand of correctness to give their jargon a deceiving stamp of authority – as if it is biblical... and sinners will be punished.

Having been admonished, little Annie asked her mother why she was not allowed to use the politically incorrect words "a chink". Her mother responded, "The people won't like it." Indignantly Annie retorted, "But I am also a people!"

Political correctness is probably one of the biggest obstacles to finding real solutions for real problems in our everyday real life. How often have you yourself perhaps told a person of authority that something was unfair, not right, only to get the response, "I know, I agree, but that's the law." If something is really unfair, shouldn't we apply our minds to finding a solution?

In the same vein, how many times when you wanted to do something were you told you shouldn't? And when you asked why, the response was, "That's life."

Since the turn of the millennium South African politicians have been blatantly cheating the people who voted them into the legislature: after the elections they switch their party allegiance without the voters' approval and without giving up their seats. The people feel the pain of injustice, but they are helpless.

If you confront the PCs, their feeble response is "I agree with you, you are absolutely right, but that's the way it works in politics." If you confront the politicians with allegations of swindling, they arrogantly say, "It's not cheating, it's the law, it's within the constitution."

Are we now supposed to leave it be and be happy just because "that's politics, that's the law" – a stupid law created by PC imbeciles and accommodated by a ludicrous constitution – and because "that's life"? I wonder if the red liberals are ever going to confront the PCs about this and save us – the people, Jimmy, Tarentaal and Gnu.

It is typical of the PCs to be evasive and vague, and to indulge in double talk, with the result that genuine problems lie in the pending tray for ever. They are the gods, the governors, the propagators, the policemen and judges – the Political Commissars – on what is good and bad.

Virus alert

PC is like a virus. You don't see it, but it is there.

It's almost unbelievable, but I have it on impeccable authority that a new [PC]² virus (Personal Computer Politically Correct virus) has been developed. It belongs to the same group of viruses as the Trojan horse.

It is malignant and deliberately planted. It ensconces itself somewhere between your server and your computer. All the electronic messages you receive come via this virus and are cleared of all political incorrectnesses. It is a peculiar virus that also delivers a service of its own, supplying you with lots of information, probably from a hidden PC propaganda source.

The dangerous part is that you are totally barred from responding to its messages or sending any of your own. If it did allow any of your transmissions to go through, they would be properly cleared of all improprieties.

This politically correct virus cannot be destroyed. The only remedy is to clear your mind and your computer altogether, and start from scratch.

*   *   *

Jimmy: Uncle Joe, what about PC tricks in the real world?

CHAPTER 7

PCs and Concubines

The Real World – The Secret is Out

One silly PC contrivance in the real world is that you are not allowed to use the words "convict" and "prisoner". Have you ever in your life heard of anybody who has been convicted?!

If you use the word "prisoner", it may just arouse the suspicion that the so-called person's current place of abode may actually be a prison. That, of course, is a malicious statement and totally void of any truth, explicit, implied or otherwise.

All politically correct and therefore civilised people know that prisons and therefore prisoners do not exist anymore. The so-called person, since not actually in the employ of the government, is in fact a guest of the Department of Correctional Services on sabbatical leave of absence from society for the purpose of re-education.

Another practical example of the stupidity of political correctness is that it is now forbidden to use the word "chairman". A chairman or chairlady will henceforth be called a chairperson. There may be two reasons for this important trivial novelty – important to the PCs and trivial to all others.

Firstly, situations may arise where there may be uncertainty as to the actual gender affiliation of such a person because it may be dressed in unisex clothes. It may not be known whether the presiding human being is handling, in other words, managing the chair or womanaging the chair.

Secondly, even in the event that you have privileged information that leaves no doubt about the masculinity or femininity or otherwise of the said person, it is still not within your rights to intrude into the privacy of such a person. You may unwittingly reveal his, her or its gender affiliation to others. How can you blatantly, and for every Tom, Dick and Harry's cognisance, reveal such a personal secret as the gender identity or preference of a person?

But the one constant factor about PCs is that they are never consistent. In the dignified and stately South African parliament the presiding person is politically correctly addressed as "Madam Speaker" – the secret is out!

When dealing with political correctness and incorrectness one cannot shy away from the gender issues of the millennium.

Hide and Seek

At this stage I feel I must interrupt to declare my own interests so as to immunise myself against the possible false PC accusation of chauvinistic preferences. I am not a women hater; in fact, I am a women's libber and I still feel aggrieved that the movement petered out. Women never completely achieved the dominant position in society they so rightly deserve. And since this is such an important matter, I give it all the attention it deserves.

I fully endorse a letter by Ms Lesley Illingworth to the editor of *The Weekly Telegraph*, which I quote for your entertainment:

> Sir – It would appear that UN weapons inspectors have not yet found any weapons of mass destruction [in Iraq]. I note that nearly all the inspectors are men. It recently struck me that, if my husband is anything to go by, they stand little chance of finding anything.[1]

It is not PC to say so, but we all know that, embarrassing as it may be to the poor arrogant men, women are far superior. They have more stamina, live longer, get things done more so than men do, are more meticulous, better at sex, and so on.

Let's look at nature. It is well known that in certain species of spiders the female devours the male immediately after copulation. He has by then outlived the reason for his existence. A spider sexpert told me, "That's exactly what happens – if he doesn't get away quickly enough, that is," she added. Overseas these spiders are very aptly called the black widow spider, and in South Africa we have the black button, *Theriidae Latrodectus spp.*

But make no mistake, females are not as unromantic as it may seem. Dragonfly ladies and beautiful petite Cape damselflies mate only in flight; that's the only way to travel, they reckon.

Perhaps the answer to all the injustices of the past against human females would be to reappraise the status quo and globally implement a modern type of Amazonism which tolerates male existence to some extent.

---

1 *The Weekly Telegraph*, 18 February 2003.

Amazonism should be fast-tracked to give women a superior position in human society so that they can continue doing all the difficult chores for which they are so well equipped. Like the lion king, males should be left to their world of majestic loafing, the only thing they are good for. I (and probably the greater majority of all males) am sick and tired of doing all the work anyway. It is high time that women took their rightful place.

Empowering women is not a new idea at all. To find out more about women I consulted the writings of a very wise man. He was none other than King Solomon. He had 700 wives and 300 concubines – he knew about women! In the sixth chapter of Proverbs he urges the reader to go to the ant... consider her ways, and be wise.

To find out more about ants I visited another expert, Dr Caryl P Haskins. She (or he) said: "Since they first emerged on the earth, more than 100 million years ago, the ants have been learning, in human terms, how to be social.

Ant colonies are female societies. The queen lays unfertilised – or male – eggs as needed. But the sole job of these drones, when they mature, is to mate for a few moments with a young queen. All worker ants are female. So basically the ant world is a mother-and-daughter universe.

...The ants did have to meet, throughout their long evolution, many of the same problems human societies later had to face. These problems involved both war – intense competition within and between species – and peace – coping with hunger and environmental stress. Surely we humans are but mere neophytes, compared with the ants, in solving these problems."[2]

Women should take over. You may say that they already have, but many people say so only because it is PC to say so – the right thing to do. Let's not be pretentious. We cannot incessantly treat women as aliens on a man's planet. I have it on good authority that most other planets have matriarchal systems – women are the bosses.

But PCs are not only anti-prisoners and pro-ants; they often have hang ups about the treatment of aliens.

Aliens

Early in 2003 a PC friend told me that in that day's newspaper there were no less than three reports of aliens who had committed crimes in South Africa – in one and the same paper!

I was a bit puzzled, so I looked up the word "aliens", and this put me on the right track. To make doubly sure, I decided to buy that particular newspaper and read it myself. I found that my PC friend was quite correct, but not very specific. The aliens were not from outer space – they were all from Nigeria.

On another occasion a compatriot once presented two foreign African visitors to me. They were looking for business opportunities in South Africa. The first one introduced himself, "I am not a Nigerian..." The second one followed straight away, "I am a Nigerian, but I am not a crook."

I haven't the foggiest notion what motivated them to say what they did. Whatever it was, it would be politically incorrect for me to speculate on the matter. When you have the PC campaigners on your track, treat the aliens with kid gloves – they have rights. When they become legal, handle them like you would anyone else.

This is not where PC ends; the saga continues.

---

2 Haskins, *National Geographic*, June 1984.

CHAPTER 8

PCs and a League of Gentlemen

Howzat

Another way of looking at PC is to refer to the English and the games they play – as long as we don't talk about soccer. The English invented a noble form of political correctness more than a century ago, long before it got its bad name in the form of the modern, useless and offensive PC.

Their useful old-style political correctness embraced two aspects. The one concerned fairness and good manners, and was characterised by phrases such as "It's not done", or better still, "That's simply not done." This aspect was quite useful for bringing up decent English children and for aliens adapting to the English culture even if they were never really regarded as part of it.

The other aspect had to do with pride, self-respect and honour. Strange as it may seem, in those days these values were actually regarded as commendable until present day PCs tightened their grip on such arrogant and foolish notions.

To promote these qualities, the English invented the game of cricket. To discourage shamelessness and unscrupulousness, the sages of the Marylebone Cricket Club would describe a dishonourable deed on the cricket grounds, fields of battle and the playing fields of life as "that's not cricket". This saying appealed to a gentleman player's sense of righteousness and decency.

If the bowler bowls a ball to the batsman and it touches his bat, and a fielder catches the ball before it touches the ground, the batsman is out – caught! And he should walk like a gentleman, without further ado. If he doesn't, then "that's not cricket"!

If a batsman touches the ball bowled to him with his bat and a fielder catches it when or after it has touched the ground, then the batsman is not out. If the fielder then, knowing that the ball touched the ground, nevertheless appeals to the umpire hoping for the umpire to declare the batsman out – caught – that would not be honourable. Then "that's not cricket"!

Cricket is a gentleman's game played by gentlemen. Its noble principles appeal to a person's sense of decency and honesty. This obsolete political correctness had honourable intentions. RIP.

The matter of honour and decent manners found a keen exponent in Robert Mugabe when Prime Minister of Zimbabwe. "Cricket?" he said, "It civilises people and creates good gentlemen. I want everyone to play cricket in Zimbabwe. I want ours to be a nation of gentlemen." [1]

In Praise of the Swiss

A few brave people even dare to smile, but PCs have a fit when it comes to the matter of stereotyping that is supposed to be funny. It doesn't matter what the joke, the anecdote or the witty retort, the PCs will find fault. In the end it seems you can joke only about your sibling provided he, she or it is of the same race, gender, age and standing as you.

1 Exley, 1994.

Oscar Wilde said that a pun is the lowest form of literary art. Someone else said that jokes are the worst form of humour. George Mikes said all jokes contain an offensive sting. Be all that as it may, a joke could be meant to hurt an opponent; but on the other hand, the offensive element could be only in the ear of the listener.

In the film *The Third Man*, Orson Welles says that in Italy for 30 years under the Borgias they had warfare, terror, murder, bloodshed, but they produced Michelangelo, Leonardo da Vinci and the Renaissance. In Switzerland, they had brotherly love; they had 500 years of democracy and peace. And what did that produce? The cuckoo-clock.[2]

KUKU
KUKU

---

2 Rees, 1980.

It reminds me of the BBC series *Yes Minister* in which the Rt Hon James Hacker stereotypes the average European Common Market official in Brussels thus: "He has the organising ability of the Italians, the flexibility of the Germans, the modesty of the French topped up by the imagination of the Belgians, the generosity of the Dutch and the intelligence of the Irish."[3]

On another occasion someone drew a parallel between heaven and hell. In heaven the chefs are the French, the engineers are the Germans, the policemen are the British, the lovers are the Italians – and everything is run by the Swiss.

In hell, the cooks are the British, the mechanics are the French, the policemen are the Germans, the lovers are the Swiss – and everything is run by the Italians.

The Swiss are an accomplished lot. They have one of the best forms of government in which the emphasis falls on the lowest tier, the canton, where we find the people. They are culturally and religiously mixed with four main languages and they all live in harmony. They have approximately zero population growth, a high standard of living, and very little poverty.

They are a proud but modest nation. They have a proven and widely acclaimed record of excellence going back many centuries; they are mature and they make damn good chocolates. They have the legend of Wilhelm Tell – and they don't worry about jokes ridiculing them.

Then there was Wagner, Goethe, Hitler, Michael Schumacher, the Beetle – car of the century. Isn't that what you would expect of Germans?

They don't care.

The French have croissants, Napoleon, Bizet, Brigitte Bardot, Bordeaux, the Eiffel Tower and the Louvre.

The French, they don't care.

The English have good manners, Wimbledon, Royal Ascot, The Beatles, and the best meal ever invented – the English Breakfast.

They don't care.

The Italians have Rome, Venice, Marco Polo, Caruso, pasta, Garibaldi, Gina Lollobrigida and Pinocchio– neither do they take offence.

The time has now arrived for us to make up our minds about political correctness and its perpetrators, and where we position ourselves.

*   *   *

3 *"The Devil You Know"*, The Complete *Yes Minister* Collector's Boxset, DVD, BBC, 2002. 1120.

This leads to the red cutting edge of political correctness.

CHAPTER 9

Something Else Ghastly

He is a great believer in changing countries – Luttwak on George Soros.[1]

My first major undertaking was in South Africa, but it was not successful – George Soros.[2]

If this isn't meddling in the affairs of a foreign nation, I don't know what is – Soros on his activities in the Ukraine according to Connie Bruck.[3]

If You are Right You are Wrong and if You are Left you are Right

The aggressive governors and perpetrators of PC are like the writers of law. They prescribe a punishment for the crime of *political incorrectness*. But that is where the similarity ends. The PCs will punish you without proving your guilt beyond the slightest suspicion of a doubt.

Such PC governors are Scandinavian and other nations who are quick with donations for countries that are "in", and equally quick with boycotts and sanctions for those who are not "with it". The big PC perpetrator is George Soros who will sponsor you for toeing the line or withhold funds for not doing so.

We have seen what a Red Liberal is, and now also what makes a Political Correctivist (PC). The worst of the lot is when you have these two all in one, a Red Liberal PC.

---

1 Luttwak, *George Soros Bankrolls Door-to-Door Voter Hunt in Swing States.* http://www.pantera-designs.com/worldnews/2004/10/george-soros-bankrolls-door-to-door. 3/16/2007.

2 Soros, *The Capitalist Threat.* http://www.yuricareport.com/Economy/CapitalistThreat_Soros.html 3/16/2007.

3 Bruck, The World according to Soros. *The New Yorker.* 23 January 1995.

A typical example of the modern red liberal PC is the haughty one who, with blinkers on, aggressively moves and shakes for a cause, mercilessly eliminating any opposition in his path; one who would, for example, fervently support democracy and steamroller others into becoming democrats too; one who wouldn't think twice of lashing you with a sjambok until you also became a democrat – voting for parties. Anyone may have an opinion as long as he is a democrat voting for the right party.

In practice, if you want to identify or emulate a red PC liberal, the arch red liberal PC operator George Soros is your role model. He goes beyond lashing with a sjambok. When money talks, people listen. Money is Soros's tool – his sjambok. Soros is a doctrine unto himself. He will pursue his ideals with all his might and money.

He has a network of philanthropic organisations that are active in more than 50 countries. His Open Society Institute claims that his political activities are wholly separate from the institute. These claims are disputed all over the world.

After failure in South Africa he turned his attention to Central Europe where he claimed successes. In 1989 he shut down in China. The wise Chinese probably wouldn't tolerate his brand of PC. He was also active in Russia and became heavily involved in the Ukraine.

Former Georgian president Eduard Shevardnadze accused Soros of orchestrating the campaign that led to his downfall.[4] Connie Bruck, who is clearly not a great admirer of Mr Soros, states that Soros made no bones about the interventionist nature of his role in the Ukraine.

In 1997 the Malaysian prime minister accused Soros of attempting to destroy South East Asia's economy, an allegation Soros denied. Soros is the type of red PC liberal who would argue that if you are right, you are wrong, and if you are left, you are right.

Jimmy says, "Whether you look at him from the left or the right, he remains Soros, a red PC."

Of Self-Respecting Social Misfits

PC in everyday terms means that if you ask the right but unwelcome question, or tell the embarrassing truth, you are guilty of an act of political incorrectness. It *ipso facto* constitutes a crime against humanity. As punishment you will be tagged with a combination of the following labels:

---

4 Bruck, 1995.

42

You are not well travelled.
You are not well read.
You are not well informed.
You are not intellectual.
You are extreme right.
You are a social misfit.

One welcome blessing accompanying such punishment is that you are also prohibited from any further participation at any PC NGO workshops/seminars/think tanks and jollies.

If you find yourself in South Africa, Zimbabwe, East Africa, the UK, Belgium, Germany, Italy, the Netherlands, or in any one of a number of other countries and continents, take extreme care of what you say! You may be branded as one who clings to old values, is not agreeable to change – in other words you are a racist, a xenophobe, or something else equally ghastly.

"That's life" – or is it? In my opinion, to be PC is a less than doubtful honour. Granted, if you become PC you have a good chance of making a lot of useless friends, but I would advise you against joining their ranks.

I don't deny that being PC has its rewards especially for people who suffer from inferiority complexes. Becoming PC gives them the same kicks as those who were born know-alls and know-betters. It gives them the feeling of intellectual superiority. They feel so good because they are so good.

The prerequisites for becoming PC are the following:
Be incapable of thinking honestly for yourself, or of caring about doing so.
Have nothing to say apart from your PC doctrine.
Don't care about integrity and self-respect.
Be lackadaisical about political principles, if you have any.

Red liberals use political correctness to satisfy egoistic needs. It is sometimes unconsciously practised by dear, innocent and uninformed well-meaning do-gooders. It is never correct. It is human society's way to self-inflicted destruction.

Do you really agree with the PCs? The PCs are a completely disorientated bunch:

They advocate taking danger out of adventure
Standards out of qualification
War out of armed conflict
Profit out of gains
Pride out of achievement
Accountability out of responsibility

Femininity out of womanhood
The he-man out of masculinity
The desire to win out of competition
Melody and harmony out of music
Common sense out of logic
Argument out of debate and
The fun out of humour.

PCs are putting sameness into equality, and restricting ripostes and retorts to parliamentarians – they are protected by immunities and privileges.

A man and a woman are equal before God, and before the law, but it would have been a most disastrous matter if they were the same. If the PCs succeed, what a drab world it would be!

The PCs have missed the golden opportunity of taking the wrong things out of the right things – they have never attempted to take politics out of governance!

We have to decide whether we are going to stick to the rules of political correctness as laid down by Stalin or Churchill, Jean-Marie Le Pen or Mugabe. Or, in the case of South Africa, as laid down by the minister of sports, Mr Stofile, the leader of the Democratic Alliance, Tony Leon, or radio presenter John Robbie, or who?

"Why don't you just ban PCs – the whole bloody lot?" advises Gnu, and promptly performs his ritual. Flicking his noisy tail, and with a snort and a jerk, a twist and a turn, he goes into a maul of little circles. His high kicking hind legs send highveld dust and tufts of turf flying. Then suddenly he takes off, galloping away in comical flight to disappear over the nearest ridge.

Jimmy smiles. "That's Gnu," I comment.

Tarentaal sighs, "Daisy is probably waiting for him."

*   *   *

There is life beyond political correctness. Nevertheless it remains an impediment to finding a solution for the imploding democracy. Democracy is about the People and their elected Leaders. Let's meet the key role-players in the drama of life, in and out of politics.

CHAPTER 10

Dramatis Personae

I hold the view that the leader must know what he himself wants. He must see his objective clearly and then strive to attain it; he must let everyone else know what he wants and what are the basic fundamentals of his policy. He must, in fact, give firm guidance and a clear lead. It is necessary for him to create what I would call "atmosphere", and in that atmosphere his subordinate commanders will live and work – Montgomery of Alamein.[1]

Apart from the Almighty and Nature it has been people and their leaders who have shaped the planet's recent past and present, and who will shape its future. But there is a big difference between political leaders – on a stage all of their own – and leaders in the world at large.

Leaders – What you Want

The Platinum rule of leadership is: Whatever politicians do – don't!

Why not? Because –
The Golden rule is: Excellence through Truth.
Political Correctness is your enemy.

A *leader* leads people – not personnel or human resources. He fills the top ex-ecutive post in the central line of authority; he is the executive chairman or chief executive officer, the CEO.

A *director* or *staff officer* manages functions, systems, and procedures, such as a director of logistics. He fills a senior post but is not in the central line of authority.

---

1 Montgomery, 1958.

A successful leader and his people consistently accomplish their goals over a long period. They develop a winning culture.

To achieve success continuously, a leader reconciles his people's personal aspirations with the company's objectives.

He will inspire and assist those who report directly to him to accomplish their tasks. He will then give them a pat on the back, and brag to others about how good they are.

He combines all the available resources to achieve the desired end result.

He is a problem solver. He has vision; he looks and plans ahead. He becomes a man with a mission.

The leader assumes responsibility for setting his organisation's strategic goal.

He assumes responsibility for planning, and sets objectives for his subordinate leaders to realise the goal.

He is an organiser. He creates the structures, systems and procedures required for getting the job done, reaching the objectives and accomplishing the goal.

He is a team builder.

He creates the right atmosphere in which his people will operate, and which will be conducive for them to achieve the company's goal and objectives.

He will motivate them.

He is a communicator.

He will monitor the execution of functions and plans and make timeous strategic interventions if required.

He is just, fair and even-handed.

He is a leader of people. What more do you want?

A business leader has a social conscience, but his core business is to make money. As Robert Townsend said, "If you're not in business for profit or fun, what the hell are you doing here?"[2]

Furthermore, the business of every business is to remain in business.

Business leaders are realists. Facing the true facts, they solve real problems. They come up with sound plans, execute them dynamically and achieve success.

But a person leading people in the interest of a bad cause may still be an effective leader of people.

---

2 Townsend, 1970.

And a leader of people is not necessarily a person who makes a lot of money, and vice-versa.

Politicians – What You Get

Governors and politicians are not synonymous with leaders and directors. Leaders and directors are decent people.

As for politicians:

Some presidents prescribe
Other presidents preside
A prime minister comes first
Other ministers lurk in the shadows of the queue.

A politician seeks power. He grabs it, or deviously collects votes for the same purpose. He remains in power by organising more votes, or amending constitutions, or eliminating opponents – a power seeker has no conscience.

A junior party politician uses every trick in and out of the book, even pretending to be humble and without ambition to convince his party bosses to appoint him to higher office.

A politician is wary of the future. Like a diplomat he tries to maintain the status quo, making the least possible waves, unless that future is guaranteed to turn out in his favour.

Politicians play games. It is all about perceptions. They create perceptions of their own and fight those of their opponents and the media. Busying themselves with perception games, they lose sight of the real problems and start to fight the next election, creating more perceptions among the voters.

A politician has an impossible job.

To get the votes he must tell the people what they want to hear.

He must also be dignified and respectful – able to walk with kings.

He must appear to be humble and have the common touch – kiss babies on their cheeks.

It cannot be done – but he does it.
He likes it. How does he manage?
He is kind to all his supporters, and sometimes more so to would-be supporters, fair to some of the others, and he ignores the rest.
He deals with the truth in an uncanny way.
He is good with words.
Most if not all of his work is done by talking.

He is a good actor.

He never takes governance seriously. He is always mindful of the fact that politics is only a game.

A politician never cares about the affairs of state. He leaves that to the bureaucracy and the NGOs.

Whether you like it or not – that's what you get.

Tit for Tat

Jimmy claims that KwaZulu-Natal presents a microscopic reflection of the global problem in the first decade of the third millennium – the battle of the politicians versus the people.

In KZN, like many other places in the world, nature is under serious threat. Jimmy's wetlands and the littoral are in dire straits. Man, plant, Tarentaal and Gnu struggle for survival.

During this grave crisis – a matter of life and death – what do the politicians do? They bicker. Bicker, over what? Over the *floor*. They harangue for days and weeks and months over whether councillors on the provincial level should have the right to change their political party affiliations in mid-course – between elections.

While everything else comes to a grinding standstill, the politicians spend all their brains, less of their energy, more of their time, and most of our money on deciding whether to legalise the swapping of parties or not – *crossing the floor* in search of power, status and wealth.

The people, Jimmy, Tarentaal and Gnu, and their well-being are out of sight and out of mind – totally forgotten!

If one looks back, these circus acts by politicians happened while crime, corruption, fraud and public safety deteriorated because of a lack of proper attention. Imagine if instead of spending all the time promoting their own personal aspirations, the politicians had spent the same time, effort and money on the well-being of all KwaZulu-Natalians.

Of course, we wouldn't want to neglect other human beings and creatures. After all, in South Africa the Amabokoboko and the Proteas also need some care and affection, as well as the Amagluglug and the Amakrokokroko and all the other Amas, and Jimmy, Tarentaal and Gnu.

The time-wasting and useless sideshows of prominent public figures are endless. Here is another random titbit from South African newspapers during the course of the battle of words regarding floor crossing:

First, ANC[3] spokesman, Smuts Ngonyama, criticises a prominent businessman's presence at an opposition *political* party meeting (Anglo's CEO Bobby Godsell). Then the leader of the UDM[4], Bantu Holomisa, reacts by calling the ANC hypocrites because business tycoons Cyril Ramaphosa, Saki Macozoma, Matthews Phosa and Tokyo Sexwale are actually members of the ANC National Executive! Where does all this tit for tat politics and squabbling lead us?

It leads us nowhere, but the political animals lap it up...

Gnu gives me a nasty look. I apologise, and Jimmy continues, "You see guys, there's no honourable place for us among that lot."

"A bunch of lowly plebs," adds Tarentaal.

Maybe no harm is done, but it costs a lot of money, and who cares for us decent people.

---

3 ANC: African National Congress.
4 UDM: United Democratic Movement.

CHAPTER 11

Decent Busybodies and Bunglers

There is no such thing as a below average student – Eddie Murphy, in the film *The Distinguished Gentleman.*

It's the Sheep that count

Leaders and people in the non-political world are not always all good. Their endeavours are not always crowned with success, but they really try their best in their own interest and that of the organisation and society at large.

Over the years I have observed many of them in action and noted their successes and failures. I have my own ideas on the causes behind such outcomes, and would like to share some of them with you.

Let's kick off with something the PCs have declared as one of the most deadly sins – stereotyping. I'll hide behind the skirts of Kurt von Hammerstein. It was he who said that an officer possesses a combination of certain qualities; he is either:

Intelligent and Industrious
or he is Stupid and Lazy
or Stupid and Industrious
or Intelligent and Lazy.

The intelligent and industrious young officer will in all probability climb the ladder to become an excellent high level *staff* officer – he is an asset to the organisation.

The stupid and lazy should not be summarily written off – he may be of some use.

The stupid and industrious young officer is a menace to the organisation – watch out!

The intelligent and lazy young officer is destined for the highest level of *command!*

Intelligence – A Much Overrated Asset

My uncle was a lazy, intelligent and successful farmer. His many assets included several hundred sheep. He told me a long time ago about how the sheep used to be counted and checked into their kraal every evening. If you have ever had the opportunity to try to perform this type of feat, you will know it's helluva difficult. So difficult that the farmers rub it in by jokingly telling inexperienced youngsters: "It's easy – count the number of legs that go by and in the end divide the sum by four!"

In his case he saddled Jonas with the responsibility. Jonas was his shepherd, decent, loyal and faithful – and illiterate. Although he performed this routine daily he could not count much further than ten.

With a sense of companionship, my uncle sometimes accompanied Jonas on his daily trip to check in the sheep. He told me that such a session would almost without fail end on the following note: "Jonas, I'm missing three sheep tonight. What do you say?" Whereupon Jonas would respond: "No, I miss only Poenskop and Moffie; they are sometimes a little late, the others are all home." And my uncle would accept his superior ability.

Laziness – A Much Underrated Virtue

I caught Jimmy lecturing Tarentaal and Gnu on heavenly blue blissful laziness:

"To excel in laziness is a rare achievement.

To do nothing is one thing; to do it well is quite a different matter.

Not just anybody can do nothing well. If you haven't got the guts, rather leave it be as it can cause unbearable stress. It is not for sissies.

Achieving a high quality of doing nothing is an extremely rare gift of nature. But very few people inherit this ability. You have to work at it.

The norms you have to observe are:

You have to be able to do nothing without feeling guilty. Anybody can be lazy, do nothing, and feel guilty, and what's more, guilt is counter-productive and self-destructive.

It is vital that you don't solve any problems and/or achieve anything while you practise this virtue. You don't take your goals, hang-ups and other baggage to your doing-nothing-well sessions.

You don't draw undue attention.

You don't apologise for inactivity.

Professional idlers do not misuse periods of idleness to pursue entertainment and sports, or to practise their favourite hobbies. The key is to plan and programme your periods of doing nothing properly. You may blissfully meditate provided you don't reflect for a cause," Jimmy ended.

"You don't have to tell me, my little cousin is an expert on laziness," said Gnu.

"Who's he?" asked Jimmy.

"She is Inxu, from down south, she is *Connochaetes gnou transkeiensis*."

"And you Tarentaal?"

"I am an upstanding country lady, but my haughty aunt in the Western Province is the expert."

"Who's she?"

"Ms Poelpetater. Her mother was French and Spanish/Portuguese, Mademoiselle Poule Pintade – *Numida meleagris capensis*."[1]

"My goodness! Has she got teeth?"

"Only when pigs and gnus fly!"

Gnu butts in, "Don't be nasty, you are a lesser species. You're not a Crested Guinea-Fowl, *Kuifkoptarentaal*, *Khaka*."

---

1 *Poule*: hen; *pintade*: painted. Boshoff & Nienaber, 1967.

"That's a gutter bird you're talking about. At least I've got a helmet on my head. The *Guttera edouardi* only has a few curling black feathers on his. That's why they stick to the woods."

Jimmy cuts the conversation, "Listen you guys, all for one and one for all. Watch out for my cousin Seamus Crystal O'Leprechaun from Waterford, Ireland!"

And that brings us back to the more light-hearted discussion about laziness and industry.

Shovel and Spade

To be industrious can be extremely hazardous. Imagine a lot of workers on site digging up a stretch of land. Loyal men have done this enthusiastically for many years and with all the gusto they could muster – with shovels.

It was this situation that really needed a new, young overseer. When the new, good and lazy foreman appeared on the scene, he replaced the shovels with spades, and the men did the same job in less than half the time.

A lazy person will always be on the lookout for better methods and implements with which to complete any task quicker and with less effort. And if he is also intelligent he will probably find an answer.

The lazy man may well defy Parkinson's Law (in which I firmly believe), namely that work expands to fill the time available for its completion. He would rather get it over and done with, and go to bed sooner, or play golf and have a drink or two.

However much I like the blissful idea of being stupid and lazy, I strongly recommend that these characteristics be accompanied by other apparently more commendable attributes. Jimmy reminds me that we meet Parkinson in the next chapter.

So, employ and inspire the intelligent, but don't expect too much of him. Do not despise the lazy. He may be more useful than you think. Get the most out of those who are intelligent and industrious. They are the intellectual grinders.

The intelligent and lazy is your best performer. He may replace you as managing director and push you further up the ladder. Don't forget, you can identify the best leader by the achievements of his subordinate leaders.

The intelligent and lazy is your most productive asset. Productivity is normally expressed as output divided by input. "To me," Jimmy says, "productivity means finding someone who can do the job for me better than I can, and in less time, and cheaper."

You go to a junior executive, he tells you:

"I enjoy my job immensely. My company knows exactly where it is going and so do all of us. I know what my division's objectives are and I know exactly what my part is in realising them. My divisional boss monitors our performance, but he doesn't look over my shoulder. He sometimes visits me and asks me about the constraints that I experience. He often removes obstacles and also gives me a pat on the back for my performance.

He has sense of humour.

They treat us fairly here and everyone is compensated according to his achievements. I might say my perks could perhaps have been a little better, but it doesn't really enter my mind very much because I'm quite happy – I get lots of kicks out of this job. I do well, and they know it, and I know it too. I'll continue to give it my all because in this job I am also still on course towards fulfilling my own aspirations."

This man's boss is a good leader. If a leader enables his people to enjoy their work, he has achieved the ultimate in motivation.

*　　*　　*

Jimmy has the last word: "A good leader brags about his organisation. If he doesn't, there may be a suspicion that he has nothing to brag about, and if he does he becomes self-obliged to maintain his high level of performance."

CHAPTER 12

Best Practice

Business leadership is all about being just, fair and even-handed, it's about taking calculated risks and accepting responsibility. It is about people, passion and achievement. The more tax you have to pay the greater the fun – and we like fun! Jimmy the Reed.[1]

Everybody is Nobody

I am especially annoyed and deeply concerned with the typical management of financial institutions in South Africa, and their haughty attitude towards the public – and they don't contribute towards creating employment and combating poverty.

On at least two occasions big business consultants from overseas told me that we have the best banking systems in the world, but they are criminal! I queried the accusation and they said that our client banking charges are extraordinarily excessive.

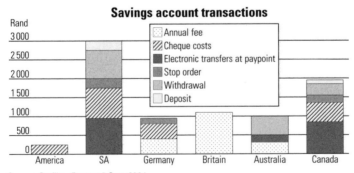

Source: Grafika: *Rapport* 3 Sept 2004.

---

1 De Umhlanga, J the Reed. People, Passion & Profit. *The Tokoloshe Times* 21 March 2005.

"Fighting with financial institutions is nothing new – it's probably a worldwide tradition. Yet, financial services companies laud themselves in their advertising, pat themselves on the back and proclaim their products will change your life and their service will leave you smiling. Basically, they lie." That is what Kim Penstone wrote in *The Citizen*[2], arguably the second best daily in South Africa.

What happened to their leaders? Where do the managers slip up?

Seminars, workshops and jollies that are supposed to promote "excellence in management" use a number of clichés overtime. One of them is to handle a matter according to "normal sound business management practices" or "best practice".

I am sad to tell you that until very recently nobody, but nobody, could present me with a piece of paper listing these *normal sound business management practices*.

Then my lifelong friend and successful international businessman, Richard Walker of Malta, suggested I consult the King II Report on Corporate Governance released in South Africa early 2002. I did.

If you are happy to stay put as a fat cat with no scope for initiative, and if stability and keeping your nose clean is your only ideal in life, this report is for you.

For a start, the word "governance" does not create the right climate for a business enterprise in which to perform miracles. It is more suited to a governmental or parastatal organisation in a rigid autocracy where business is centrally planned and governed.

We don't need rigid business "governance" in a free market economy within a democracy. It seems as if business is falling into the trap that upset one Franz J Strauss who said that an army cannot be administered; it must be led! We all know that a general in command of an army should not behave as if he is a mere administrator. But it would appear that the top business executive is now fast becoming a mere straight-jacketed manager, instead of a creative and passionate leader.

King II is supposed to apply to South African companies listed on the stock exchange, banks, financial and insurance entities and public sector enterprises. It could well serve real big businesses like Shell and Coca Cola who make millions of dollars per hour, and they just can't help it.

2 *The Citizen*, 3 July 2004.

I want governments to organise themselves more like business, while King II wants to organise business more like governments.

The report is of special importance to big businesses that removed all traces of the profit-making motive from their visions, missions and goal statements. This has been replaced by higher priorities such as promoting health and safety, protecting the environment, social engineering and, hopefully, making money on the stock exchange. Furthermore, the report is meant for big businesses that like to donate tens of millions of rands to political parties for them to party and display posters.

The man in the street knows that to finance all such activities, the company must get its money from somewhere, namely by overcharging its loyal customers for their services and products, and by undercompensating its hard-working and loyal employees with annual increments below the inflation rate.

Business people whom I believe did welcome the report are those who are highly legal and audit orientated, that is, they don't mind making less profit or even losing money as long as their books are audited and found correct, and the shareholders can't get at them. It was also welcomed by those who believe there is safety in blind rigidity.

The report reads: "The board is the focal point of the corporate governance system. It is ultimately accountable and responsible for the performance and affairs of the company."

This is the most ridiculous load of rubbish that you could ever dish up to a young, decent, enterprising and potential big business leader. It is cunning advice for a loafer seeking money, status and the good life.

The best way for any person holding a top position to escape accountability is to seek refuge in collective responsibility. The worst one can do is to make a board or committee responsible and accountable – for anything. Then business becomes as bad as democratic governance. If everybody is responsible, nobody is. That's why we have Kebble and Enron fiascos.

Dick Walker agrees that King II is not for budding Henry Fords, Bill Gateses and Richard Bransons.

What the Hell are You Doing?

It is true that our exact scientists have made fantastic strides, while our social scientists have lagged far behind and are still grappling with the same problems of millennia ago. But there are a few special social scientists I'd very much like you to reconsider. Let's call them business scientists.

Time magazine described the old, but evergreen Professor C Northcote

Parkinson[3] as the Charles Darwin of the managerial revolution. Parkinson defined his law as: Work expands so as to fill the time available for its completion. He also said: Heaven forbid that students should cease to read books on the science of public or business administration – provided only that these works are classified as fiction.

Instead of the normal textbook fairytales, he came up with reality: Expenditure rises to meet income.

Then came Peter and Hull[4] with the Peter Principle: Every employee tends to rise to his level of incompetence.

Peter out-Parkinsoned Parkinson. He made significant discoveries vital for the heads of big private or public organisations.

Now we get to Robert Townsend. I believe most of you are also familiar with his book, *Up the Organisation – How to stop the corporation from stifling people and strangling profits*. As already stated, he is well known for asking: If you are not in business for fun or profit, what the hell are you doing here?[5]

Parkinson said of him: His teaching was not about how to preside with dignity over the mess you've inherited from your predecessors, or how to muddle along indifferently. It was about how to think unthinkable thoughts, and how to do undo-able things with a view to making an unusual success out of a usual situation and making a minor success out of an impossible situation.

Townsend became president and chairman of a tiny company, Avis Rent-a-Car, which he turned into a highly respected profitable international organisation in three years. When he was appointed to Avis, he was offered a salary of $50,000 – which he refused. He said: As an about-to-be substantial stockholder I insist the president be paid $36,000 because that's top salary for a company that has never earned a nickel for its stockholders.

What Townsend regards as important is very much in contrast with politicians' attitudes. He advocates humility and respect for people on the firing line; deep understanding of the nature of the business and the kind of people who can enjoy themselves making it prosper.

And lastly we get to Tom Peters. He is described as the most influential business thinker of our age. His first book, *In Search of Excellence*, co-authored with Robert Waterman in 1982, was hailed "the greatest business book of all time".

3 Parkinson, 1979.
4 Peter & Hull, 1971.
5 Townsend, 1970.

Tom Peters tells the story of how he failed to get rid of his MBA and why he doesn't think much of business schools and auditors. In 2002, he tried (without success) to induce Stanford University to retract his MBA. He explains:

"The dean of the business school when I got my degree there was Robert Jaedicke. He was also an accounting professor, and I took his advanced accounting course while I was a student. I last saw Jaedicke 30 years later, on TV. He was testifying about his involvement in the Enron fiasco. Not only was he an Enron board member – he was chairman of the board's Audit Committee. Yet he claimed he had no clue about the truckload of peculiar transactions that brought the company down!

...needless to say, my view of MBAs and of traditional business education soured even more than it already had. (Which is saying a lot.) The same goes for my view of 'accepted business practices' in general."[6]

* * *

"What do you say, Gnu?" chirps Tarentaal.

"No match for the Lion King."

Jimmy: "That's business. What I want to know, Uncle Joe, is what are we are going to do about our failing democracy?"

From leaders and people in business, we now look at political leaders and then we're there.

6 Peters, 2003.

CHAPTER 13

Not so Decent Busy-bodies and Bunglers

Strike the shepherd and the sheep will scatter – Greene and Elffers.[1]

Pose as a Friend, work as a Spy

President Mbeki fires his deputy president, Jacob Zuma, amid allegations of corruption. Member organisations of the ANC/Cosatu/Communist Party alliance and their youth leagues insist that the deputy president be charged so that he can prove his innocence. When he is charged, they urge that he be reinstated and the new incumbent sacked. When this does not happen they claim there is a political plot against Mr Zuma. The president then undertakes to have a commission of investigation convened to probe the accusation, which they in turn reject. And so it goes on.

The IFP[2] splits into two. Members of the ID[3] break away from their party. General Bantu Holomisa, leader of the UDM, seeks a court order against members of his party who might abscond. All but one of the old NNP[4] walk over to previous arch-enemy, the ANC. And so it goes on.

This is intrigue and back stabbing for Africa. But who cares about us – the people, Jimmy, Tarentaal and Gnu?

Politicians have become professionals, that is they do politics for a living. They don't care for the people.

As you will discover, professional politicians are egocentric and party-centric. The young, budding politician schemes to climb the party ladder to

1 Greene & Elffers, 1999.
2 IFP: Inkatha Freedom Party.
3 ID: Independent Democrats.
4 NNP: New National Party.

satisfy his ambitions and make a living. "After all, politics is about jobs," said David Dalling, former MP and ANC whip.[5]

It is how people who don't work make money. It is a world of brainwashing and propaganda to condition the people.

The politician is not objective, neutral and fair; he is for himself. He is also for the party, inasmuch as it serves his interests. He is never a team person.

In all spheres of human endeavour we promote team spirit and develop teamwork, all in the pursuit of excellence – except in politics. Politicians generically don't fit into the frame of teamwork, synergy and productivity.

There is a very simple explanation for this unfortunate state of affairs. All politicians are forced by our system to compete with each other. They have no motive to co-operate. Different parties are rivals in the pursuit of power. Within a party all the members contend for the same positions, for the same reason – and more money. And before elections all politicians bullshit the tarentaal, the gnu and the people – they need their vote.

Because the different parties as well as the individual politicians are in opposition to one another, they will continually

- join hands to fight their colleagues
- split a party to create more party positions
- create brand new parties to create new opportunities
- desert one party to join another.

All of these shady activities can be traced to the beginning of time. But the modus operandi has changed for the worse. The classic and literal elimination of an opponent, for example, was often performed by way of a frontal attack. This more or less noble form of political confrontation deteriorated into what became known as "back stabbing".

The figurative "back stabbing" of the modern era is the most devious and cruel of all. Deceit, libel, defamation, character assassination and psychological violence – all under the banner of noble ideals in the interest of the state – are the malicious order of the political day.

Politicians are forced to stick to the rules. If you want to become a seafaring captain, you don't venture into the political Sahara Desert with a canoe, nor do you launch yourself into the political Atlantic Ocean on the back of a camel. You have to play the game – according to the laws! Sly as a fox and ferocious as a hyena. That's politics.

---

5 *The Citizen*, 2004.

The laws are well described. Here are some of them:

- Never outshine the master.
- Never put too much trust in friends; learn how to use enemies.
- Conceal your intentions.
- Learn to keep people dependent on you.
- Pose as a friend, work as a spy.
- Keep others in suspended terror.
- Play on people's need to believe to create a cult-like following[6]

In order to deliver, non-political organisations go through a planning process and arrive at a decision; then they convert the decision into a plan and implement it. When politicians arrive at a decision, which is not necessarily the case, they say, how are we going to play this politically? Then they arrive at a plot...

A politician's business is talking – talking politics. In fact, talking is the politician's armoury. He always has words and arguments stashed in some or other cache under the mud. Talking is his strategy, tactics and weapons systems.

If you are a politician, you may not acknowledge the attributes of your opponents. You have to tell the people your opponent is useless but sly, and plotting against them. The best way to counter a truth that hurts is to ignore it. The second best way is to retaliate with a humiliating joke at the expense of your opponent.

Clever politicians stay clear of the rational. In a highly argumentative debate they never play the ball, they play the man. They argue that if you floor the man, his issues go down with him.

The preservation of the gnu, our planet and everything on it has very little chance of getting their attention. If it does feature, since they know nothing about it, they only talk about it.

The breed of politicians to which we have become accustomed hasn't the knowledge and experience, or the training, to handle these vital matters. We find the expertise only among the ranks of the non-political bureaucrats and the NGOs.

The bureaucrat has been trained for his portfolio. It is his profession. The NGOs made these matters their pet subjects. It is their passion.

6 Greene & Elffers, 1999.

Intellectuals and Sentimentals

At a typical pre-election address, the politician's audience usually comprises a small percentage of intellectuals, real or self-styled, and a large percentage of normal, good and sentimental citizens.

The political orator entertainingly floods the sentimentalists, they being the majority. He tells them that he cares for them because they are so good; he looks after their interests because he knows what is best for them and because he is so good.

He will turn on the drama and play on such topics as freedom, patriotism, tradition, sentiment, loyalty and solidarity. Politicians always cheat when it comes to patriotism. Any governing party will use the trick of calling you unpatriotic when you criticise it.

He ignores the thirsty intellectuals. At most he may crack avant-garde jokes trying to make fools of his political opponents.

It's all a matter of quantitative play-acting about emotions concerning the majority of the sentimental listeners, and little quality of reasoning about issues of interest to the knowledgeable minority. The harsh facts and real problems play no role at all.

I recall reading somewhere: A politician shakes your hand before an election and your confidence after the election.

Axel Gustafsson (Count) Oxenstierna said, "You don't know, my dear boy, with what little reason the world is governed."[7] That was in the early 17th century and it is still true.

What about international politics? That's also a mess. Yasser Arafat was awarded the Nobel Prize for peace. Then, when he passed away, the international media widely claimed that his death raised new hopes and optimism for peace in the Middle East.

I end this sorrowful valedictory with a final observation on the profile and job description of a minister of state. His, her or its duty sheet does not list Financial Accountability. Not a single minister, being the political head, is accountable for expenditure incurred by his department! The functional head, the person who does the job – the director-general of the department – is the sole accountable person.

Sad as it might be, the politicians survive. An oft-quoted adage is "The less government there is the better", but why should we be satisfied with small mercies? Why not go the whole hog and scrap governments and polit-

---

7 Mackay, 1977.

icians altogether? Problem is, if you do away with them what do you put in their place?

The answer is simple – Nothing.

Actually it's not a matter of doing away with governments and politicians; we actually put them there. We continue to vote them into power!

"Just stop doing it!" Jimmy says. "There is a solution..."

* * *

We have come a long way since we focused on the looming dilemma of a failing democracy at the UN. Our journey was a necessary excursion for gathering the relevant background information for analysing the problem of the Great Divide and the solution, namely the New Design.

Now that we know exactly what we are up against, we can face it head on. Previously I blamed the red PC liberals for our predicament. Now, during the next leg of our travels, we come up against their blue-eyed boys, the MAD democrats. And I have yet another confession to make...

CHAPTER 14

A Near Extinct Concept

Democracy is the worst form of government except all those other forms that have been tried from time to time – Winston Churchill.

Pre- and Postmodern Democrats

I confess: I am a democrat, a democrat with a difference, a democrat with a very big difference – I care for the people.

There are two types of democrats, the bad ones and the good ones.

Except for me, all those you know are probably the bad ones – they care for the party. They are the adherents of contemporary ancient democratic systems, MAD for short – Modern Archaic Democracy. It is an antiquated system still being practised today.

I am a follower of the advanced Sovereign People Democracy – SPD for short.

Aliens will never believe it when they hear that on planet Earth the bad MADs still stubbornly continue to cling to their outdated practices:

They vote en masse once every five years for a political party;
Relinquish the people's sovereignty to that party;
Have their decisions made for them by parties; and
Refuse to change because they fail to find an alternative.

The good SPDs recognise the vital need for a new political culture:
They treasure and endeavour to uphold the peoples' sovereignty;
Rely on an elite and ethical peoples civil service especially at grass roots level;
Consider proposals by experts on affairs of state – issues and projects;
Make decisions by voting as individuals on any such matters of importance; and Promote the sturdy pillars of democracy: science, logic and the sense of nature.

Examples of the MADs are all the parties and politicians who practise voting-for-parties democracy, supported by red liberal PCs. The SPDs are yet to surface – the sooner the better – before the big crash. They promote a system of voting – without sacrificing their sovereignty.

The Curse of Modern Civilisation

First there was classic democracy, then the modern, then came Churchill – the beginning of the end. Now the ultimate in people's sovereignty awaits us.

Classic democracy was started by the Greek blue liberals. Modern democracy began in the era of the French Revolution, and then the red liberals forced it on other people all over the world – left, right and centre.

In the meanwhile Churchill came to light with those well-known words destined to save our dark world. They mean democracy is not good, or at best contains serious flaws. Stating the truth like Churchill did is a sign of wisdom; it is also a confession of goodwill. It is like turning over a stone for all to see – and it takes guts. It is easier to leave a stone unturned and waffle around it, leaving the truth obscured.

But neither Churchill nor anyone else has come up with proposals for a better form of societal living. The dilemma is we've got used to what we have. That's why we no longer entertain alternatives for the voting-for-parties democracy. Traditions, customs and conventions blur our thinking. We stay put apathetically, oblivious to where the fallacy of democracy is towing us.

What's happened to the red PC liberals? Have they chosen the option of "let sleeping stones lie"? Or are they dumbstruck and scared because they are incapable of finding something better than Modern Archaic Democracy?

We are now forced to turn to the true blue freethinkers for a solution. Let's be positive. Churchill lit a little torch that is now, half a century later, about to enlighten the whole world.

A dictionary definition of democracy claims it is a system of governance by the population. That is not so! Modern democracy is government by a party, or two – perhaps. It is all about a voting system. The people vote for a party and relinquish their sovereignty for a long period of five years at a time. The people don't get the government they deserve. They get the government the defective system deserves.

We confuse "Governance by the People" with "Democracy". Jimmy told me, basically, if we vote on the issues of a) the death penalty, or b) the basics of the shape, size and content of the African Union, or c) the issue of floor crossing of politicians in legislatures, then we have governance by the people. If we vote for a party, and the biggest party makes all the decisions on all these matters, then we have a bad representative democracy.

We may just as well at present regard genuine peoples' sovereignty as a new, unknown, theoretical concept that we have to develop. We have become used to associating democracy with ministers and politicians. Why? They are not prerequisites for governance by the people – they are the flies in the ointment.

Stated simply, there were countries where people on the local level voted for a private individual (who may have been a member of one of a number of local parties) to represent them in the local government council. Then at the national level they also voted for a candidate (who may have been from one of another number of nationwide parties) to represent them in the national parliament.

This was still not good, but much better than voting for parties. Voting for parties is the modern but bad application of the archaic custom, and by allowing the selfsame parties to operate on all levels of government, we have allowed the system to create political monstrosities. Is it desirable to vote for some unidentified person that the party will appoint and who will make decisions for you regarding both the potholes in your street and international nuclear pollution?

It is better to vote for a person than for a party, simply because it is much easier for the people to exercise some of their sovereignty by holding an individual responsible, and bringing him to book, if necessary. This is especially so in the case of third-tier governments.

Incidentally, nowadays in South Africa, most, if not all, of the local governments are elected by less than 50% of the voters – they are apathetic; in other words, we have *minority* governments! The anomalies of modern democracy are endless.

Instead of voting for a person or party, I would rather cast my vote for something entirely different. On a matter of state that affects me, I would like to vote for what I think is the best one out of a number of *projects*, or the best out of a number of *plans* or the best out of a number of *solutions*, presented to me by experts.

In the US, for all practical purposes, the poor voter has only one of two choices. He can vote either for the Democratic Party or the Republican Party.

In the end it doesn't really matter, the one party is as good or as bad as the other. I believe that their conservative Democrats are more conservative than the liberal Republicans, and the liberal Republicans are more liberal than the conservative Democrats – they are all the same. Most people are born into a party, grow up there and die there.

Cheats and Liars

All over the world many democrats are quietly but very much aware that they have been trapped in an absurd political system from which they seem unable to escape. Why do I say that?

To begin with, a democracy with one dominating party is not a democracy. Period. It is a *unopartocracy* (with the most sincerest of apologies to the highly commendable Fiat). There are many serious issues and policies that affect matters of state, and every one of them potentially holds more than one option regarding how it should be handled, but you as the voter have no choice. The majority party will make the decisions on how all issues and policies will be handled.

Where only two parties dominate the political scene, it is ridiculous to think that for each of the many issues or policies under consideration there will always be only one or two options. Furthermore, are you convinced that only one out of the two parties will satisfactorily represent any one voter's overall opinion on all policies and issues? No.

The *popularity of a policy* is not truthfully reflected by the election results. In simple terms, if you agree with Party A's agricultural policy, but Party B's immigration policy, then for which party do you vote? If you now sacrifice your convictions about agriculture to vote for Party B whose immigration policy you prefer, it means that the election results will not correctly reflect the popularity of the agricultural policy.

The *preferences of voters for parties*, individually and collectively, are also not truthfully reflected by election results. If Party B wins the election, it should mean that all the people who voted for it support all its positions on all issues and policies, which is not true.

Instead, if the voters could regularly (more frequently than only once every five years) vote on issues and policies rather than for parties, the outcomes would be a much fairer reflection of the opinions of every individual and of the total electorate, for example if there were separate elections on agricultural and immigration matters, and on home affairs and foreign affairs!

Even when we vote for a person, as opposed to a party, we are still voting for a politician, and politicians are renowned for being deceivers of the highest order. Politicians agree.

The South African politician Frederik van Zyl Slabbert once said, "There is no way you can get an electoral system that will force a member of parliament to be honest. They lie and cheat in every conceivable electoral system. You will find them, some of them, in any electoral system in the world."[1]

Democratic representative politics is based on numbers, not quality. Politicians and parties have no option but to play the numbers game. It is high time we transcended the borders of our conventional thinking by considering alternative political systems.

* * *

Jimmy asks, "Have you ever thought of the usefulness of voting not only for the person you favour, but also voting to state which person you definitely do NOT want, or LEAST want, in public office?"

"Or the party you least want in public office," Gnu adds.

---

1 *The Citizen*, 14 March 2003.

CHAPTER 15

How the West went Wrong

You earn your rights when you accept your duties and your responsibilities – HRH Princess Anne.

The Question

Pondering the matter of modern democracy, I recalled a chat some time ago with my friend – soldier, writer, naturalist and thinker – Jan Breytenbach. He told me his brother, internationally acclaimed writer, poet and anti-apartheid activist, Breyten Breytenbach, had asked him some tricky questions a while before.

Breyten apparently had been involved for some time in humanitarian and developmental work somewhere in Africa. He was befuddled and disappointed with the behaviour of some of the people for whose benefit he was devoting himself. He then asked Jan, "Where has the West gone wrong?"

What a question to ask, especially against the backdrop of democracy. Democracy is a crazy world. We have TVs, landline and cell phones, sms text messages, walkie-talkies, fax machines, computers, electronic communication through the Internet and email; we have the most sophisticated means of establishing the needs and wishes of the people via attitude and opinion polls. And what do we do?

We vote with a pencil on a slip of paper!

Have you ever heard of any serious investigation into the possibility of adapting such technologies to officially determine the public's opinion on issues, plans or policies, instead of giving assemblies and governments a mandate every four or five years to summarily do what they like?

It would be very interesting if we could stage a technological state-of-the-art referendum on the question of, say, the reinstatement of the death penalty – yes or no. If it were possible, it should be done without too much warning – before the politicians have a chance to brainwash the people.

Can you imagine the calamity and utter confusion in the red liberal PC ranks if the people manifested their choice in favour of the reinstatement of the death penalty! In South Africa I have no doubt that this would be the case. (Whatever the outcome, you'll find that the opinions thus expressed will produce a completely non-racial opinion.)

Why the consternation? Since the PCs oppose the death penalty, it would mean that they would be wrong vis-à-vis the majority of the people. Furthermore, while they persist in claiming that righteousness is on their side, it would mean that the majority is wrong – and that can't be because democracy is based on the principle that the majority opinion is always right in the sense that it must reign supreme! The red liberal PCs and the politicians deny us Real People's Sovereignty and the opportunity of making the decision on this particular issue. They fear defeat and prefer to decide for us that the death penalty is wrong.

There are many other topics on which the public would like to have the right to exercise sovereignty, such as municipal borders – real Governance by the People! The politicians commit treachery by denying us the right to vote on such issues. What we have now is NOT governance by the people.

Ipochreosicracy and Kathikoncracy

Modern democracy has retained only one pair of its essential elements – *freedoms and rights*. The other pair, namely *ipochreosicracy* and *kathikoncracy*, has become obsolete; the red PC commissars have branded them as politically incorrect. That was, and remains wrong – democracy should also embrace governance through citizens' *obligations* and *duties.*

We have charters, bills, manifestos and codes on the citizens' freedoms and rights; and we have a vast number of constitutions, official commissions and NGO institutions, lawyers and other professionals overseeing and safeguarding the citizens' freedoms and rights. This is necessary, good and correct, but lopsided – how many citizens will pass a quick and easy test on their obligations and duties towards society and the state? Our system of governance fails to correct the imbalance. We have a commendable rights culture, but we score badly when it comes to our responsibilities and obligations.

As a matter of fact it is not only the essentials of freedoms and rights, obligations and duties that are important, it is the overall culture of a people that counts. It is of paramount importance that the *essentials of the political system* be in harmony with the *culture of the people* in order for a style of governmental management to be successful.

What happens in practice is that through evolution a people produce a political system naturally in harmony with their culture. So if any political system has to be forced upon a people, then the only way it can work is for the enforcer to bring about a political system in harmony with the people's culture. Failing that, the enforcer must facilitate change in the people's culture in order for them to accept and support the new political system; failing that you have what is known by the man in the street as a balls up.

If the people's culture is to want a strong leader, that is what they will get; and the strong leader, and his government, if any, will suppress them, such as in Zimbabwe. And that's that. So, if you want the people to have a democracy, then the culture of the citizens should change or be changed to enable them to exercise their people's sovereignty properly – it's a matter of do or die.

Democracy has served the British well. This was not necessarily so because of their generic culture, but rather because of their *acquired culture* over the centuries – and because of the English Channel. There were revolutions all over Europe, but they didn't spill over into the UK. However, the British did get the message of the times – democracy – and aligned their ways.

So "Where has the West gone wrong?"

The Answer

Jan told his brother the problem was that the relentless (Western red) liberals enforced the Western model of democracy upon the Africans.

Africans did have cultures and they did have a properly governed civil society. However, instead of facilitating the development of these systems and aligning them to the "modern" times that had suddenly been forced upon them, the colonial and postcolonial West insisted on imposing their own, quite different, brand of political ideas on Africa – different even from their own.

After the French Revolution, a number of significant Western powers democratised. The abolition of slavery soon followed. After the two World Wars they hastened to get rid of their overseas colonial possessions.

Having destroyed Africa's kingdoms, the now PC European colonial powers replaced them with republics – many of whose presidents became little Hitlers – while they themselves retained or reinstated their own monarchies: the UK, Spain, Belgium, and the Netherlands. Sweden, Denmark and others also retained their monarchies.

What would have been wrong if the Western PCs had enabled and assisted the African countries to empower their own royalty and nobility in the modern era? Then these institutions could have survived for the benefit of their people in the same way as King George VI and Queen Elizabeth II, and Queen Wilhelmina and Queen Juliana.

Destroying Africa's royalty is by far not the only sin that the red PCs committed. Busying themselves with all sorts of typical petty PC nonsense, such as gender terminology, they blinded themselves to possible new concepts of democracy.

Exit the Reds, enter the Blues – the Ultimate Ps

It is high time that the aggressive red liberals have introspective, freethinking sessions about their unreasonable and irrational hang-ups and obsessions, or make way for the Blues.

The red liberals have had their chance. They started democracy and then left it to rot. They have added little value to it. Do they, or anyone else, really think that the present type of democracy will last for centuries and millennia?

Are we going to stay in control and develop something sensible and workable, or are we going to be overtaken by disastrous events, international bloodshed and global misery before we wake up?

The red PCs have continued campaigning and stopped thinking. They have no new ideas. Sophisticated fine-tuning of ultra-developed democracies and international laissez-faire will not save mankind from conflict and disaster. The time for the Blues to take over is overdue.

As a Sovereign Peoples Democrat I wish to impress upon you that it is not so much the voting-for-persons-and-parties democracy that we want, but genuine people's sovereignty. The final proof of people sovereignty can be gauged by *who makes the decisions* in the affairs of state at any level of its structures.

Sometimes the people vote for Persons – *persons who will make the decisions* for them. This system is better than the current one, but is still far from satisfactory.

At present in South Africa we vote for political Parties – this system is really bad. For all practical intents and purposes the *governing party makes the decisions.*

The neo-PCs propagate what they call "voting for Principles". There is nothing wrong with this except that it serves very little purpose. It will probably still leave us in the hands of political monsters, albeit parties with principles, which, granted, are better than parties without them. Principles mean nothing, as the saying goes, "If you don't like my principles, I've got others."

We, *the people, should make the decisions.* Those of us who are affected by an issue and those who are knowledgeable on the matter must vote for the last three Ps; we must choose the best one from the optional Projects or Plans or Policies – with no Persons, Parties or Politicians in between.

What the Greeks intended to be the most suitable form of governance has turned into a **DEMONCRACY**. We have strayed far away from the classical Greek concepts of democracy, following trendy notions from time to time, but without adding any value of substance.

Now, if at the UN, we agree that a system of one state one vote is not acceptable, why would one person one vote be acceptable within a national state?

Instead of being overtaken by the Great Divide, let's manage it. We are searching to replace the shambles of the present democracy with a new future dispensation – the New Design. The miracle is over.

*   *   *

Churchill not only indicated that democracy was seriously flawed, but also pointed out that there were "other forms of government that had been tried from time to time". We should review these before hastily coming up with something new.

CHAPTER 16

Excellence in Anarchy and Laissez-faire

Up the Irish

Before we entertain the idea of designing a new "best form of government", let's at least briefly survey some forms other than democracy.

One thing man has not been able to master has been how to organise or unorganise society properly. He has never known how to conduct himself when in a position of authority, or how to behave when subordinated to authority. I suggest we consult the Irish.

The Irish, a small nation, are known for St Patrick, the leprechaun (Jimmy's cousin), Irish stew, *I'll Take You Home Again Kathleen*, Galway Bay and Irish whiskey. The Irish can confuse you. Instead of saying, "That is Greek to me", some people say, "That sounds Irish to me."

The Irish can do what we need to do so much – think unconventionally. Sigmund Freud said that the Irish are one race for whom psychoanalysis is of no use whatsoever. No one can deny that they have produced wise people like George Bernard Shaw, Oscar Wilde, Patrick Fitzgerald, Gerald Fitzpatrick and Paddy.

However, more often than not it is the Irish man in the street or the man on the rail, if you like, who comes up with wit and wisdom.

The Irish actor-manager Anew McMaster was travelling with his company by train one Sunday when they stopped at an isolated rural station. Lowering the window and revealing his extravagant hat and other thespian garb, McMaster inquired of a porter, "What country, friend, is this?" Being an educated Irish railway employee, the porter recognised Viola's opening lines from *Twelfth Night* and promptly gave Shakespeare's own reply: "This is Illyria – lady."[1]

1 Rees, 1980.

The wisest of them all was Paddy, who was shipwrecked and eventually flushed out half-drowned and unconscious onto the beach of an isolated island. The friendly locals came to his rescue and resuscitated him. When he opened his eyes he looked at the inquisitive faces around him and demanded, "Is there a government on this island?" They looked at him in silent amazement. He blinked and asserted, "Well, if there is, I'm against it!"

So the Irishman Paddy is against government, and the Englishman Churchill said that democracy is the worst form of government except for all the others. What now?

Of course, Churchill and Paddy are both right, especially Paddy. There is no such thing as a good form of government. The first and last good one was the government of the Garden of Eden. Let's call it Utopia. This lasted until the Fall of Man. After the Fall all other forms of government became bad for some reason or another – various dystopias.

Dystopia is the evil twin of Utopia, and a synonym for Cacotopia, meaning a form of government where something is as it shouldn't be, or something is not as it should be. Most dystopias evolved because strong governments weren't penalised for their successes in becoming strong, and where the people will be happy whether they like it or not.

I will courteously refrain from labelling governments according to their different brands of dystopia and stick to their flattering conventional names.

Up the Dictators

Supposedly some of the more popular forms of government are dictatorships, anarchies, monarchies, theocracies, bureaucracies, technocracies, plutocracies and ochlocracies.

Perhaps we shouldn't talk of *popular* forms of government; we should more correctly refer to forms of government *most used* or even more precisely, forms of governments *most abused*. All governments have one most common characteristic – they have no built-in protection against becoming abusive, even in the unlikely event of their trying to avoid this folly.

It is generally accepted that a dictatorship can be bad. A dictator operating under the guise of democracy is evil. But many people agree that a *benevolent dictator* can be the best. This type of ruler can do long-term planning in the best interest of the country and its people because, unless he is assassinated, he will probably govern for a long time.

President Bongo is such a benevolent dictator. He has already been in power for 38 years. Danny Kaye and the Andrews Sisters used to sing his praise a long time ago: *Bongo, Bongo, Bongo, he don'wanna leave the Congo, o no no no no-no ...I refuse to go... I'll stay right here...*[2] He donated lots of his own money to the people, especially to needy students. At the end of 2005 he started a new term of office for another seven years. We meet him again later.

A democratically elected party and its leader plan only for the period until the next election, four or five years in advance, if they are so inclined. They may be ousted. However, if you run a business according to such short-term planning, it will probably run into serious trouble.

Those who really carry the can in a democracy are the civil administrators – the long-serving bureaucrats. Bureaucracies usually plan for approximately the next 15 to 40 years, but monarchies plan for dynasties in the future.

Dictators sometimes have the habit of forming their own international cliques. This arrangement is good for international order and stability, but bad for the suppressed people.

The uninformed may indignantly ask, "With benevolent dictators and whatnot, what's happened to freedom?"

---

2 Sigman & Hiliard. *Put It There Pal!* Compact disc, Bourne Music, 2000.

Laissez-faire

There isn't really such a thing as freedom. If there were, and it is absolute freedom you want, I recommend a kind of anarchy. The highly commendable feature of *anarchy* is that it has no rules and rulers, only token guides at worst. Man performs at his excellent best in an environment and climate of freedom and competition.

It is unorganised anarchy that provides the highest level of freedom – freedom of movement, free enterprise, and whatever you can think of that can be free.

In modern times, anarchies strangely became quite unpopular with spoil-sport intellectual red liberals. As a result of their uninvited interference, anarchy lost its excellent advantage, in fact the very reason for its existence – excellence through unrestrained freedom.

In return for the PCs' imposition of constraints, such as the abolition of free trade, which includes such lucrative capitalistic practices as corruption and fraud, the outgoing anarchies were inundated with lots of human rights. Sadly, however, they had to forfeit some of the rights they previously enjoyed:

the right of the individual to guaranteed successful self-defence;
the right of the citizen to take pre-emptive action to safeguard life and property;
the right of the individual to effective retaliation;
the right to self-organised collective community protection; and
the right of choice of association

"And," says Tarentaal out of the blue, giving Gnu a nasty look, "choice of dis-association."

There are encouraging signs though that anarchy may already be making a comeback:

laissez-faire is speedily becoming rampant;
crime is winning the war against outmoded restricting police practices, while security companies are taking over;
dictators are falling out of favour;
restricting international borders are disappearing, illegal aliens are exercising their rights to become the friends of the people – and rob them;
merit and worth are being sidelined and are beginning to disappear; and
the abhorrent human weaknesses of pride and self-esteem are becoming outmoded.

On the other hand, unfortunately, it seems as if the remaining traditional and self-respecting anarchies are fading. The last one to succumb, to a highly questionable type of magnum democracy that centralises vastly spread diversities, is the Democratic Republic of Congo.

A cunning set-up is the anarchy of Somalia with its government in Kenya.

Organised anarchy also looks quite attractive, as long as it is not organised by warlords, but sadly, by its very nature, it curbs freedom somewhat. You may actually have to stop at red traffic lights, regardless. You may also, although it may seem quite unreasonable, be charged if you burnt down the mayor of Pretoria's house should he persist in supporting the Western Province Stormers and in adopting the name "Tshwane".

* * *

"I have a friend who prefers a monarchy," says Jimmy. "He told me, 'I like a strong leader. We had very successful true blue-blooded kings in our history. They didn't take any nonsense. It suits our culture.'"

"Unfortunately they are now outmoded," replied Jimmy.

He was not entirely right, as we'll soon see.

CHAPTER 17

The Yak and the Gnu

Up the Danes

Jimmy's friend had his say about his version of a strong leader, a monarch. A friend of mine, a metropolitan Portuguese, Manuel Chorão de Carvalho, also favours a monarch, but a democratic, non-executive or constitutional monarch, somewhat like the British monarch. He said a king is a national symbol, and even if it so happens that he is infantile or a moron, it doesn't matter, because no one can grab power – that's paramount. The constitution remains protected; it ensures the smooth transition of power.

As in the case of dictators, it is not necessary for me to promote monarchies too much. In spite of democracy having become a magic word in liberal circles, dictators and monarchs are still very much alive and well and living in many parts of the world.

Ms Tarentaal says, "I don't like just any common king. I prefer a stately queen such as the one in Denmark."

Popular Queen Margrethe comes from the Danish royal house dating back to before 958 AD. Her code for successful royal governance is:

accept your destiny;
go to your people and show them you care, but don't be shy or conceited;
be positive;
be wholly engaged in what you are doing;
be philosophical about the press. don't waste time on political correctness;
be yourself; and
know what you are and believe in what you are doing.[1]

---

1 *Hello* magazine, January 2003.

What more, or less, do we want? Long live the queen!

Denmark is only one of 43 monarchies existing in the world in 2003. Queen Elizabeth II and King Juan Carlos I reign over parliamentary monarchies. There are 23 monarchies listed as *constitutional*.

Only three are *absolute* monarchs: Sultan Qabus ibn Sa'id of Oman, King Fahd bin 'Abdulaziz of Saudi Arabia and King Mswati III of Swaziland. Emir Sheik Hamad ibn Khalifa al-Thani is the *traditional* monarch of Qatar. If you criticise King Mswati III and you're an honest person, you have no excuse for not challenging his other two big blue-blood brothers.

One of the greatest nations, the Japanese, has the oldest existing monarchy. From his Chrysanthemum throne Emperor Naruhito reigns over one of the most successful and best run countries in the world. And the monarchy is destined for long life. A government panel of ten members from academic, legal, business and political circles recommended that the emperor's first-born child, regardless of sex, should be next in line to the throne. The legitimacy (of the emperor) will not weaken as long as succession by the imperial line is maintained.

Much like dictator cliques, many monarchies are interrelated or they sometimes form a happy international royal elite. This could be good for regional stability, but bad for their subjects.

Theo-, Pluto- and Other -cracies

A *bureaucracy* looks like any other form of governance. As a matter of fact, a bureaucracy is much like a government and its civil administration without the government. It may have a head of state, preferably a monarch, but definitely not a conventional council of ministers.

There were times in the not too distant past when nations such as the Italians and the French lived through long periods with no government. No one cared, and life went on as usual – and they prospered. The bureaucracies kept functioning and so admirably administered these countries that the citizens were mostly not consciously aware that they had no government.

A *technocracy* is government by experts. It could combine well with a bureaucracy observing the rule of law. Both maintain continuity and are facilitated by well-trained people with lots of experience.

Another form of governance is *theocracy* such as we had in Tibet and still have in many Muslim countries or provinces. Gnu claims the Dalai Lama cared more for the yak than the government of KwaZulu-Natal cares for the wildebeest.

A theocracy does not necessarily mean that the ecclesiastical authority is also the government of a country. It could simply mean that whoever the government is, it reigns in accordance with the national religion – it is the constitution, laws, rules and regulations, such as in Iran.

A *plutocracy* by definition is governance by the wealthy. There are two types. The *genuine* plutocracies are the less dangerous of the two. Examples may be found among Eastern and Middle Eastern countries ruled by the rich and super rich. In some instances the plutocratic form of government is combined with royalty and/or religion. Although they are not necessarily democracies, these countries have a reputation for good governance – except among people who dislike Muslim laws enforced by the religion police.

Some heads of state use money to govern, others govern to make money. The following is a list from Forbes.com showing the richest heads of state.[2]

Name	Country	Est. Net worth
King Fahd Bin Abdul Aziz Alsaud	Saudi Arabia	$25 billion
Sultan Haji Hassanal Bolkiah	Brunei	$14.3 billion
Hans Adams II	Liechtenstein	$2.2 billion
Saddam Hussein	Iraq	$2 billion
Queen Elizabeth II	United Kingdom	$660 million
Yasir Arafat	Palestinian Authority	$200 million
Queen Beatrix Wilhelmina	Netherlands	$260 million
Fidel Castro	Cuba	$150 million

Some haven't much to brag about; they inherited their money through generations, such as Hans Adams and Queen Beatrix. Others earned their money through hard work in their own lifetime only after they had reached the top, such as Hussein, Arafat and Castro. They are the star performers.

P.S. *The Weekly Telegraph* crossword no. 642 posed the following clue: "Government by thieves". You will find the answer a little later; it contains 11 letters. I don't know if I am helping you or throwing a red herring in your way, but the thieves will deny that anything like this exists.

The *pseudo* plutocrats are the real menace. They are not found in the top executive ranks of governments or political parties. They are gutless, selfish people who refuse to accept the responsibility of public office.

2 Royals & Rulers. 15 March 2004. http://www. Forbes.com 3/17/2007.

These super influential moguls achieve their political aims through the power of money. They are semi-covert operators who finance governments or projects through parties, institutes, heritages, foundations, associations and other NGOs. A good example is, yes you guessed it, George Soros. They also use financial resources against governments.

Second from last we have the *ochlocracy*. This is also known by the experts as *mob rule*. It is a cousin of *populistocracy* – like some people in South Africa who want the courts to be accountable to the masses.

And finally there are the quite commendable *race federations*, and *canton* systems.

At this point it should be noted that some of these styles of government could come in *combinations*. It also happens that different forms of government have some common features, while some countries have basically the same system, but show different characteristics.

One obvious example of a combination is a monarchy with a democracy such as in the UK. An example of a common feature is a technocracy and a bureaucracy both upholding the rule of law – a good call, a good combination.

In the case of the same system with characteristics differing from country to country, there could be a democracy in the form of a unitary state with centralised political power at the top like Zimbabwe and South Africa. On the other hand, there could be a democratic country in the form of a federation or confederation with political power decentralised to lower levels somewhat like the US, Canada, Germany, Spain and Switzerland.

What appears to be the ideal would be a constitutional monarch heading a combination of a techno-bureaucracy that respects the rule of law and has decentralised authority. Unlike a conventional democracy, this form of government scientifically forecasts the future and uses trained and experienced experts to plan ahead for the country in periods of up to four generations and more.

In such a dispensation what is it that you have in mind for the politicians?

Nothing. Jimmy, Tarentaal and Gnu nod in unison, "Politics must disappear, and that is a prerequisite for any happy society."

Two countries nearly got this form of governance right, but it's a matter of so near and yet so far. Both their heads of state succeeded admirably in abolishing political parties. They are Museveni's Uganda and Mswati III's Swaziland.

Uganda unfortunately has no monarch. There can be little doubt that Museveni would amend the constitution to enable him to remain president – for how long? How is he going to be succeeded? I don't have to remind you of the horrors of some of Museveni's predecessors, Milton Obote and Idi Amin.

Already towards the end of 2005 at Valletta, Commonwealth secretary-general Don McKinnon expressed concerns about *democracy* in Uganda, where Museveni, aiming to extend his 20-year rule, charged the opposition leader with treason before a military tribunal. At the same time at Midrand in South Africa, the High Commissioner of the UK, Paul Boateng, told the Pan African Parliament "things have fallen apart". He said that the evils of colonialism in Africa had been replaced by ignorance, corruption and despotism.[3]

Swaziland has a monarch, but unfortunately he is an absolute monarch.

It is a pity Uganda didn't have a constitutional monarch. Can't Museveni restore Uganda's royal family? It is a pity Swaziland's Mswati III isn't a constitutional monarch with an elected executive prime minister. If there is anything wrong with these two countries, it is not because they don't have any political parties.

We may now be tempted to go to the drawing board to begin The New Design for better living. However, if we tackle this head over heels, we may fall into the same traps as the architects of democracy of the past. They could never have come up with the nonsense they produced if they had given nature and science due consideration. We don't want to make the same mistake – let's be circumspect.

*   *   *

P.S. Answer to crossword clue: KLEPTOCRACY – a mere hypothetical concept.

---

3 *The Citizen*, 26 November 2005.

CHAPTER 18

Man of the Veld

Exit Science – Enter Politics

Okay, Churchill was right. In Western and some other countries democracy has probably been a more acceptable form of government than the alternatives – up to now. However, do we honestly think that, unlike most other man-made arrangements, ancient democracy was custom made to serve the world at large until eternity? We have already seen that the adaptation of the old democracy to the modern world constitutes a serious trap for mankind.

Are we just going to pirouette around the political landmines in the field of international globalisation, or are we going to apply our minds? We need a new system, but let's not be too hasty. We shouldn't make the same mistakes as in the past. Do we know who and what was responsible for democracy – ancient and modern – stagnating and outliving its usefulness, and why?

G.A Rauche identifies exactly why democracy, if not political science as a whole, became completely bogged down. He maintains that historically "democracy" changed from a scientific concept to a political concept. He is absolutely right and that is where the problem started![1]

Democracy in its present form is not the end result of a planned and scientifically developed process. Granted, through the ages science did play a role in influencing types of governance, but where and how did political science fit into the overall science scene?

My uncle taught me about science. He was not a man in the street. He was a man of the veld. He said science was the search for knowledge of the truth. God created the cosmos, the galaxies, and our own solar system and planet Earth with everything on it. From this point of departure he broadly

1 Burgess, 1988.

divided science into two branches. Based on God's creation, nature, we have the *natural sciences*, and based on man's way of doing things – his culture – we have the *cultural sciences*.

The natural sciences embrace the physical and exact sciences. I have heard some people calling them the pure or perfect sciences: astronomy, physics, chemistry, mathematics and the like.

The cultural sciences include all the human and social sciences, also called the inexact, imperfect and impure sciences: sociology, psychology and such others, and of course political science – the most imperfect of the lot.

On planet Earth the *exact* is generally a true science. It does not vary. Whether an Inca, Russian or Japanese drops a stone from a building in Central America, Moscow or Tokyo 50 or more years apart from each other, the laws of gravity remain constant and valid.

In contrast, the perceived truth found in the human sciences is inconsistent. It varies from place to place, from people to people, and from time to time. An Englishman and a Cantonese in more or less the same situation may behave totally differently.

In the past, everyone, including scientists, accepted that women were inferior to men. Now they are regarded as equals – they never get it right! However, a 2003 survey revealed that nearly half the Chinese people believe it reasonable for husbands to administer corporal punishment to their wives – when they won't listen.[2]

The exact scientists progressed. They excelled. The social scientists marked time. They muddled.

The natural scientists, past and present, hailed their predecessors and progressively built on their discoveries – and continually introduced new or improved products. The political scientists didn't build on the experience and knowledge gathered by their predecessors – or not that one could notice it – and only talked about them.

When the natural scientists came up with new knowledge, the technologists capitalised on the new ideas, and together with business entrepreneurs they devised practical applications for their use – like motorcars and radios in lieu of buggies and smoke signals. The political scientists only researched, observed and reported. They didn't look for improvements. If they did, they never had them implemented.

The reason for this tragic state of affairs is that the natural scientists were only slowed down from time to time by PCs such as certain religious practitioners, while the political scientists, by contrast, got completely stopped in

2 *The Citizen*, 11 December 2003.

their tracks and kept there by the PCs. The crux is that the poor political scientists were, and are, completely dependent on the ruling politicians to implement their ideas. Now, can you imagine any self-respecting politician demolishing his own livelihood and holy ground! This is still our problem today. However, the main problem remains PC.

Toe the Line and Die

During the days of Galileo (1564–1642), the politically correct PC philosophers incited the clergy into believing that Galileo's scientific theories were blasphemous.

While Galileo was professor of mathematics at Pisa, he demonstrated to his students that Aristotle's belief that speed of fall is proportional to weight was wrong: he dropped two objects of different weight simultaneously from the Leaning Tower of Pisa. They hit the ground at almost the same time. During his life he built a thermoscope and a geometrical compass; he invented the microscope and built a telescope, discovered the satellites of Jupiter and observed the sunspots. That was too much for the PCs; they stepped in and eventually he was sentenced to life imprisonment commuted to permanent house arrest. He was compelled to solemnly abjure his theories.

He wrote his last book, became blind and died.

Let's now start our research on how the political scientists dropped us and got bogged down, while the natural scientists made steady progress.

Classical scientists from the East, Middle East, Asia Minor and the Mediterranean set out to prove some of their predecessors' theses incorrect, and at the same time to build on those that they regarded as correct, and to come up with new ones. Socrates (c. 470–399 BC) was an outstanding and versatile scientist. Plato was Socrates' pupil, Aristotle was Plato's pupil and, incidentally, Aristotle was the tutor of Alexander the Great – the greatest general of all time.

One remarkable feature was that some of these scientists, such as Aristotle, directly or indirectly left a heritage of knowledge of the natural as well as the social sciences. Aristotle excelled in studies of methodology and nature, and produced doctrines on physics and natural philosophy, biology, psychology and ethics, logic and metaphysics.

Every one of the more modern scientists has had a favourite classical forerunner. Darwin remarked that the intellectual heroes of his own time "were mere schoolboys compared to old Aristotle".[3]

Aristotle was a "walkie-talkie" – he conducted discussions on the walk. His Lyceum became known as the strolling school. ("Not to be confused with the Troll School for Higher Learning," Jimmy interjects.) Many present-day scholars still honour him as an initiator of the modern natural sciences.

Aristotle observed that it is generally the poor who place a high value on human rights, whereas it doesn't much concern the rich, and many social scientists even today regard him as a forerunner of modern political science.

He was not "with it" and "in" with the red PCs of that time, and they got hold of him: at Alexander's death, 323 BC, Aristotle found himself connected to the wrong crowd; he fled Athens – just in time – for charges of "impiety" were brought against him; the same charges, which, 76 years earlier, had led to the death of Socrates. He did not live long in exile: he died within the year.[4]

The natural scientists have come a long way. They are now continuously exploring space. Millennia have gone by and what do the political scientists explore? The rich and the poor.

3 *Aristotle*. Encarta online encyclopaedia. Microsoft. 2005.
4 Landry, *Aristotle* (*BC, 384–322*). 2004. http://www.blupete.com/Literature/Biographies/ Philosophy/Aristotle.htm 3/17/2007.

The natural scientists used rational thinking as an instrument to analyse the law of nature – and achieved success. The political scientists set out to determine how corrupt societies should be demolished and replaced by newer and better social orders – and failed.

Political scientists' thinking was restricted by the petty red PC demands of the day. They repeatedly thought that if you replace an *evil* dictator with another sort of *good* government, everything would come right. We know now that the chances are very good that the *new* government will also in time deteriorate to the same level as the previous one, and the longer it stays in power, the worse it will get. The liberals' theories could work only if the new government was something like a god, but power, wealth and status corrupt the best human beings or governments on earth. We need something new!

* * *

Medical scientists have found preventative and curative measures for the major diseases of our time – yellow fever, cholera, polio and tuberculosis. They are working hard at HIV/Aids and they will find a solution...

"Uncle Joe," Jimmy asks, "when are we going to reveal our cure for the diseases of political governance?"

"We're getting there, my little friend. You undoubtedly noticed that we have concluded all we had to say on forms of government, and now we can move on to functions of government."

"Of course – there is a solution."

CHAPTER 19

Man in the Dock

People need service providers, not political controllers – Jimmy the Reed.[1]

Protecting Criminals and Robbing Society

We, the people, should force PC governments to relinquish the firm political control they have over our sociocultural activities. They pass legislation that is supposed to restrict criminals in a soft manner "so as not to destroy society's normal civil liberties".

However, through Information Acts of parliament, politicians intensify their collection of spy data about innocent citizens without thinking twice. In this way they invade our privacy more than ever before, making George Orwell's ominous prophecy of "Big brother is watching you" a real threat.

Governments have robbed communities and societies of their right to manage their personal, communal and societal affairs. The Soviet Union and Cuba were notorious for this type of behaviour. Ministers of state now control the games people used to organise and play, like cricket, swimming, hockey, athletics and football. To this end, they misuse the civil service departments, which they wrongly regard as their property.

We didn't have a minister of sports until recently. I suppose a political minister of religion, or religious minister of hobbies and leisure time utilisation could be the next. I have it on good authority that chess and chequerboard colours are also being reviewed.

At present we sponsor governmental structures accommodating presidents, deputy presidents, prime ministers (or chairpersons of councils of ministers), cabinets and cabinet committees, assorted parliaments, higher

---

1 De Umhlanga, J the Reed. 2006. PAFS for grass roots. *Tokoloshe Times.* 1 May.

and lower houses, councils of provinces, congresses, senates, madam speakers, madam chairs, and the like – the monuments of political decadence. If we are not happy with these political controllers, what do we do?

Actually we don't have to do much. It's more a matter of undo. We should merely empty the structures that accommodate the redundant politicians. (I have a proposal for the utilisation of the so vacated edifices, but we come to that a little later.)

We need service providers, not political controllers. If governments disappeared overnight, it would take a long time before we noticed it. But if the civil-municipal services vanished, we'd start crying early in the morning.

Once we have undone the archaic political structures, we should privatise many more of government's functions. We could assign some of them to independent permanent commissions. Many functions and tasks of the civil departments could be allocated or subcontracted to the private sector. This process has already begun, such as with the issue of roadworthy certificates; we must just accelerate it.

You will probably ask how then do we go about finding the few essential structures that we do need?

We don't just create organisational structures and build office blocks simply because it seems to be conventional to do so. We first have to decide what society *needs* and *how* it can best be served. Then we must establish what *functions* should be performed, and consequently what *structures* will be required for doing the job.

Many years ago society didn't need to be organised much because it consisted only of Adam and Eve, and later family groups and clans. But with growing concentrations of populations, the people had to develop some system to perform the basic functions of community and societal living for them.

I don't like calling the system "government". So Jimmy, who is an expert at conjuring up new words, hit the nail on the head with the "People's Administrative Facilitating Service" – PAFS, to perform these functions. Well done, James!

Let's now have a closer look at the basic functions this facilitative service should perform.

The Rights of Sperm and a Roof over Your Head

What we want to achieve in the idyllic scenario where politicians no longer exist is the *well-being of the people* – the people must be happy. All the functions of the PAFS should be directed towards this goal.

Reflecting on the basic truths about what the people need I recalled a television interview I had seen quite some time ago. The man in the dock was Lee Kuan Yew, the prime minister of Singapore, and the interviewer may have been Larry King.

Until shortly before this interview, Singapore had been an almost unknown city-state not highly rated as a member of the international community of countries in that part of the world. However, under the leadership of Lee Kuan Yew, the Singapore Committee on Productivity had been formed on 23 April 1981. Following the prime minister's example and philosophy, Singapore achieved the world's fourth highest per capita real income in a very short time and became one of the four economic "Tigers" of South East Asia together with South Korea, Taiwan and Hong Kong.

At one stage during the interview Lee Kuan Yew had to answer some queer questions, mainly regarding the finer Western PC-type concepts of democracy, human rights, gender issues and so on. He listened in silence before responding.

At the end he replied. He said he had a dream, and when he assumed office he set himself goals: every household in his country should be able to attain the position where the family could care for itself and everyone would have

food to eat
a roof over their heads
clothes to wear, and
suitable education.

In fact, he summed up all the basic necessities of human life – and the priorities of a facilitating service.

He continued by asserting that only after he had achieved all these goals would he be in a position to think about the secondary PC whims of modern democratic values.

This type of argument about vital basic requirements versus seemingly superficial social PC issues bothered me for some time. A do-good international activist with a social conscience that he, she or it developed on home territory must analyse the country targeted for his, her or its benevolence very thoroughly. The activist should appraise the country's circumstances and available resources for his charitable work, and should acquire a comprehensive appreciation of the peoples' culture, their state of mind, emotions and essential material needs. There may just possibly be more important things for them than the rights of sperm, of unborn babies, of same-sex married couples and their rights to adopt children, or the right to in-vitro fertilisation.

By the turn of the millennium South Africa had become the playing field and testing ground for zealous Western-driven legislation – PC castles – from trying to persuade pipe-smoking Xhosa women to gently refrain from this vulgar habit, to trying to convince cattle farmers – victims of cross-border stock theft – to surrender their arms.

The PCs will use this legislation as models, together with other devious arm-twisting tactics to achieve their aims elsewhere in Africa. They will tighten the PC screws of gender terminology, as well as refine restrictions on health and safety, and professional hunting, on the rest of Africa – a continent in dire need of nourishment, shelter, clothes, jobs and education.

Once people have roofs over their heads and enough food, then you can try to tell them to call the presiding official of the local town council a chairperson instead of madam chair.

So now we can categorise the functions of the facilitating administrators of earthling societies into five main domains. Let us start at the beginning – well almost.

The second priority of the People's Administrative Facilitating Service (PAFS) would be Bread and Butter issues, as well as shelter, and all the essential municipal services, such as the provision of lighting, potable water and sanitation.

The third priority should be the Preservation of our immediate natural surrounds. (If every community preserved its surroundings, we would safeguard our planet, our moon, our sun, our galactic system and the others.) Our planet Earth should be secured for the infinite future with all its living creatures, flora and fauna.

"We have not inherited this planet from our fathers; we have borrowed it from our children," interjects Gnu, but Jimmy whispers in my ear it was actually Ralph Waldo Emerson who said that.

The fourth priority should be the Upbringing, Education and Training of our species for its own pleasure, and to promote our survival and our role in the preservation of the planet. This should include how to live as an individual, and in communion with others, including all animals and plants, as well as how to adapt to forthcoming changing scenarios caused either by nature or mankind.

The fifth priority would be to Protect what we preserve. A community or society cannot accept responsibility for National Security and Public Safety. For this function we need a national defence force and a police service, run by the government.

However, the first priority would be to facilitate Growth and Development to produce and preserve the resources necessary for achieving the other priorities.

The new local, provincial, and national people's facilitative administrations are vitally important service providers, no more and no less – for the people, by the people and responsible to the people. These new civil administrators (of PAFS) will be paid by the people. They will not work for the government, nor will they be responsible to it.

* * *

Tarentaal: "Now we know what our New Design should deliver, but we need a bit more detail starting with the Preservation of our environment."

Gnu: "Ms Tarentaal, have you got children, chicks?"

Tarentaal: "I said 'preservation', not 'procreation'. And I have no chicks."

Gnu: "Jimmy, have you got a chick?"

"Yes, I have a bevy."

"Beverley who?"

"A bevy of beauties."

"Are you polygamous?"

"No! I'm a monogamist; I have only one bevy, and you?"

"I have none."

"And what about Daisy?"

"Well, what about her?"

Tarentaal: "My goodness gracious me, too-teu, too-teu, too-teu...chit-chit-tchirrr-tchirr-tchirrrrr."

And she starts her take-off roll for the woods in the grassland for a good night's rest.

95

CHAPTER 20

The Lion King and the Mantle

The environmental pressures of our time could be the very pressures behind a new evolutionary leap – not another expansion in brain size, but of a consciousness and an intelligence that can redefine our sense of history, our sense of Nature and our sense of co-existence – Ian McCallum, the amazing medical doctor, psychiatrist, naturalist, and rugby Springbok fullback[1]

Johnny Come Lately

Creation put us all here on planet Earth, one after the other.

First were the plants and then the animals. They are naturally quite ignorant and thus innocent.

Gnu claims animals came before birds. Ms Tarentaal says, "No, Mr Gnu, *Numida meleagris* were first."

Jimmy puts his foot into it: "To kill two birds with one stone, you are both wrong, the fish were first."

Tarentaal insists Jimmy retract his offensive statement, and continues: "Yes, the fish were first – flying fish!"

Gnu snorts and concedes, "Yes, I believe you, flying fish and birds of a feather flock together!"

Jimmy puts an end to the bickering with his favourite quote of the oath of Alexandre Dumas' three musketeers, "Come on guys, one for all and all for one – people came last."

Man came much later than plants and animals. He is endowed with a higher intelligence. Man, the Johnny come lately, reigns supreme. He super-

---

1 McCallum, 2005

vises the animals, plants *et al*. But man isn't better than the animals because he is more intelligent. In fact, it makes him worse. Dangerous.

Jimmy says that intelligence is as good or bad as its possessor. And I am sure you too will agree that a clever villain has a very good chance of being a better thug than a stupid one.

"The denuding of tropical forests, acid rain, air and water pollution, and diminishing wilderness areas, the introduction of alien vegetation and green house warming all have one thing in common – the human factor," states Ian McCallum.

Through agriculture, industry, mining, urbanisation, and communication networks, man has left a ruinous mess in his wake. He has destroyed a horrifying number of plants, animals, and whole nature systems.

It is a terrible self-confessed shame, but there is no doubt that planet Earth would have continued to exist in a much better way without man. The more people we continue to make, the more animals and plants we continue to kill.

It's a fact and it's evil.

My other uncle said he sometimes found it difficult to believe that it was God who created Earth and everything on it, because an authentic god wouldn't have put a being here who is obsessed with destroying it all.

Why shouldn't the animals rule and un-rule themselves and the world, as they did for millions of years? With their sense of freedom and natural rightness – live and let live, die and let die – they would do a better job without our fantastic level of intelligence.

How much longer can Africa's virgin habitats survive brutal rape by ever-increasing ravaging hordes of *Homo sapiens*?

> Good versus evil is ever present –
> The animals are good we are not
> We domesticate animals, such as cattle
> We breed them as fast as we can
> We make them stand still
> And feed them as fast as we can
> To get them as fat as they can
> So that we can butcher them
> As soon as we can
> And devour them –
> Every day!
> We tin the bloody leftovers and sell them
> To satisfy the appetite of other humans
> Who haven't easy access to dripping flesh of young cows
> Or we deliver the tinned meat free of charge
> To other people we breed
> Unable to survive on their own
> We are not only dispensable, a liability –
> We are the undesirables.
> Let's put things right.

The great apes ought to have the protection of the same laws that forbid the murder, abduction, assault, rape and torture of humans. Morally, the boundary between them and us is indefensible. Chimpanzees and their close relatives, the bonobos (dwarf chimps), should be reclassified as members of the genus *Homo*. We should all be members of the same genus, *Homo sapiens*, *Homo troglodytes* and *Homo paniscus*.[2]

In Nepal, the law protects rhesus monkeys and for over 2000 years they have had complete free reign in the temples of the capital city of Kathmandu. And Nepal didn't come to a standstill. And neither has India with its holy cows.

---

2 *The Citizen*, 26 May 2003.

The boundary between us is indefensible.

Source: *Rodney Brindameur/National Geographic Image Collection*

The Lioness Queen and the Potion

However, I have a more comprehensive idea for stopping the abuse of chimps and all other living creatures, fauna and flora – one that will have lasting results.

My idea entails persuading red PCs in South Africa with contacts in the government to contrive legislation involving every nature reserve and game park of whatever kind. New laws will require that every one of these areas will rapidly and progressively be expanded in ever-widening concentric circles until they cover the entire land. The animals will rule the whole country. His Majesty King Lion takes the reins.

Animals were always well organised, but they never had any use for political parties. The Lion King, as suggested by the Lioness Queen, will establish completely new isolated territorial enclaves – exclusive unnatural reserves for human habitation, politicians excluded. Being a king he will put traditional human royalty in charge of every enclave.

For the entertainment of the royal feline family and their animal subjects, including those liberated from the reserves and game parks, the king will furthermore establish a number of smaller, especially selected, eco-friendly confines. These will accommodate the politicians in environments to which they should easily acclimatise, such as the present Union Buildings and edifices housing parliament, as I promised in an earlier chapter. These restricted areas will be homological gardens, not to be confused with Zoocracies, and will be for the benefit of holidaymakers.

His Majesty will approve a Reorientation and Development Programme contrived at a series of PC workshops called "*bosberade*". The aim of the programme will be to re-empower and fast-track the de-domesticated animals such as cattle and pets, as well as those liberated from the zoological gardens.

The deserted structures at the now defunct game parks will be declared national historical monuments.

The Lion King has hinted that he will not wear a mantle of human skin around his shoulders.

The Lioness Queen also is not mad about mantillas, but what worries me is that according to confidential information obtained by Ms Tarentaal, Her Royal Highness believes that human testicles with peri-peri make a potent potion – with Afro disiacal qualities.

* * *

In preserving our natural heritage the PC governments and do-gooders haven't got their priorities right. Instead of advocating the restriction of the population to promote sustainability, alleviate poverty and preserve nature, they prefer to harass harmless anglers, professional hunters and gun owners. These people in their wildest dreams could not wreak havoc on the environment like the creators of more cities and more slums for more people. Nature is not an impediment on human existence, it is our lifeline.

In 2004, tourism made up 11% of the national economy and was the second largest contributor. However, man's disregard for his environment is evidenced by what has happened since the signing of the protocol at the first Earth Summit Convention in Rio in 1992: there has already been a lamentable loss in species worldwide, and our wetlands have decreased by 50%.[3]

Politicians don't care! They say all the right things and sign all the right papers, and that's all. They may be around for five years only. Have you ever heard of a party losing an election because of preservation issues in Africa? This is the problem we face – Jimmy, Tarentaal, Gnu, you and I.

Gnu whistles and snorts. Jimmy says, "We need long-range planning and solutions. Politicians never do it. They are the people whom we should subject to the long-term plans. Care of ecology and the environment should be wrested from political claws. We should place this responsibility in the understanding embrace of competent experts, in the same way as we put macro-finance in the hands of governors of the central banks."

Tarentaal adds, "Perhaps then the Americans will be more cooperative about global air pollution, so that Gnu can breathe fresh air and I can fly the clear skies."

* * *

Legislation can do much for the Preservation of the environment in the short term, but Upbringing, Education and Training are absolute musts for the long term.

---

3 *The Citizen*, 20 May 2004.

CHAPTER 21

Grannies are Better

The first half of our lives is ruined by our parents and the second half by our children – Clarence Darrow.[1]

The Scientech Fast Lane and the Social Slow Lane

The Peoples Administrative Facilitating Service (PAFS) should help us maintain harmonious cohabitation. We should all know how to play our roles in a free, competitive and productive society.

We should acquire this know-how through Upbringing, Education and Training. When a person leaves home, school and college, he should be armed with the will and ability to think. He should be prepared to make decisions and to accept responsibility for the consequences. He should also have gathered a basic general knowledge and some important skills – ready to survive and enjoy life.

Jimmy: "Why don't you just say:

We should keep our young alive – until they do it themselves.

We should encourage our children to use their brains – until they begin to tell us to use ours, which happens quite soon.

We should help them to align with nature, life and living – until we need re-adjustment ourselves."

Together with the coming generations we travel the dual carriageway of life, sometimes in the fast lane of *science* and *technology*, but mostly along the slow, taxing road of societal coexistence.

"Scientech" has provided the lifeline for man from time to time in the past and will do so again in times to come. Jimmy invented this name for the fast

---

1 Prochnow & Prochnow, 1979.

lane. It is an imperative among the mainstream of formal educational disciplines.

The lifeline:
"It is science alone that can solve the problems of hunger and poverty, insanitation and illiteracy, of superstition and deadening custom and tradition, of vast resources running to waste, of a rich country inhabited by starving people... Who indeed could afford to ignore science today? At every turn we have to seek its aid... The future belongs to science and to those who make friends with science." – Jawaharlal Nehru[2]

But scientech demands that we negotiate the waves that it creates.

The waves:
During the past 75 years the world has experienced more and bigger waves of scientific and technological innovation than ever before in the history of mankind. "Ninety percent of all the scientists who have ever lived have still not died," said Alan Lindsay Mackay in 1969. And since then the tempo of new discoveries has continued to rise at a rate never before experienced. The effects of every wave are so sweeping that man continually and in quick succession has to struggle to adapt to the consequences of these in everyday life.

Our spiritual and cultural adaptation, however, lags far behind scientific and technological developments. As a result we find it progressively more difficult to negotiate the successive waves of scientech innovations. What now? Our salvation is at stake. Effective upbringing should instil the values we need for successful living; progressive education should present essential new knowledge, and continual training should provide the necessary vocational skills.

The Real Life Lane
So who does the Upbringing? Older people know everything better than younger people because they have experience; younger people know everything better than older people because they haven't.

I always thought that Education and Training started with upbringing at home, until I read George Bernard Shaw. He said: "There may be some doubt as to who are the best people to have charge of children, but there can be no doubt that parents are the worst."[3]

---

2 Mackay, 1981.
3 Prochnow & Prochnow, 1979.

I believe Mark Twain said that when he was a boy of 14, his father was so ignorant he could hardly stand to have the old man around. But when he got to be 21, he was astonished at how much his father had learnt in seven years.

I concede that parents are much too stupid to raise their offspring properly. Children's grandparents are much better suited to the task. They are settled, bored and they love grandchildren. They have more spare time, and are too decrepit to swing or rock and roll. Most important of all, they have experience of life and people, young and old.

If we switch the responsibility for raising children in this manner, we should see a great improvement after one generation. Parents have a habit of bending over backwards to give their children what they themselves didn't have, and they tend to be overprotective. They also tend to focus their children's attention on finding happiness in the world, as it should be; and they don't equip them for the real bumpy roads and breakers ahead, only for the smooth sailing. Grandparents know better than to rob the kids of life's vital experiences.

A personal email I received puts it in proper perspective. Here is a condensed and adapted version of the contents:

According to 21st century PCs, we kids of the middle 20th century should not have survived:

our baby cots were covered with brightly coloured lead-based paint, which was promptly chewed and licked;

when we rode our bikes, we wore no helmets;

as children, we rode in cars without seat belts or air bags;

we drank water from the garden hose and not from a bottle – it tasted the same;

we played all day, as long as we were home before dark. Nobody could reach us, and no one minded;

we fell out of trees, cut ourselves and broke bones and teeth, and there were no lawsuits – these were accidents – we learnt not to do the same thing again;

the idea of parents bailing us out if we broke a law was unheard of – they actually sided with the law!

This is the generation that has produced some of the best risk takers, problem solvers and inventors ever. In the past 50 years there has been an explosion of innovation and new ideas. This generation had freedom, failure, success and fun, and learnt how to deal with it all.

After upbringing we move on to consider formal education. This should be facilitated by PAFS according to the wishes, and with the cooperation of parents, including Parent Teacher Associations. Skills training should be done according to the needs and with the cooperation of the employer organisations.

Here are a few worthwhile remarks from Bill Gates to school kids I received in another personal email:

> The world won't care about your self-esteem – the world will expect you to accomplish something *before* you feel good about yourself.
>
> Your school may have done away with winners and losers, but life has not. In some schools, they have abolished failing grades and they'll give you as many times as you want to get the right answer. This doesn't bear the slightest resemblance to *anything* in real life.
>
> Life is not fair – get used to it.
>
> If you think your teacher is tough, wait till you get a boss.

However, the progressive educating of our offspring, as a function of society, is much easier said than done. When you reduce it to the simple truth it becomes feasible. Like everything else it has to be planned.

The Future for a Start

You've got the whole world to live in! There's beauty all around you! There are things to do... great things to be accomplished! No man treads this earth alone! We are all together; one generation taking up where the other generation has left off! – that's what Lucy told Charlie Brown.[4]

---

4 Schulz, 1970.

We can plan the education of the young for their future after school by generations – but this creates more complicated questions than it provides simple answers. For one thing, people's concept of a generation differs: some say it is the average time in which children are ready to take the place of their parents, usually reckoned at about 30 years.[5] Others put it at 20 years.

All time-period based formulae are confusing: every day launches a new generation! Planning for the future generations would make sense only if we could forecast particular future periods in terms of their main characteristics. Let's call them "future eras".

Looking back we talk about eras... of seafaring discoveries, of rising nationalism, of the industrial revolution, of decolonisation, of the Cold War, and the new era of terrorism after 11 September 2001. Looking forward, what future eras do we visualise in the real world-to-be for which we have to prepare the young through education and training?

The Future, for Now and Ever

The writing of future scenarios is a profession. The forecasters can apply a variety of models and indicators. One such indicator is music.

In the early 1990s musical genius Nico Carstens told me a new romantic era was dawning. In the early 2000s it seems that sentiment, romance, soft light and sweet music, serenade, melody and harmony, dearness and goodwill are something of the past. What awaits us is volume, clamour, speed, lightning, thunder and sparks, aggression, electrogressive-zukunftsbewälti-gung, Götterdämmerung and screaming in praise of drugs.

Jimmy: "And what about Bryan Adams' 'All for One and All for Love'"?

To plan for the future in South Africa is easy. The future already exists; it lies beyond the skyline. We'll get there in due time. In the meantime, we can reconnoitre; beyond the blue horizon we'll find scenarios that we will have to face a decade or more from now.

Jimmy (whispering under his breath): "Just follow the guiding star."

If you study what has happened in the US, Japan or Scandinavia, you will find many situations that were created by scientech and which society has already negotiated. We will catch up in a decade or two. So we can get quite a good idea – with regard to upbringing, education and training – of what we have to prepare our young people for. Let those countries try out their new ideas, make mistakes, and correct them. Only then should we implement them here with the necessary modifications.

5 Tulloch, 1992.

Tarentaal cocks her head, "You guys are ignorant: a single hen lays a dozen eggs at a time and raises the chicks single-handedly to become handsome citizens."

Jimmy responds, "It's easy to talk if you have no chicks."

Then he concludes, "Through upbringing and education we should instil values in the young, irrespective of what the future may demand. I am talking of those vital intangibles that are so important at any time, any place, in real life and the real world – permanent values."

CHAPTER 22

The Good, the Bad and the Children

I am the state – Louis XIV of France.

Seven Deadly Sins

Values and codes of conduct can sometimes be as important, if not more so, than scientech. Knowledge, aptitude and skills alone cannot maintain our society; we should foster and further develop our values and virtues for all times, present and future; this is the task of parents and teachers, and of grandparents. Sometimes it is more important to unlearn bad old habits than to develop good new ones.

Moral and ethical values are common to non-theists and to the religious. They are nearly all the same. Jews, Buddhists, Hindus, Muslims, Christians and other believers all have sound doctrines. The problem lies with sinful man's interpretations and applications that go awry and may even become evil.

Examples of bad traits to unlearn are the well-known seven deadly sins: Vanity, Envy, Gluttony, Lust, Wrath, Avarice and Sloth. To corrupt an old adage: If you don't like my sins, I've got others – those identified by the fascinating Mohandas Karamachand Gandhi:

Wealth without Work
Pleasure without Conscience
Science without Humanity
Knowledge without Character
Politics without Principle
Commerce without Morality
Worship without Sacrifice.

To acquire good virtues you needn't look much further than Professor Nic

Wiehahn's seven values of life – humaneness, honesty, modesty, purity, sanity and tidiness, diligence and self-discipline.[1]

Jimmy mentioned an important bad attribute that should be unlearnt, but seldom gets any attention. It is hero-worship. This is an undesirable and extremely dangerous activity irrespective of whether you are the worshipper or the worshipped. We should rid ourselves completely of this nasty weakness within a generation. Hero-worship is a cancer that provides the manure for cultivating evil politicians.

Jimmy says: "In the beginning hero-worshipping is like money: The more you get it, the more you'll need it. The more flattery you get, the more you'll believe it. The more you believe it, the more you'll insist on it – and the more you'll be persuaded that you are irreplaceable, a demigod. And in the end your supporters will suffer – all because in the beginning they worshipped you."

The King of France, Louis XIV, said "*L'état, c'est moi*" – The state, it is I. Then came Louis XV and Louis XVI and the French Revolution. In those days taxes were paid to the king. In fact, money belonged to the king, and gold coins of one pound were called sovereigns.

I met Mobutu Sese Seko many years ago. He was the president of Zaire, now the Democratic Republic of the Congo (DRC). He gave me the impression that, just like Louis XIV, he believed he was the state, and that all revenues were due to him; he would decide what bits of his fortune would go to the government and what to the people.

Mobuto is an example of how a ruler can become a tyrant as a result of the sustained hero-worship accorded him by his people, and of how the tyrant's ways can change normal society into a corrupt culture.

For more than a generation, people in the employ of the state seldom received their salaries. They had to ask for money from the public for services rendered, and the public became used to giving it. Ignorant Westerners describe this practice as corruption and bribery, but for the Congolese it was the normal way of making a living. The practice became part of their culture.

Many other heads of state have also been acclaimed at first before they became despots. Today's hero is tomorrow's villain. Decent people become inebriated with power through hero-worship; they turn into demigods and tyrants. They really come to believe that they are divine saviours of their countries and peoples, perhaps not unlike Uganda's Idi Amin and Zimbabwe's Mugabe.

---

1 Wiehahn, N. *Lewenswaardes*, Compact disc, RSG, nd SABC Johannesburg.

It may be unfair to accuse the people of corruption, but one can rightly blame them for creating corrupt presidents through hero-worship. Perhaps you'll tell me it is a natural and inherent part of the human psyche to hero-worship, and that you can't change or destroy this. You may have a point, but is that really so? Didn't the Swiss change the habit of putting a president on a pedestal? Anyway, for a start, instead of hero-worshipping people, I suggest you worship your God, and find yourself a constitutional monarch like the Swedes.

Crown Princess Victoria of Sweden, the latest in a long line of successful Swedish royals.
Source: *Scanpix.*

History of the Day

As you have probably noticed over and over again, as soon as politicians appear on whatever stage, the trouble starts. When teaching is about the natural sciences, you are on pretty safe turf because it is not arguable. For example, Newton's laws of gravity are the same, all the time, all over the world. But when you teach values and social subjects like history and religion, every minister in government becomes his own little political Newton, Pythagoras, Louis XIV or Mobuto.

What happens with history is that governments prescribe the History of the Day for teaching at schools. This type of political indoctrination is best illustrated by using the example of the old Soviet Union. People used to say you couldn't forecast Soviet history because every time the communist party, and therefore the state, got a new boss, the country's history would be rewritten.

When the subject is religious tuition, governments tend to push their favourite brands of theism, atheism and non-theism. The people cannot allow that. The ANC's policy on religion used to be atheism. They are now in government. What is the latest?

In South Africa, 85% of primary school learners actually attend school. This is the highest percentage in Africa, but actually very sad because the government's grip on schools and children is getting tighter and tighter. Schools and parents are being deprived of the right to determine the nature of tuition, for example with regard to language and religious subjects.

Many Afrikaans-medium schools have had to resort to the law and courts to protect their rights – and they have won.

Lawrence Schlemmer is a much respected, top socio-political scientist. He wrote (in an article in *Focus*, published by the Helen Suzman Foundation, and quoted in *The Citizen*), that the people in South Africa suffered (and continue to suffer) because of contrivances by the department of education under minister Kader Asmal. He continued, saying that the latest victims were conservative and religiously inclined parents: The problems of conservative brown and white Afrikaans-speakers today are perhaps the unsexiest and least politically captivating issues in these times of transformation, but liberal democrats should spare more than a passing glance at them because they are giving the game away in key areas of our politics.

Possessions of the State

Schlemmer said that mounting dismay had been voiced at Asmal's proposal that religious instruction in public schools be replaced by doctrinally neutral instruction on all major religions – a proposal suspended belatedly under pressure from churches in late May 2003.

He continued, pointing out that the policies were squeezing dominantly Afrikaans schools out of existence in the name of greater access for all learners. Many people saw this as an inevitable sacrifice to transformation, he said. This attitude could be found among many other opinion leaders, including people easily mistaken for liberals – trendy and upper middle-class people of the super-contemporary, secular and cosmopolitan variety. But what they are missing is a matter far bigger than old-fashioned moral and ethnic sensitivities. Former conservative MP Cassie Aucamp raised it in Parliament with these words, quoted in the television news: Children at school are being treated as if they are possessions of the state.

Schlemmer believes that when the zeal to transform extends to deciding, for the people, that certain religious practices, values and cultural rights are not in their best interests, we are well on the way to destroying freedom in the name of democracy.

I agree with him that if the government thinks that it "owns" schools, and schoolchildren, it also thinks that it owns all of us. Both liberty and hegemony are indivisible.

This is typical of what happens when the people relinquish their sovereignty to a political party when they vote it into power.

The parents should rightfully make the decisions. They should do so in the absence of undue political interference, but in conjunction with independent experts, the parent-teacher associations and the education department of PAFS. Then these problems would be solved without friction, animosity and the courts.

* * *

The penultimate function of government that we are going to discuss is to be ready and able to maintain and protect what we are not prepared to sacrifice. We need National Security and Public Safety, and the main players at the cutting edge are the military and the police.

CHAPTER 23

War and Peace – Woes and Weals

It is useless for the sheep to pass resolutions in favour of vegetarianism while the wolf remains of a different opinion. – WR Inge, Dean of St. Paul's Cathedral, London,[1] seconded by Gnu.

War – The Second Best

No government can afford to divest itself of the function of National Security. The closely associated function of ensuring Public Safety can be delegated to a certain extent, but it remains the responsibility of government. Be-

---

1 Prochnow & Prochnow, 1979.

cause, in fact, governments tend to deprive the citizenry of their weapons needed for self-protection.

When it comes to you and your country, decide what is valuable and dear to you – that which you rightfully are not prepared to sacrifice:

Determine if any of these are being threatened, now or in the future.
If there is nothing you cherish, and no dangers – emigrate to a better place.
If there are challenges – invest in a secure future.
Mankind lives through times of war interrupted by periods of peace.
Whenever there is more than one person, there will be personal quarrels.
Whenever there is more than one country, there will be international disputes.
Individuals sort out problems among themselves, or seek legal adjudication –
Or they resort to violence.

Between states, war may be the last resort for settling disputes. It could however, be one of the warring parties preferred ways of doing it – usually the dominant one. The aim is to subject the other party to one's will through victory on the field of battle. Fighting it out is not the best way of doing it, but having exhausted all other avenues, an alternative for war has yet to be found.

War is waged to achieve a political aim, but warfare itself should be conducted by the military. It is governed by international law, more specifically by the laws of war, the Geneva and other conventions as well as UN and other international resolutions. The laws and conventions are aimed at the military and stipulate what is acceptable practice and what not. They also protect innocent civilians.

A national defence force is there to defend a country. To do so, it has to prevent war. The main way of preventing war is through deterrence. To deter a foe from war, the shape, size and quality of a country's military force should constitute a credible deterrent – and potential aggressors must know that there will be no hesitation in using it.

If a country has to fight a war, it must win. I believe it was Wellington who said that the biggest human tragedy after winning a war is losing it.

Pick and Pay – The Swiss versus the Lebanese Option

The old adage is still very valid: A defence force is like an insurance policy. You pay for it, but you may never need it. However, should there come a time when you need it and you haven't got it, it's too late to get it. You can buy a custom-made military insurance policy or the closest to it that you can afford. It's a matter of pick and pay.

Switzerland has been neutral for as long as I can remember. Basically, it has had the same constitution for centuries. It hosts the head offices of many international organisations such as the Red Cross and UN agencies – and hasn't fought a war for ages. Yet it is renowned for having one of the best and well equipped defence forces in the world – prepared and ready to make war.

Switzerland has an impressive but mostly part-time defence force – the most economical way of maintaining an effective defence force in a country that is not in a state of war. I'm told that even Roger Federer, the Australian Open and Wimbledon tennis champion, had to do national service.

While Europe has constantly seen various wars, such as the Hundred Years War, Thirty Years War and two World Wars, over the last few centuries, Switzerland has not been militarily challenged for centuries. Why not? The reason is the exact opposite to why a country like Lebanon has been invaded.

The Lebanese have been incessantly ravaged by foreign military aggression. Why? They are a peace-loving people.

Some years ago I was listening to the early morning news about the situation in Lebanon. It was all about war. Everyone was having their say; the Americans, the French, the Syrians, the Israelis, a spokesperson for the Blue Berets, the UN – but there was not a word from a Lebanese! They had no say.

Why did they not have any say? It was their country! The reason is they did not count – they didn't have a defence force of note. If they had had one, they probably would not have been invaded in the first place.

War is waged by the application of movement (manoeuvre) and firepower to destroy the enemy's military capability to resist.

The victor imposes his will on the loser.

Two Tales of One Country

Erstwhile fellow senior officers of mine, Generals Jack Dutton, Mike Muller and Denis Earp, were members of the South African contingent in the Korean War. The latter two were fighter pilots of a sizeable air force complement (and were both later to become Chief of the South African Air Force). Jack Dutton, then a lieutenant, served in Korea as a troop commander in the British Royal Tank Regiment.

Denis told me long ago he was once confronted with the statement: It served absolutely no purpose to have made war in Korea.

Now, before I tell you his reaction, you should know that Denis does not talk lightly about war and its tragedies. During that same war, on 20 September 1951, his aircraft's cooling system was shot to pieces. For 23 months and 3 days he was a guest of Red China's political commissars – a horrific experience. He was released towards the end of August 1953, after peace had been concluded. That was the war in Korea.

During South Africa's border war against Angolan/Cuban forces his only son, helicopter pilot Lt Michael John Earp, was killed in action in January 1982. Denis knows about the tragedies of war.

To the statement about the purposelessness of the war in Korea, he replied: We saved a country and its people from communist domination, which in other countries had caused so much grief and misery to so many peoples over so many decades. And look where South Korea is today – one of the most dynamic and prosperous industrial countries of the world. North Korea, its neighbour, by way of contrast, is one of the most miserable, one of the cruellest and most suppressive of all the Stalinist countries. It is also one of the poorest. How can you say it served no purpose?

Jack Dutton revisited that country in 2005 to attend a United Nations Korean peace forces memorial convention. He said that in the 50 years since the war, when the South Korean nation had been on its knees, they had recovered and built a national spirit, an economy, and technologies second to none. Their shipbuilding industry is the largest and busiest in the world; their motor vehicle industry is the fastest growing; and their IT and electronics are way on top.

"The country is certainly the power house of the East," he concluded. That was war.

Peace – The Best

Peace is the preferred way of maintaining sound international relations. It is conducted by politicians. Like war, peace can be disastrous. "How governments wage peace is highly questionable," said Fareed Zakaria, editor of *Newsweek International*. One has only to recall, for example, the mass peacetime killings of millions of people by Stalin in Soviet Russia and Mao Tse Tung in China.

And then there were other peacetime rulers like Idi Amin who earned himself the official title of His Excellency, President for Life, Field Marshall Al Hadji Doctor Idi Amin, VC, DSO, MC, Lord of all the Beasts and the Earth and Fishes of the Sea, and Conqueror of the British Empire in Africa in General and Uganda in particular, and King of Scotland. He never waged war, but his victims of torture and murder were reported to have numbered between 100,000 and 300,000 Ugandans.[2]

Far greater figures are quoted for the genocides in the Great Lakes region of Africa, the Sudan, and during unrest in West Africa and elsewhere.

Our problem is that politicians can't make war, and soldiers can't make peace. Politicians don't declare war anymore, and soldiers hang around regions earmarked for Peacemaking and Peacekeeping. The politicians fail through lack of integrity and courage, and the soldiers fail because they are supposed to achieve the exact opposite of that for which they have been trained.

In the old days governments used to declare war. They had guts. All the people in the world knew exactly where they stood. What is important is that the soldiers who did the fighting also knew. The last such formal declaration of war of which I know was at the beginning of World War II. That doesn't mean that people have stopped making war. It only means that the politicians have stopped declaring it.

Ever since then violence has gone on the rampage. Political transparency has disappeared and the responsibility for war has become blurred. Honour and pride are under pressure.

*   *   *

Let's now analyse how governments have handled National Security and Public Safety in practice, to learn lessons for future application. We first adopt a global perspective, and then go on to the ever mystical and intriguing Middle East and East Africa.

2 www.wikipedia.org.

CHAPTER 24

A Sneaky Affair

Israel should be wiped off the map – President Mahmoud Ahmadinejad of Iran.

Society and War

In modern times much attention has been focused on the effects of war on society both with regard to securing national interests as well as maintaining international security.

Geoffrey Best said, "War and society normally means no more than armies and society."[1] He was wrong. No army has ever declared a war, only politicians do. True, armies wage war to accomplish political objectives, but war and society means nothing more than politicians and society.

Since the end of World War II, war has become a sneaky affair. Whereas declared wars were largely waged between national states up to and including World War II, they have since been replaced by undeclared "armed conflicts" between states and political movements. Outside countries or organisations sometimes support these movements, clandestinely and otherwise. In the Middle East there are intricate webs of such affiliations.

Declaring and waging such a war is one thing, but it is another – cowardly – thing not to declare war, but to go ahead anyway, as became the custom during the Cold War. Here the bravest political performer of recent times has been George W Bush senior. He went through all the legal procedures, and if he stopped short of making the honourable old-style declaration of war, then at least he went as far as going up to the UN Security Council to obtain a mandate for evicting Saddam Hussein's invading Iraqi looters from Kuwait.

---

1 Best, 1982.

During the second half of the 20th century, armed conflicts were being waged in 25 to 40 countries at any given time. They were mostly initiated by, or happened as a result of, the big East–West power struggle – inappropriately called the Cold War by politicians: they were the only ones out in the cold.

Strategies and tactics became *unconventional* and *irregular*, and modes of application of movement and firepower changed, *guerrilla* warfare being a prime example. However, flying passenger aircraft into buildings, and blasting civilians to smithereens in restaurants with human suicide bombers are not acts of war by any definition or stretch of the imagination.

Such methods do not attempt to secure national interests or safeguard international stability in terms of the relevant conventions. They are violent criminal activities against non-military targets for personal, political or religious gain, using non-military methods and equipment and performed by non-uniformed agents. The 9/11 attacks are prime examples and contrary to any acknowledged legal convention.

Nuclear warfare has not been practised since Hiroshima and Nagasaki in 1945. It is dormant at present. Where nuclear capabilities do exist, they are exclusively a political weapon used mostly for international posturing and deterrence.

Furthermore, peacemaking operations and peacekeeping troops are the exact opposite of warfare and military combat forces. Such activities should be outsourced to private security companies. In 2006, more than 5000 South Africans in the employ of NGOs were active in various parts of the world, including the Sudan and Afghanistan, where they performed life-saving mine-clearing, medical and protection services.

Society and Peace

For conducting general international political relations, monarchs, presidents and prime ministers used to deploy ambassadors, high commissioners, consuls general, special envoys, and rank and file diplomats. They did rather well – jollies and all.

Nowadays, with modern communications, romantic old-style diplomacy has become outdated. Presidents and ministers have not much use for ambassadors anymore – apart from posts for pals and square pegs. They prefer to struggle through the sweat and tribulations of the travels and jollies themselves.

The effectiveness of this nouveau genre of tour de force diplomacy by the avant-garde presidents and ministers has not yet been fully determined.

Nevertheless, the people have given them the green light – the absence of ministers at home is not really noticed since they don't give the people enough time to get used to their presence.

However, during the conduct of peace talks presidents and ministers do not expose themselves too much to frontline peace negotiations. If the talks don't succeed, they should not be blamed. Apart from limelight events such as stately appearances at ceremonial signings of agreements, they leave the play-acting to special envoys and appointed facilitators – usually all PC.

Peacemaking is the domain of the red PCs. While not necessarily creating any incidents, they go all out to turn the slightest occurrences into sob stories, and publish them to shock the international public at large and to ensure that they will continue to recur. These incidents are regularly splashed in the media because the PCs have made them into so-called "key events". And so the international world becomes involved.

The red PCs aim to secure peace in a particular region, or more correctly a "peace agreement", by a certain date. They couple this step to a programme with benchmarks, or "road maps" if you wish. If the predetermined schedule is not accomplished (which is usually the case the first few times), they call it a problem.

For example, Palestine and Israel are not a problem. They are barely a pinprick in a coffee table atlas of the world. These two half-brothers have been happily fighting one another for many millennia – since time immemorial. What is all the fuss about? Why can't we leave them to fight in peace?

The reason is obvious. The PCs have turned this conflict into a key event and a problem. Some or other crank wants to establish peace between them before he retires. Yet another dimwit politician wants to do the same within the four, five or eight years he is in office.

A certain country assists a Palestinian suicide bomber to kill an Israeli policemen and/or civilians, and Israel gets support for its soldiers who level the Palestinian's house. The red PCs are in business. By internationalising the incident, and keeping it alive and flaming in the global media, they turn this tiny scrap of real estate into a monstrous conflict – a complex complex.

In the meantime, hundreds of thousands more people get killed, maimed and assaulted in other parts of the world, but that's okay. The PCs may take decades before they turn these other sad happenings into key events. The result is that these regions don't acquire the same potential for arousing people's passions, and don't secure a place in history for the peacemaking PCs. President Mbeki highlighted this phenomenon when he pointed out that people cry out about Zimbabwe while the situation is much worse in the DRC.

And why do we worry about Haiti when the situation in the Sudan has for many years been a million times worse?

President Ahmadinejad makes a valid point when he says we should wipe Israel off the map, but why not remove both Israel and Palestine? On second thought, if you remove one of them the fighting will stop – perhaps he has selected a target for trying out his nuclear capability.

Those PCs who claim they will permanently solve this millennia-old problem within the few years of an Israeli or Palestinian premier's term of office, or that of a UN secretary general's, are unscrupulous. If they are honestly seeking a real solution – not just a quick peace agreement for short-term political gain or kudos – they must devise a long-range plan that will be executed over a period of at least one generation. Unfortunately they are more used to planning short-term failures than long-term successes.

The modern trend is that the PCs want to find a solution without removing the cause of the problem. This is where they make a name for themselves quickly, to make way for others to make their names quickly, to make way... They are not Dag Hammarskjolds.

Victories, such as the signing of ceasefire agreements are prerequisites for international diplomacy, securing donations and development funding, kudos, and a place in history. The PC facilitators are not interested in *peace*, they want a signed peace *agreement* – and they want it now!

In the case of the Burundi peace negotiations, *The Scotsman* reported that the South African principal, ex-president Nelson Mandela, "instructed the women of Burundi to refrain from providing their husbands with 'marital services' until their men agree to sign a peace treaty to end the civil war."[2]

Having secured a signed agreement, the facilitators lose interest. To illustrate: the government of Burundi and three of the four Hutu rebel groups signed peace accords; an AU peacekeeping force was to be deployed in the country to supervise the ceasefire; the force would consist of Ethiopian, Mozambican and South African troops.

Then many, many months later, during March 2003, President Pierre Buyoya of Burundi visited Pretoria. He lodged a complaint with President Mbeki, chairman of the African Union: the promised AU peacekeeping force was already three months overdue! President Mbeki undertook to send troops soon.

The PC peacemakers shouldn't ignore the root causes of the friction while demanding the signing of a peace agreement. More often than not the

---

2 *The Scotsman*, 24 July 2000.

real issues have to do with deep-seated cultural, religious, ethnic, business and border problems. Unfortunately these matters are regarded as holy cows, non-starters, so the PCs skirt around them. That's where we fail – all because of the red PC politicians. They are not serious; they haven't the guts to give these matters the attention they deserve – for a better Africa.

That is why we often read in the newspapers that soon after the dignitaries have signed the accords and treaties, hostilities break out once more. And this pattern will continue indefinitely until real statesmen take the African bull by the horns. The PCs must stop praying to God that there never should have been clans, tribes and cultures, business and borders.

Jimmy whispers to Gnu, "PCs don't pray – they *are* God. The crux of the problem is they don't deal with the crux of the problem... by the way what happened to Ms Tarentaal?"

"She offered her apologies; she's gone off to Durban to watch the Sharks donnering up the Falcons."

"Good for her; she's got no chicks that need babysitting."

* * *

And yes, Jimmy, we haven't escaped the comings and goings of war and peace. Our next stories begin with a European perspective and end up with war and peace in Southern Africa. This is the backdrop:

122

The Soviet Union and its satellites supported one of the three revolutionary movements in Angola, and those in South West Africa/Namibia and South Africa. The Soviets also sponsored the Cubans who were never far away. The latter operated in the American surrounds, the Middle East, Central Asia and Africa, and they had more than 52,000 troops in Angola. The often-aired warning, especially among military correspondents, was that one had no chance against an insurgent movement that had the support of the Soviet Union plus the physical participation of Cubans.

The South African government's brief to its military regarding South West Africa/Namibia was to maintain order, peace and stability to protect the political peacemaking processes. A violent revolutionary takeover was not an acceptable alternative. Its brief regarding South Africa was basically the same, but here military involvement was minimal in comparison with Namibia and Angola.

CHAPTER 25

A Place in History

Enter the Young Major

We are discussing National Security as a function of government. I would like to entertain you with real stories starting in Europe of the hot World War II, and ending in Namibia during the global Cold War. They illustrate how warfare deteriorated from the noble art of manoeuvre and valour to the messy mixture of politics, propaganda, deceit and terror. The first story is about the young British major, a flashy Swede, and a big Finnish commissioner.

During World War II the allies were planning a parachute assault operation at Arnhem. An intelligence officer, a young major, had serious doubts about the reliability of the information on which the senior commanders and staffs had based their planning. His intelligence, backed by aerial photography, unmistakeably showed the presence of menacing, strong German tank forces in the zones where the paratroopers were going to be dropped.

He became increasingly alarmed at what he saw as a desperate desire on everybody's part to "get the Airborne into action", regardless. "It was absolutely impossible," he related later, "to get them to face the realities of the situation; their personal longing to get into the campaign... completely blinded them."

The superiors were unmoved and conveniently pretended that the young major might be suffering from nervous exhaustion. General Montgomery wasn't going to let a young upstart abort his operation! The result was 17 000 Allied and Polish soldiers killed, wounded or missing, considerably more than during the D-Day landings. The Dutch civilian casualties might have been as high as 10 000.

The story of this disaster is well documented in a book by Cornelius Ryan as well as by a movie of the same title, *A Bridge Too Far*. You will meet the young major again later.[1]

---

1 Ryan, 1974.

Jumping from the 1940s to the next century, I now introduce the next actor.

The Flashy Swede

During November 2005, out of the blue, reports hit the press, radio and TV news fast and furiously. They announced the sinister discovery of "bones and mass graves" near old South African military bases in the north of Namibia.

This was not my first experience of "massacres". In 1972 the secretary of information for Swapo (the revolutionary South West Africa People's Organisation), Andreas Shipanga, visited TV man Per Sanden in Stockholm. He told the Swede about a village in Namibia that had been destroyed by South African soldiers. So Sanden and his crew met with Shipanga at his office in Lusaka, Zambia. From there Shipanga sent the Swedes on a conducted tour across the border to the village in question. They took reels and reels of film of skulls, skeletons and gutted houses. When they were all back in Lusaka, Shipanga staged an international press conference and showed Sanden's films of the village that had been wiped out by the South Africans. The story spread around the world in a flash.

In South Africa, under great pressure, the minister of information, Pik Botha, referred the matter to the military who told him it was not true. So the minister took an international press group on a helicopter trip to visit the place in Namibia. Before they got there, however, he got cold feet and instructed that the flight be aborted.

Fifteen years later, in 1987, at a social occasion in Cape Town, I prompted Shipanga to tell Botha about his 1972 village massacre in Namibia. When Shipanga related his story, Botha was completely flustered.

As the hoax unfolded of how Shipanga had tricked Per Sanden and the whole bunch of international journalists, and the world at large, Botha's face became redder and redder. It had never been into Namibia that Shipanga had sent Per Sanden and his TV crew, but into a derelict place in old Portuguese Angola!

Reporters and political commentators like to believe whatever suits their causes. Some, even if they do become aware of the true facts, wouldn't let that spoil a good story. But Sue Armstrong has told the whole story in her book published in 1989, *In Search of Freedom: The Andreas Shipanga Story*.[2]

The Big Finn

We return to November 2005 and the newly discovered "secret mass graves in Namibia". The red PC journalists and political commentators went to

2 Armstrong, 1989.

town as they had during the days of the Cold War. They kept up a regular flow of accusations and agitated for further investigations: Why had the SA military kept mum on these graves all this time?

Then the truth slowly started to emerge. The bones were those of members of the armed wing of Swapo, the People's Liberation Army of Namibia (PLAN), who had fallen in armed skirmishes many years previously. Peter Stiff gives an account of the episode in his book, *Nine Days of War*.[3] The whole story is well known:

All the parties concerned with the Namibian peacemaking process agreed that 1 April 1989 would be the date of implementation of the ceasefire in accordance with UN Resolution 435 (and the Geneva Protocol).

The Big Finn, Mr Martii Ahtisaari (special representative of the secretary general and head of the UN Transitionary Assistance Group - UNTAG), declared that all the safeguards were in place to ensure that all parties would obey the rules of the agreement. The whole world awaited the historical event with bated breath and crossed fingers.

That very morning, in flagrant violation of the ceasefire, the first wave of 1600 heavily armed, shooting Swapo insurgents – wearing uniforms for the first time ever in Namibia – crossed the border from Angola into Namibia.

The UN had failed bitterly. Following interventions at a high level, they thankfully agreed that South Africa should be assigned to save the day. Fortunately, a small contingent of South African police, elements of the South West African Territory Force, and a tiny air force complement that were still in Namibia – within the provisions of the agreement – restored law and order.

With UN authorisation and supervision, and under the UN flag, they shot more than 300 invaders, but also lost 26 of their own men. The skirmishes lasted nine days, of which the first two were the fiercest, with the policemen bearing the brunt.

There were probably more international journalists in relation to the Namibian population than on any other similar occasion. The UN regularly briefed the correspondents who also witnessed the burials. This is the story behind the "secret" mass graves in Namibia "rediscovered" during November 2005.

However, in 2005, apart from the accusations that the military were covering up these occurrences, there were also those like ex-minister Pik Botha, and Mr Martii Ahtisaari who, according to the media, claimed with convic-

---

3 Stiff, 1989.

tion that the violation of the ceasefire by Swapo in 1989 had come as an utter surprise! And this leads to the most astounding part of this whole story...

During that time, in 1989, I was the Chief of the SA Defence Force. Before the invasion I and other spokesmen officially as well as publicly reported that we had reliable intelligence that the terms of the ceasefire agreement were not being adhered to and stood in grave danger of being violated, and this would have dire consequences.

Closer to D-Day, my last monthly briefing to the media was dedicated solely to the now imminent threat to the implementation of the peace process in Namibia. Senior South African diplomat Glen Babb and I conducted it jointly.

Desperate, I told the well-attended conference that if they wanted to make a positive contribution, they should publish our information to put pressure on the parties to obey the rules. The media did their job well, to quote only a few:

"Angolans not keeping pact: Defence Chief" – *The Citizen*, 17 February 1989.

"Angola must say now if it does not want to, or cannot oversee Swapo's withdrawal." – *Beeld*, quoting me on 17 February 1989.

"The Deputy Director of Foreign Affairs, Mr Glen Babb, said the Cuban-backed Angolan government had not honoured an undertaking to urge SWAPO to withdraw from southern Angola by September 1 1988. Mr Babb warned this put SWAPO in a position to interfere with the Namibian elections and could 'affect independence'." – *Pretoria News*, 17 February 1989.

This peacemaking operation launched Mr Ahtisaari on his way to becoming president of Finland.

Encore the Young Major

We now recall the young major of Arnhem.

Montgomery didn't heed the young major's alert about the German tanks because he wanted "to get the Airborne going" – vainglory. The peacemakers did not want to be bothered with Glen Babb's and my warnings. It was as the young major had said, "It was impossible to get them to face the realities of the situation; their personal longing to get *the peace plan* going...completely blinded them" – in search of kudos and a place in history.

After World War II the young major worked closely with a man for whom he developed the greatest respect – the secretary general of the UN, the great Swede, Dag Hammarskjold. You may recall that he died tragically in an air crash on 17 September 1961 at Ndola, in then Northern Rhodesia, while on peacemaking missions.

When the major eventually retired, the diplomatic correspondent David Landau addressed him in an open letter in *The Jerusalem Post*:

"I need not tell you, nor the readers of this newspaper, that of all the many shuttlers and would-be peacemakers, you have come through with an unblemished record for dispassionate compassion..."

"Nor are you a politician, present or past, concerned with the 'place in history'".[4]

I quote from an autobiography, *A Life in Peace and War*, presented to me by the author, former long-serving under-secretary general of the UN, the "nervy" prophet of doom – the young major of *A Bridge Too Far*, signed "Brian Urquhart 24.vii.89".

Jimmy: "I hope your second story, Uncle Joe, is the one about the rivers."

4 Urquhart, 1987.

CHAPTER 26

The Rivers and the Firing Squad

War goes through six phases: Enthusiasm – Confusion – Disillusionment – Searching for culprits – Blaming the innocent – Decorating the non-participants – Quoted by JJP Erasmus.

A young tree doesn't grow in the shadow of the big one – Jonas Malheiro Savimbi.

Part 1 – Battle: Failing the Lomba

During the Cold War, armed conflicts went hand in hand with the intensification of psychological warfare, deceit and terror. I believe the dictators came out tops with regard to propaganda, but they often caused military underperformance through undue political interference. The democratic politicians, by comparison, were the palookas of the propaganda war, but were less inclined to spoil military outcomes by political interference. This story illustrates these phenomena.

Millions of people fell victim to the hoax of the "massacred villagers" of 1972 in Angola; and the 2005 hullabaloo over the 1989 "mass graves" in Namibia turned out to be a farce. However, those with hidden agendas rekindled these past fiascos to recall another supposedly sinister happening, the so-called *Battle of Cuito Cuanavale* of 1987.

The red PC propagandists claim that the whole story has never been told. They allege that South Africa suffered a disastrous defeat including the loss of more than 1000 South African soldiers and over 40 South African fighter aircraft, and that "the generals" swept the military dust under the carpet.

An instinctive response to these allegations is that anyone familiar with South Africa in the 1980s will tell you that losing more than 1000 soldiers and 40 fighter pilots in an operation would have been regarded as an absolute disaster, and hiding it would have been impossible. These allegations are lies!

Southern Africa was one of many regions all over the world in the grip of the Cold War, caught up in the biggest propaganda atmosphere of all time. Moscow and Havana, and specifically Fidel Castro, were regarded as among the most skilful and ardent practitioners in this field. The events are publicly well documented.

The Soviet Union sponsored Cuba's overseas military adventures during the Cold War. However, the 1970s and 1980s were the prelude to events that saw the total collapse of the Soviet Union's economic and financial capacity. At the extreme west of the Atlantic Ocean, the island of Cuba had to sustain a force of more than 52 000 troops (their own minimum figures) for military operations on the opposite side of the ocean in Angola. This is how it happened:

During 1975 there was no smooth handover of Portuguese colonial authority to the Angolans in Angola. The MPLA[1], supported by Cuba and financed by the Soviet Union, grabbed power and fought against the other Angolan parties, the FNLA[2] – America's neglected pet, and UNITA[3]. The latter two soon sought to resume their freedom struggle from their familiar territory, the African bush. The Soviet Union and Cuba supported the MPLA on a massive scale and with physical intervention. By comparison, South Africa's aid to UNITA was minute. The Cubans later conceded that in 1975 they thought that the *coup* would be settled, over and done with, within the year. But it didn't happen that way – almost 15 years later they were still in Angola.

The military struggles continued, but by the mid to late 1980s the Soviet Union's economy was on its last legs. Only a short while later the world saw the pathetic Soviet president, Boris Yeltsin, in tears on television, saying words to the effect: I'm the head of state, my mother is ill – and I can't afford to buy her medicine.

The Soviet collapse was no surprise. As early as September 1979 I had predicted, "... Soviet Russia has moved so far out of its sphere of influence and area of interest that it is now running the risk of burning its fingers in Angola such as happened to the United States in Vietnam."[4]

Cuba became desperate; it had to get out. During all those years the Cuban soldiers also faced other enemies, HIV/Aids and worse – malaria and

1 Popular Movement for the Liberation of Angola.
2 National Front for the Liberation of Angola.
3 National Union for the Total Independence of Angola.
4 *Die Suidwester*, September 1979.

TB. South African families who experienced national service at that time may have a slight idea of the ordinary Cuban families' hardships back home. Our own servicemen served for a continuous period of two years. A small percentage did one or two operational stints of about two months at a time across the border in South West Africa/Namibia during the latter half of their two years. It was quite a different matter for the Cuban soldiers, as you can imagine. They did operational service across the ocean for one to three years at a time.

By the mid-1980s the Cubans had reached the end of their emotional stamina. However, as they told us later, they couldn't leave in a rush; that may have created the impression back home that they had lost the war – after all those years, for what? During late November 1987 they approached the South African mission in New York and put out feelers about the possibility of negotiations. In the final analysis the Cubans wanted to get out of Africa, but they sorely needed a quick victory before doing so.

So the Soviet Union came up with a plan to solve both its own and Cuba's problems: the Soviets would reinforce the MPLA/Cuban forces to the absolute maximum to give them all they needed to conquer Jamba.

Jamba was a place in the south-east of Angola where UNITA's headquarters was located. It was the movement's home base, cultural centre and *capital*. Historically, the onslaught on Jamba had become an annual affair, but the offensive always petered out before it reached the halfway mark. This time the Soviets would give it their all – one last go, the mother of all offensives that would end the war, once and forever.

Thus it happened that in 1987/1988 the joint MPLA/Cuban/Soviet forces launched their final offensive. In Africa, this campaign would turn out to be Moscow and Havana's swansong of the Cold War. And in Europe, the Berlin Wall would crash in 1989.

The Cuban/MPLA forces crossed the start line near the confluence of the Cuito and Cuanavale Rivers, on their way to Jamba in the east. The Soviets provided the logistics and air support, and the Cubans the rest, including chemical warfare aid, pilots and missile support. Their intermediate objective was Mavinga. To reach it they had to cross the Lomba River.

Facing this formidable offensive was a UNITA force, comprised overwhelmingly of infantry, with South Africa providing limited air support as well as artillery and armoured support under the command of Colonel Deon Ferreira. The same troops did not remain in this operation from beginning to end. We had three sets of relief troops in Angola for the duration of the campaign, but never more than 3000 at any time. This is what happened:

Cuito Cuanavale →   Lomba River →   Mavinga →   Jamba

The advancing forces, as had happened before, didn't get anywhere near Jamba. In fact, they never even came close to Mavinga! They tried to cross the Lomba River several times, over and over again at the same place, but suffered disastrous defeats every time.

These were the decisive battles of the whole campaign. They determined the course of history. Squadron commander Major Hannes Nortman and his men knocked out many Russian tanks with their Ratel 90s (infantry fighting vehicles). He was one of a number of heroes to be decorated for bravery during this campaign.

The MPLA alliance retreated westwards from whence it had come, and the last throes of the armed skirmishes took place at Tumpo, a minefield on the eastern side of Cuito Cuanavale. These clashes occurred during the UNITA and South African forces' classical "mopping-up" phase of the operation – back at the threshold of the retreating forces' launching pad. The Cuban and MPLA forces had set out to capture Jamba, but were defeated with catastrophic losses at the Lomba River.

In retrospect, this was the turning point of the Cuban Cold War armed hostilities in Africa. The final battles were soon to follow.

The Cubans faced a crisis, and Moscow had no option but to quit supporting the war. Havana needed a victory so that it could pull out of Africa with honour.

To escape, Fidel Castro pulled off a strategic hoax. As a postscript, he concocted a propaganda "victory". Following the failure of this offensive, he explained afterwards that his allies (the Soviets and the MPLA) had lost the war in the south-eastern region of Angola, so he feigned and claimed victory at Cuito Cuanavale, and then immediately forced international attention away from that mess towards the south-west of Angola.

Here he re-assembled all the available Cuban forces he could muster from inside and outside Angola and had them redeployed in the far south-west, not far from the Atlantic Ocean – roughly the same distance away from the eastern region as Denmark is from England across the North Sea. He had hoped to assume a threatening posture vis-à-vis north-west Namibia.

For all the Cubans' trouble in the south-west they got a bloody nose. Combined army and air force operations destroyed much of their modern Soviet missile/rocket/radar systems with typical South African ingenuity, and in the end Commandant Mike Muller's 61 Mechanised Battalion group knocked out a number of Soviet T55 tanks and 302 Cuban soldiers. That finally persuaded the Cubans to settle down nicely. They retreated northwards to a place called Techipa. This had been the last encounter, including the biggest battles between pure Cuban and South African forces in Angola since 1976.

Part 2 – Words: Singing the Blues

In among the hot air of the Cold War propaganda, the MPLA issued its usual media releases of South African losses. Characteristically its claims were so wildly exaggerated that neither the public nor the troops batted an eyelid. Had their figures been true, it would have meant absolute consternation in South Africa. However, it was a joke; such "national disasters" couldn't possibly have happened without a massive public outcry in South Africa – and the government would have tumbled, for sure.

Two typical examples of their claims were that 40 SA Air Force aircraft had been shot down (*Angop*, official Angolan news agency, 22 January 1988.) And that South Africa had lost 140 men, 6 aircraft, 47 tanks and diverse armoured cars during the previous 45 days (President Dos Santos, 19 February1988.)

These news bulletins were the joke of the day for some time, until they became monotonous. That was **1988** – but hold your breath!

13 May **2004**! A *Beeld* newspaper report claims that way back in December 1987, South Africa had suffered the following losses at Cuito Cuanavale: 1230 men, 41 fighter aircraft, three helicopters and 31 combat vehicles. Thousands(!) of South African troops that had been encircled on the banks of the Cuito River had all been shot dead!

These allegations had been regarded as preposterous during the 1980s. Now in 2004 (and into 2005) the plotting PCs were using much the same figures, as if they were new revelations and worthy of serious consideration! During a radio panel discussion that started with the topic of the "secret" mass graves in Namibia, the panellists ended up by clamouring for investigations into Cuito Cuanavale. One of the panellists even asked whether it was Castro or the "generals" who were telling the truth?[5] It seemed the PCs either wished the newspaper allegations to be true, or if they knew (as they must have done) that they were lies, they nevertheless pretended that they actually believed the statistics might just have been true, and that it was of great national importance for the public to know!

Actual Data of losses sustained in the fighting between September 1987 and April 1988 are as follows:

---

5 *Rekenskap*, radio programme, RSG (*Radio sonder grense*) 2005 SABC, Johannesburg.

Cuban/ MPLA combat losses:

Tanks	94
Armoured troop and combat vehicles	100
BM21/BM14 MRLs	34
Artillery, rocket and missile systems	15
MiG21/23 combat aircraft	9
Helicopters	9
Personnel	4785 accounted for

South African losses:

Tanks	3
Infantry fighting vehicles	5
Radars	5
Mirage F1 fighter aircraft	1
Light reconnaissance aircraft	1
Personnel	31

Two questions often recur: How could it be that the Soviet/MPLA/Cuban forces persisted in crossing the Lomba River, time and time again at the same place, after taking a beating each time with the same calamitous results?

One possible answer is that commanders who follow Soviet teachings are inclined to make exactly that type of mistake. They tend to stick rigidly to set doctrines and patterns – if they have decided to cross at point x, they will cross at point x! (Indeed, the Soviet influence was strong. Soviet General Constantin Shaganovitch, the chemical warfare expert, was supposed to oversee a victory for his allies.)

On the other hand, that approach is exactly contrary to the tactics for which the astute General Ochoa Sanchez became famous. He was the general in command of the Cuban/ MPLA forces and was known for his flexibility and unorthodox methods. He would definitely not have been in favour of hammering a classical river-crossing operation to the point of exhaustion. He was known for daring operations behind forward enemy lines.

However, another possible explanation subsequently emerged: at a much later date Castro established a propaganda tour for the gullible in Havana. It included a display of his planning room from where he commanded the operations in Angola! Now, an arrangement whereby a politician, albeit a president, dictates operations in the field from his armchair in a planning room far away over the sea is courting disaster! This was probably the reason for the Cuban failures.

On the South African side, there is no one with better first-hand knowledge of the interrelated international military and political events during that part of the war in Angola than I. With regard to the military, the buck stopped with me.

On the Cuban side there is no one with more experience and knowledge of the military course of events than General Ochoa Sanchez. He was there, the commanding general. He was a famous man of many Cold War proxy campaigns – Syria, Afghanistan, Ethiopia, Nicaragua, and so on. And he was the popular holder of the exclusive title "Hero of the Republic of Cuba", Cuba's highest award. He used to be cheered in the streets.

Wrapping Up

Cuito Cuanavale was another typical Cold War story of deceit. The Cuban allies were decisively thrashed in the east at the Lomba. And the strategic Cuban manoeuvre in the west ended in disaster for them – their last military hoo-ha of the Cold War in Africa. But that's what I claim, so to help you to make up your mind, let's see what the other experts found.

Bridgland, in his book *The War for Africa*: "[Castro]... tried to dress up political, economic and military failures in Angola as glorious triumphs... Cubans will surely someday trample his grave and destroy the monuments erected to him..."[6]

Freelancer Fred Bridgland is an expert on military aspects of the Cold War in Africa. He called his book on the Cuban intervention in Angola "the unofficial story of the war through the eyes of the men who fought it, not those of generals and politicians hundreds of kilometres from the blood, sweat and dust." He "... pieced together the course of the war for Africa through scores of interviews with the fighting men." He boasts there were no interference from the military or government, and no censorship.

Heitman, in his book *War in Angola*: "The defeat inflicted on the Fapla (MPLA) forces... was so crushing that it changed the strategic situation beyond recognition."[7]

Heitman is a professional writer on military affairs and correspondent of the *Jane's Defence Weekly*.

Renwick, in his book *Unconventional Diplomacy in Southern Africa*: "Stopping the massive Soviet- and Cuban-backed advance in October 1987 required some quite heroic actions by 32 Battalion and the other heavily outnumbered South African forces involved... The South African force never exceeded a

---

6 Brigland, 1990.
7 Heitman, 1990.

brigade in size... Huge quantities of Soviet equipment were destroyed or captured... a most impressive military exploit."[8]

Super diplomat and erstwhile British ambassador to South Africa, Sir Robin Renwick, had intimate knowledge of the big five Western powers that concerned themselves with the region, and painstakingly followed events in Southern Africa.

In his book, *High Noon in Southern Africa*, **Crocker**, US assistant secretary of state for Africa, poses the question: "The Soviets and Angolans... had been thoroughly defeated. How, then, did the fighting at Cuito become a heroic Cuban legend?" He answers his own question, "By proclaiming to a credulous world (*and South African red PCs*) that the town of Cuito Cuanavale... was the 'prize' over which the entire campaign was fought, and then by crowing when you have managed not to lose it... the South Africans were no match for Castro in the battle of perceptions."[9]

US assistant secretary of state for Africa and peace negotiator Chester Crocker was the one person who knew more than anyone else about the political/military scene, including the goals and objectives, strategies and tactics, decision-making processes, and the likes and dislikes of all the role players – the Soviets, the big five Western powers, the Angolans, South Africans, Cubans, the lot. He had full use of state-of-the-art satellite photo surveillance. He published a voluminous book, *High Noon in Southern Africa – Making Peace in a Rough Neighborhood*.

And there was Simon **Barber** with "Fidel's fight not to lose face – Castro explains why Angola lost the battle against SADF".[10] He said "... the 'heroic' defence of Cuito was therefore a vainglorious fraud, designed to cover a retreat that had already been decided."

Southern African statesmen were well informed. Soon after the crushing defeat of the Cuban/Angolans, Southern Africa's so-called front-line state presidents of that time encouraged the ANC to enter into negotiations with the South African government.

The Ultimate Conclusion

The last question is: What did the popular General Arnaldo Ochoa Sanchez say about Cuito Cuanavale?

---

8 Renwick, 1997.
9 Crocker, 1992.
10 Barber, 1989. Fidel's fight not to lose face. *Business Day*, 27 July.

He didn't say anything. In 1989, after Cuito Cuanavale, this national hero of the Republic of Cuba was executed by firing squad – he was dead.

The Cuban air force commander in Angola couldn't be executed. General Rafael Del Pino Diaz, who, like Ochoa Sanchez had fought side by side with Castro, had defected to the US during 1987.

*　　*　　*

War and lies are bad. What do peace and truth bring?

CHAPTER 27

Unpopular Peace

The fight against crime is being lost and crime is out of control – Michael Howard.[1]

Let the People kill Burglars

How do democratic countries react to crime?

Now that the war against crime is steadily being lost in Europe there is a change of heart. In the UK in 2003, *The Weekly Telegraph* quoted the metropolitan police chief, Sir John Stevens, who said it was time to let the people kill burglars; householders should be able to use whatever force was necessary to defend their homes against criminals, even if it involved killing the intruder, and that they should be allowed to do so without any risk of prosecution.[2] That's the UK, and only 211 people were murdered in London during the year!

In South Africa in 2006 there were over 16 000 murders! The Sunday newspaper, *Rapport* (16 April), which is not inclined to antagonise the ANC government, splashed this headline across its front page, *"Here, so kan dit nie aangaan nie"* (Lord, it can't go on like this). This is the SOS from the hearts of millions of South African victims of violent crimes after a spate of murders, farm attacks and cruel assaults. A header reads:

52 murders per day, 1 566 per month, 6 793 per year.

Immediately after this emotional public plea, violence took the streets of Cape Town by storm, as seldom if ever seen before.

The years 2005 and 2006 saw the South African police hiring security companies to protect their police stations. Then in mid-2006 these private

---

1 *The Weekly Telegraph*, 14 December 2004. Michael Howard was leader of the Conservative Party in the United Kingdom in December 2004.
2 *The Weekly Telegraph*, 7 May 2003.

security guards went on strike: marches, protests, demonstrations, looting, damage to public and private property, assault and shooting. And the police warned the public to stay out of the central business districts of Pretoria, Johannesburg, Cape Town and other cities because it had become too dangerous. What had happened to the country?

The following was the lead up to the crisis:

- The protracted low-intensity insurgency war in the Namibian-Angolan border regions came to an end in 1989.
- National service was terminated and the territorial forces dismantled.
- Racial quotas were haphazardly applied in the defence and police forces.
- Public safety rapidly eroded and made way for an unpopular peace.

Violent crime became a dominant factor in South Africa. Owing to various types of official restrictions on the release of crime statistics, the situation is never absolutely clear. During 2003 South Africa had one of the highest murder rates in the world at 48 murders per 100 000 people as against, for example, the US with six murders per 100 000. An average of 59 people per day were killed in South Africa, and more than 50 000 rape cases were reported annually, with no signs of improvement.

Veteran journalist Stephen Mulholland reported that "A sort of low-grade civil war has broken out on the Highveld with armed gangs brazenly attacking banks and shopping malls and ramming armoured cash-in-transit carriers before seizing their cash boxes. Bullets fly and people are killed and wounded."[3]

Our jurisprudential system is diabolical. Cases referred to the high court take up to 553 days from first appearance to the passing of sentence. Only 6% of violent crime cases end in a finding within two years.

Preparing for Iraq

The staggering truth is that the UK sends its military surgeons and nurses of the United Kingdom Defence Medical Services to the Johannesburg Hospital to gain much-needed experience before being deployed to Iraq. Ward 163 sees more than 1200 gunshot wounds a year. "These surgeons and nurses see more injuries in three weeks at the Johannesburg Hospital trauma unit than they would in their life-time in the UK," said Professor Kenneth Boffard of the hospital.

"Trauma surgeon Lieutenant-Commander James Badden said the experience he gained would stand him in good stead should he ever be deployed to

3 *The Citizen*, 3 November 2005.

a war zone. Major Mark Foster said, "At first I was a bit apprehensive about going to Iraq, but now with the experience I have gained I am more confident."[4]

Life-threatening ordeals are taking their toll. The number of police suicides is a cause of great concern. It's okay elsewhere to be super strict on "minimum force" and police decency, but in South Africa, where the crime rate is over the top, we need a different approach. Cops get little sympathy from the authorities.

When violent crime and the killing of policemen reach atrocious levels, it means that we are losing the struggle against crime: we have succumbed to living with it – we have acknowledged defeat. Public Safety has ceased to exist.

We sorely need a state of emergency. Law enforcers should have more freedom of action in the execution of their duties, and the judiciary more powers to impose harsher punishments, until the situation normalises.

I don't mean to curb the citizen's normal liberties; to the contrary, I advocate the restoration of the citizen's liberties, freedoms and rights. But, we are not safe anymore. Within a decade everything has changed: children used to walk to the nearest café at night without fear, and there were few security companies. Now –

We can't walk outside at night – the dark belongs to the criminals.
We isolate our homes – those who have homes.
We fence our homes – those who have homes.
We electrify the fences – those who have fences.
We have double doors and lock them both – those who can afford it.
We always look over our shoulders.
We are a captive society.

Those who are worst hit are the township dwellers and the farmers in the rural areas. No other country in the world has had or is having as many farmers killed as in South Africa.

Our government sits back. Jimmy says the people hear that the government doesn't want to stop the killings. He may well be right. In Muslim states, you just don't kill a policeman or a soldier. In Israel, if a soldier were shot in the street, the house from which the bullet was fired would literally be flattened. In the US, if you kill a cop, you are dead meat. Police are effective deterrents. In South Africa police officers are easy targets.

---

4 *The Citizen*, 1 November 2005.

The Nordic countries have an average of only 60 murders per year, while in South Africa there are nearly as many per day! These countries have donated funds to South Africa for use in the safety and security environment. They should cease such financial assistance forthwith until such time as their governments and people have a better understanding of what's happening in Africa. I propose instead that our government invites other countries with a proven record to come and give us a hand: China, North Korea, Iran, Haiti and Zimbabwe.

Tragically our police service is depleted. Those that still try their best often haven't got the means to function properly. A citizen reports theft or robbery only to be told: "We can't investigate the matter because we haven't got transport."!

Our government can't argue that it hasn't the financial capability. That is nonsense! The defence budget was drastically slashed. South Africa's military operations of the last number of decades in Namibia, Angola and elsewhere in Southern Africa ended in 1989; the research, development and manufacturing of a nuclear capability, artillery weaponry, tanks, aircraft and ships have been scrapped; national service has been terminated; the citizen force has all but disappeared; the territorial force has shrunk immensely. What has happened to the money that we have saved on all these activities?

Meanwhile embargoes and boycotts against South Africa have been lifted. Billions of dollars are pouring into the country like never before! Why can't we afford a suitably equipped police service? The frightened man in the street wants to know!

At the same time, the private sector security industry is booming like you cannot believe. The only industry showing better growth than this is the crime industry.

Instead of the politicians mollifying the public with bravado clichés of "declaring war against crime", they should declare a state of emergency, be constructive, and give us real hope. We want to level the playing fields so the policemen can do their job without fear, and the judiciary can adequately protect the freedoms and rights of citizens and victims, and regain the respect it deserves. There comes a time when you don't fight crime, you fight criminals.

Just as one cannot declare war against warfare, you cannot declare war against crime. War is declared against an entity.

Some people will undoubtedly tell you they don't like what I say. That's fine. You can respond that they should tell the politicians to quit play-acting, to stop deceiving the public and to fight criminals on level grounds. Can a politician declare war against terror?

CHAPTER 28

PCs foster Terror

We have made a paradise for terrorists in our own backyard – Alasdair Palmer[1].

What Apostles said

How do democratic countries react to terrorism?

On 3 January 2004, 148 French holidaymakers were killed when an Egyptian charter plane plunged into the Red Sea. The Islamic Ansar el-Haq, the Apostles of Truth, claimed responsibility. They threatened the French government with another attack should they not change their policy on religious headgear in French state schools.

This is terrorism – that is true. Some people call it terrorist warfare – that is not true. It is not warfare by any definition; it is criminal action perpetrated by civilians against women and children to promote pseudo-political, religious and other self-righteous aims.

The terrorists' *tactics* are continually to assault private individuals, singly or en masse. Their *strategy* is to demoralise the people. Their idea is that the cumulative effect of many murderous incidents over a period of time will cause a people to succumb; and the nation will sacrifice its values and eventually exert pressure on its government to accede to terrorist demands in favour of peace – a peace they would have enjoyed if it had not been for the terrorists.

In warfare the government and military leaders operate, or endeavour to operate, within international laws and conventions. Terrorists violate laws as a matter of policy and boast about doing so. There is no remorse – the more publicity they get the better.

---

1 *The Weekly Telegraph*, 7 May 2003.

Terrorists fight for causes which they claim are ordered by, or are in line with, God's will. In the process they use relatively cheap gadgets to cause major disruption and bloodshed. For example, by paying a suicide bomber's family a few thousand dollars they aim to force another country to change its laws.

The people, led by its government, must resist organised terror. This conflict will tax the mental and emotional stamina of a nation for a long time, maybe even generations. However, displays of long-term resolve demoralise terrorists.

Terrorists, like criminals, have the initiative. The criminal will decide when and where he will snatch a lady's handbag. The terrorist will decide when and where he will roll grenades down the aisle of a church.

In the US, on 11 September 2001, terrorists crashed two commercial aircraft carrying civilian passengers into the New York World Trade Centre's Twin Towers and destroyed them, killing approximately 3000 people.

George W Bush Jr. then declared war on terrorism. A declaration of war against terror is quite useless, unless it is qualified by legislation. Legislation is quite useless, unless it is effective and governments have the will to enforce it.

What Palmer said...

In the UK, in May 2003, Alasdair Palmer said, "Political correctness and policy errors have made life easy for them [the terrorists]." He claimed Britain had given refuge to a host of Islamic fundamentalists wanted for terrorism in countries around the world. The governments of France, India, Turkey, Israel, Algeria, Egypt, Jordan, Yemen and Saudi Arabia had all protested against Britain's protection of known terrorists. These protests had had no effect.

Palmer goes on to say that men such as Abu Qatadar, who had instructed Richard Reid, the shoe bomber, and Zacharias Moussaoui, who, in 2006, was sentenced to life in prison for his part in planning the attacks of 11 September, were allowed to remain in Britain, preaching and organising terror.

There was ample cause for taking counter measures. One video distributed by Islamic fundamentalists advised, "Your task against the infidel is to kill their children, take their women, destroy their homes."

Palmer concludes that the paralysis created by fear of offending the Muslim community in Britain had induced a kind of institutionalised political correctness that had prevented government departments from taking the vigorous action that was needed. He added that the "fear" was complete-ly misplaced since more than 1,8 million Muslims in Britain are not insulted if action is taken against firebrands such as Abu Qatadar.[2]

And then it happened – the infamous London terrorist bomb blasts of 7 July 2005 that shook Britain and the world – 56 killed, 700 injured.

The PCs had opted for pleasing a small minority within the decent and silent Muslim community – and dropped the whole nation!

How do we react to terrorist massacres?

In 1961 South African general CA "Pop" Fraser said, "The best counter to terrorism, and the only one to guarantee lasting results, is education."

What Dad said in 2001

In December 2001, *Rooi Rose* claimed that the horrendous event of the Twin Towers in New York initiated a new era of unrest for South African parents.[3] The magazine asked a father, Schalk Schoombie, "Dad, what do you say about terrorism?" The article deals with how parents should educate their children about terrorism. It took the terrorist attacks of 11 September 2001, 40 years after his pronouncement, to prove that Pop Fraser was right.

The article concludes: Schalk Schoombie drops his two kids off at school; he hugs each one, and looking them in the eye, says: "I love you very much." – *Hierteen is geen terreur bestand nie!* Love will resist terrorism!

Sadly that's not the way it works. To the contrary, terrorism thrives on emotion, sentiment and sensation. Terrorists would rather kill the members of loving families, preferably a kid daughter, than some unknown or lonely waif.

A nation should realise that education is a long-term pre-emptive and counter strategy to terrorism. It should not be a negative approach consist-ing of emotional and defensive preaching; it should be positive and rational coaching. It should not only expose unethical terrorist methods, it is more important and lasting to instil a deep appreciation of the nation's own irre-placeable values that are being threatened.

Earlier we discussed equipping our children with moral and ethical values to enable them to face the future as *individuals*; now individuals have to be armed with additional *collective* values to resist terrorism.

People should be educated from a young age to treasure core values such as freedom and human rights. They should also be taught how terrorism is a

2 *The Weekly Telegraph*, 7 May 2003.
3 *Rooi Rose*, 2001.

threat to such assets; who and what are behind these threats, what their tactics and strategies are, and what mental and emotional strength and stamina are required to resist and overcome them.

In long-established democratic countries young people tend to accept freedom as a given; they should be taught not to take it for granted – their forebears worked hard for it. It is really only when you lose a treasure you once had, that you appreciate its real value. Freedom has many facets and it includes the freedom of a democratically elected government to make legal decisions, such as the government of 148 French holidaymakers. There is no substitute for freedom.

Then, besides universal human rights, every country also has its own values and rights. In the US for example, the death penalty is still applicable in certain states. Switzerland values its nationhood and autonomy and refuses to become a member of most international organisations. And I don't regard it as necessary to tell you that the Irish are different from other people.

Every country targeted by terrorists should decide how much it cherishes its values. When the terrorists get the message that a nation collectively treasures its values such as its religions, cultures and languages, liberty and democracy and will defend these to the bitter end, that nation will triumph. We should treasure our values with a determined passion; not the sudden-rush-of-blood type of passion, but an enduring passion that forges a lasting mental resistance.

Feed emotional stamina and starve emotional sensationalism. Fighting terrorism will be a hard, long, tedious struggle.

What Say Fathers now

When it comes to terrorism, don't be like a red liberal PC. Listen when you are spoken to, discuss when necessary, and negotiate when required. Talk, yes, but never yield to intimidation. Don't negotiate your soul with the devil for the sake of escaping terror, even when the terrorists don't like a school child being forbidden to wear a headscarf in France.

The experiences of the British and the French have taught us a lesson. The liberal British have a generous open-door policy. They allow immigrants freely to practise their foreign religions and cultural customs. The conservative and patriotic French count on immigrants to assimilate into French society. They expect of them to adapt to the culture of their new *patria*.

Both suffered terrorist attacks. The lesson is that terrorists blow women, children and themselves into bloody morsels because their God told them so. They don't care about anyone else's culture or religion but their own. However divergent the British and French policies, to the terrorists they are all the same.

To declare war against terror(ism) or crime is simply a politician's way of getting the citizen's vote by a show of resolve. War must be declared against an entity – a country, organisation or individual that performs, aids, abets or allows people to perform acts of terror. If a government is really serious about combating terrorism, it should – after all reasonable conventional methods of friendly and coercive persuasion have failed – openly declare war against such a country.

The key aspect of any legislation dealing with terrorism is to define the vital elements of the crime of "terror" and "terrorism". In the UK legislation "terrorism" used to be linked to two elements: firstly, the *type of targets or victims* at the receiving end; and secondly, the type of *implements and methods* of the *perpetrator*. In the law of evidence, *motive* is not an element of the crime of terrorism. In South Africa we have been sitting on this problem for years.

There will definitely be some people who will not like what I say. That's fine. They should tell the politicians to quit play-acting and deceiving the public with their declarations of "war on terrorism". People of all races, political persuasions, standings, sexes and ages have been killed in terrorist attacks between 11 September 2001 and 9 November 2005 in the US, Peru, Tunisia, Pakistan, Indonesia, Kenya, Britain, Egypt, Saudi Arabia, Morocco, Afghanistan, Turkey, Spain and Jordan. The killings involved all types of societies – Muslim, Christian, Jewish, African and also Hindu.

In South Africa after September 2001, Schoombie dropped his kids off at school and pondered what to tell them about terror.

In Beslan in the Russian Federation, on the 1 September 2004, some loving fathers and mothers also saw their children off to school. They also gave them a hug and a kiss – and never saw them alive again.

* * *

Professor Klrtz agrees with me. You'll meet him soon.

We have discussed preservation. We deliberated on national security and public safety. Now we move on to the government's interesting function of facilitating economic growth.

And I have another confession to make.

CHAPTER 29

Poor People and Capitalist Pigs

How to stop poverty? Stop breeding – Leonie Theunissen, Cactus Creek.

Beg, Borrow and Steal

I confess I am for the poor.

After protecting what we wish to preserve, another function of government is to enable society to do good business and to prosper. Economic growth where the rich swap shares is one thing, but economic growth that creates jobs and alleviates poverty is quite another – and that's what we need in South Africa.

I discovered a truth of paramount importance:
The problem with the poor is they do not have enough money.
The problem with the rich is they have more than enough money.
Our problem with poor people is we have more than enough of them.

We make too many people.
The rich people are not the culprits – they procreate poorly.
The problem is with the poor people – they proliferate profusely.
High population growth in rich countries is not a problem – there isn't.
High population growth in poor countries is rampant – and a disaster.

Poor people in a poor country are not a problem because they are all poor.
Rich people in a rich country are not a problem except for boredom.
A few poor people in a very rich country are not a problem because they qualify for social welfare.
Many rich people in a very poor country are a problem; if you are one, you are a selfish, exploiting, capitalist pig.

Throughout the ages we have had laws, policemen, judges and re-educationists, and we have never been able to eradicate crime. In the same way, we can do whatever we like, but poverty to a degree will always be with us.

Social services and charity are the worst and last resort. They don't solve poverty. They simply accommodate the problem by alleviating human suffering, but at the same time secure its future.

Present-day Germany is well known for its highly developed extremist socialist politics, but the gap between rich and poor in Germany in 2004/5 had widened despite six years of social democrat-green government committed to achieving the opposite. A leaked report from the social affairs ministry showed that the proportion of people living in poverty rose from 12.1% in 1988 to 13.5% in 2003.

In African countries in the early 2000s – perhaps not for the same reasons – the trend is also for the rich to become richer, and for the poor to become poorer and increase in number.

We can try eliminating the rich, then everyone will be poor and the problem will cease to exist, or we can distribute the wealth evenly, but we already know from the communist experience that that leads to the equal distribution of poverty.

We cannot let the rich live and the poor die, so we must make the poor richer. The best way to achieve this is to distribute poverty among much fewer people; we should not make more people than those for whom we can care.

I asked the Lion King about poverty. He looked at me as if I were from outer space. "We don't know such a thing as poverty in my kingdom."

You don't find poverty among animals. Nature has its own way of creating a balance between different animal and plant species. It also controls the optimum population levels of each species in any particular ecological environment.

Animals don't have contraception. Their populations are restricted in other ways.

Balance is maintained by cross-elimination between species. Predators kill other animals for food. (We do too.) In addition, within some species, their own members including the parents and siblings will destroy some of the offspring or the eggs. This they do to restrict the population to that which the environment can sustain. Their way nips the agony in the bud. Otherwise their misery is prolonged, with a slow and miserable death setting in at a later stage – as we humans do.

The further we move away from nature the more poverty we create. If we don't want to use nature's way of elimination because we regard it as cruel, we must devise other non-cruel means of managing the problem. But the more socio-political solutions we find to accommodate poverty, the more we sustain it. We can't continue in this way because at present we are crueller than animals.

Mind Your Own Business

The government is forever thinking up more labour legislation, and big business is forever streamlining its human resources. The best advice for the government with regard to promoting national economics is to stay out of it. Business excels when there is economic freedom. Politics, democracy and human rights don't bring economic growth.

To enhance growth, a climate of opportunity and competition that will attract businessmen to create small businesses should be developed. Such a situation calls for minimal restrictions. We have exacerbated poverty through political restrictions on the economy and lackadaisical immigration control – every day is a Be Kind to Aliens Day. And the government through its "kindly" legislation, and NGOs and donors through their misplaced generosity sustain and encourage poverty.

We need the dynamics that go with initiative and enterprise, as well as the productivity that goes with being smart and working hard.

I believe it was Wellington who said that a big country can't fight a little war. And nowadays big PC business cannot curb poverty.

Celestial foreigners from rich Western countries often annoy me with their naïve wisdom and stupid ideas about poor African countries. Some foreign nations have negative, or well nigh zero per cent population growth. In their annual budgets they don't have to provide for more schools and the multiple other "mores" that go with high population growth. They can use all their gains to further their growth and increase their already high standards of living for their stagnant population; they can finance the finesses of democracy and a highly cultured society.

In South Africa we constantly have to budget for more development areas, more houses, more water, more waste disposal, more energy, more schools, more medical clinics and more transport, more ministers and more overseas jollies – all because of increasing overpopulation.

Overpopulation is not a new problem. About a thousand years ago the Mayans had an empire superior to those of many old world civilisations. As they flourished, they destroyed more and more of the environment to make space for more and more construction, and to feed more and more people. The increase in population and the decrease of natural resources led to their downfall.

149

World-renowned David Attenborough sums it all up: in the same way as we used to manage the environment to sustain population growth, we should now manage the population to sustain the environment – if we want to survive.

In South Africa the macroeconomics are firmly in place and lauded by the government, the international world, the multinational companies and the local rich. Unfortunately this admirable state of economics means little to the poor people – they know nothing about it and don't benefit from it. Where did we go wrong?

Even Western countries find it difficult to rationalise the interrelationships between population growth, poverty, unemployment, job creation, taxation, charity, social welfare, making and repealing laws, and economic growth.

An excess of legislation and structuring puts the economy in a straight jacket that suits only big corporations and internationals. Big business may create nominal growth, but it does not promote real productivity and real growth, and does not create jobs for the man on the street. Between 1995 and 2002, with all the major economic factors in place, the official unemployment rate in South Africa increased from 16.4% to 30.5%.

A Wee Problem

In earlier days, only communist-type countries, whose economies have since crashed, had ministers of sports...

Jimmy interrupts. Ever since his visit to his cousin Leprechin in the Far East he has been nursing an idea, and I quote directly from Jimminese:

I suggest we take our cue from the Chinese and make a change by creating quite a different portfolio for an extra minister, and perhaps a deputy minister. They would politically manage one of the most essential inventions of man – The Thing. Without it, big cities like Rio de Janeiro and Shanghai would never have been able to exist.

The Chinese showed off their state-of-the-art Thing to 400 delegates at the November Beijing 2004 conference. Yu Debin[1] said, "... It represents a country's level of development. It reflects a place's level of material and spiritual civilisation."

That was the fourth annual World Summit on The Thing – the flush toilet.

---

1 *The Citizen*, 6 November 2004.

Singaporean Jack Sim said, "Governments realise that toilets are the competitive edge of the nation."[2] And South Africa hasn't even got a minister of toilets!

Jimmy concludes: "The deputy minister should preferably not be a woman; it is not for nothing that the men's urinal got the vote for the single most influential work of art of the 20th century!"[3]

2 *The Citizen*, 22 November 2004.
3 *The Weekly Telegraph*, 14 December 2004.

CHAPTER 30

A Professor called Klrtz

You have the right to make babies – Professor Klrtz.

Joy Rides

While shaping a new socio-economic culture, and to assist us in dealing with poverty and its ramifications, I should tell you about my true blue liberal friend Douglas Peacock. He is an academic without a cause and an expert on human living – ancient and modern. He is a self-made rich man. He invited me to join him for one of his series of interviews with a most extraordinary visiting colleague – a professor called Klrtz.

His guest was an extraterrestrial research professor working on a project about civilisations of the galaxies through the ages. Dougie first briefed him. I listened intently to the alien guest's response:

"¥¤§¢¿δ?υαβχδεφγηιφ – thank you, but your obsession with poverty leaves me dumbfounded. I refer to your lamentations about childcare, orphanages and street children.

You have to restore equilibrium in your lopsided rights culture. We have rights too, but they come with their essential balancing obligations.

Let me tell you how we manage rights as opposed to the decadent, super postmodernistic and tragic way you do it. Start with the basics. In your case everyone has the right to own a motorcar. But quite rightly you prescribe certain requirements and obligations for exercising this right; we do the same for our space vehicles.

In spite of your right to own a vehicle you have to register and license it. It has to pass a roadworthy test. In spite of your right to drive it, you have to prove that you satisfy certain driving skills requirements. And you must pass a test to prove your knowledge and application of the laws and rules before you are issued with a driver's licence.

You strictly follow the maintenance manual and keep it roadworthy. You people care for your cars...

You also have the right to own and use a weapon. But you have to obey similar prescriptions and restrictions – age, sense of responsibility, skills and mental health. Your weapon owners are very particular about maintaining their possessions. If a weapon is not in regular use, it is properly treated and put away. You care for your guns."

Lust and Disaster

Klrtz got very excited: "You are so correct in everything you do except in the most vital aspect of planetary existence – life and giving life!"

He stared into the heavens.

"With us, creating life is a joy and treasure. With you, it's lust and disaster!!

The right to own and use automobiles and weapons, although they are apparently great killers of your species, is trivial in comparison with something much more important which you virtually don't even think to manage at all – procreation.

You have the right to make babies. Yes, but in your case it is a free for all. Your prescribed requirements and obligations are for all intents and purposes non-existent. You don't have to register and take out a licence to make a baby. It's much easier to make babies than to have motorcars or weapons. There are virtually no restrictions on age and responsibility. Your males may not even know how many babies they make – you have carte blanche and no strings attached.

You are crazy about motorcars and guns, but you don't give a damn about making babies and deserting them. If some do care about their offspring, but are incapable of

153

looking after them, they naturally and as a matter of course leave them in the care of government and society.

Your lack of managing procreation is one of my biggest disappointments with you earthlings. You would appear to our people, I am sorry to say, to be extremely insensitive and self-righteous when it comes to creating life. You don't act unwisely – you are worse, you have absolutely no conscience and no moral culture!!

Like you, each of our males and females also has the right to have children. And we also have our weaknesses, but this right is coupled to certain prescribed requirements. In the case of natural conventional reproduction, every one of us must be registered after birth, the same as you, and every one gets a once-off licence to procreate when he or she requests it. And this licence is renewable from time to time.

Every one of us has to submit to a simple medical protocol at a certain age. It is very similar to the obligations you told me about. You have to be vaccinated against smallpox and polio at certain times. And also when you travel to other countries, you need to submit proof that you have had the necessary vaccinations against diseases such as yellow fever.

In our case, at a certain stage after birth, a minor procedure is performed at a local clinic where, for ease of understanding, let's say something like a microchip is inserted into every female and every male. This makes fertilisation between any partners impossible.

When a couple wants to have children, they must qualify. They must apply and follow the stipulated protocol to obtain a licence. Successful applicants then have their chips reset for the required period.

The granting and renewal of licences depend on very much the same parameters that you lay down for owning and using motorcars and guns in terms of age, sanity and responsibility. But most of all, the issuing authority must be convinced that one or both of the parents will care for their offspring properly until it becomes self-sufficient.

This is why we don't need childcare institutions, either governmental or societal.

Of course, as you well know, there are many other ways of managing sperm, and of producing babies, which I won't go into now, but the main point is: You simply cannot allow unrestricted proliferation by people who haven't got the means or even the intention to care for the young.

The crucial and strictly applied rule is that the well-being of the children must be guaranteed before a licence is issued. I'm sorry to say but you people are very unfeeling and uncaring, and worse, you don't seem to know it - ¥¤§¢¿ð?υαβχδεφγηιφ"

We all said good night. Until next time.

* * *

Earlier we reviewed the functions governance should perform. A socialist autocracy with a centralised dictatorial form of governance demands complete subservience to the state. The government controls the press and provides all the social services. We should therefore look briefly at democracy's mass media and society's NGOs.

CHAPTER 31

Mike and the Poster Girl

You who are strong and swift, see that you do not limp before the lame, deeming it as kindness – Kahlil Gibran.

The Baby

Since we have had a look at the functions of government, we can now focus on some aspects of how society functions, including the private mass media. In the administrative hierarchy of a business, every entity reports to an overseer, until responsibility ultimately rests with the senior executive who is responsible to shareholders or owners. This is also true of our public service – until we come to the government at the top. It doesn't report to anybody. It is supposed to be responsible to the people, but that is a theoretical concept; it doesn't happen that way in practice, not in South Africa's voting-for-parties democracy.

That's where the press comes in. It is not an end in itself; it is a vital instrument in achieving and maintaining a free society. It projects today's history today. It has no substitute as the watchdog over the management of the affairs of state. The press performs the important function of voicing the people's protests against unfair government practices.

Citizens abdicate their say for five years and have no influence until the day of the next election when they can, hopefully, voice an opinion once more. In South Africa we, the citizens, had no input regarding the formation of the African Union, nor did we have a say about donating R10 million to Haiti; the press had to protest for us.

The press looks after the people's interests during the political recess - the period between two election campaigns. This lamentable, flawed type of democracy cannot function properly without a brave and independent media, especially when the government dominates the TV and radio.

Tiny, black toddler Birham Woldu was barely three when she was given up for dead. BBC journalist Michael Buerk made this pathetic child famous in the form of the Famine Poster Girl. Twenty years later, reporter Angela Johnson related this story,[1] which took place during the misery that gripped Ethiopia in 1984. Enter the NGOs and Bob Geldof with Live Aid who raised money for disaster relief.

Many pop stars have staged glamorous concerts and NGOs raised funds to relieve the agony of abject poverty and to save starving infants. The splendid Pavarotti did the same. At one time, the "in" target country for charitable NGOs was Ethiopia. Later it was Mozambique, and other countries followed one after the other, including Guatemala and Kosovo. There always seems to be a new fashionable country or disaster, and the old ones disappear from central stage. We don't hear much about Ethiopia or Mozambique anymore.

I don't recall ever hearing what had happened to the babies after the concerts or after they had reached the age of four or five – or whether they ever did. And the older tots? Did they ever go to school, and to what level? If they did, did they find jobs or other ways of making a living afterwards? Are there sufficient public records of the sequel to these concerts and projects?

Wouldn't it be sad to learn that the babies did not survive? Or if they did, that they never went to school; or if they did go to school, that they couldn't find a way of making a living – and continued to make more babies. In view of all this, might we not have been cruel by prolonging the agony?

Many PC organisations and NGOs are international concerns and report to their masters overseas. They do not seem to be under much scrutiny and sometimes even appear to be secretive. Do you read about them in the press? I believe all projects and organisations should be transparent.

Charity ventures lend themselves to the system of Management by Projects. This in turn implies that every project should have a beginning and an end – and a project manager. Furthermore, it implies that every manager must report on the outcome of his project by stages – from its inception, and more important, to its final conclusion.

This means you cannot, by whatever reasoning, raise money for a project to save babies for a time only until they reach the age of two. If the post two-year age period is not planned for by one and the same project, then another project should take over from that point, or another structural arrangement should apply. If there is no such provision made then the project shouldn't

---

1 *The Star*, 6 January 2004.

be started. The long-range venture should be finalised only when the baby becomes self-reliant.

I would like to believe that this is the way it happens. I also believe that the donors and the project managers can tell us all we want to know, and that they do have long-range objectives to save babies and see them through school and ultimately to employment.

In some developing countries, NGO spending on social affairs substantially exceeds that which is provided through the national budget. We don't know to whom these organisations report besides to their donors and head offices in Europe and the US. They go about their good and evil, benevolent and vindictive operations in an unobtrusive way. Some should be welcomed and lauded, and others should arouse serious concerns.

We do know that all fund-raising organisations have to be registered; that they have to abide by financial and auditing rules and regulations, and that society's relevant "interest groups" probably know exactly what is happening in their particular domains.

Furthermore, researchers most likely have access to any documents and statistics and can probably get all the information they may need. But what about us, the public at large? Is the media failing to inform us, or are the NGOs unnecessarily tight-lipped, or overly modest?

While the media often target governments, politicians, the civil service, parastatals and big business, the NGOs live a happy, oblivious and sometimes arrogant life. A minister picks up flak fired by the press for sleeping in parliament, and a departmental director general for running a business from his office, but have you ever read about an NGO or its representative being taken to task for anything whatsoever – before they were taken to court for fraud, that is?

Recently, per chance, I noticed a newspaper article on a survey done on NGOs. My first reaction was that at last we would see who and what they are all about! To my chagrin, there was no feedback on projects. The article dealt with a typical PC topic: the issue of whether the composition of the management of the NGO correctly represented the gender and national four colour race ratios – all the old nauseating PC stuff!

Of course, the tempo of race and gender transformation in NGOs should be speeded up to the point where women dominate the scene. Then perhaps we'll come to know more about NGOs.

NGOs cannot forever remain half faceless and sneaky; they should do much more to keep the public informed about their projects and their end results. I am disappointed in them.

George Soros has NGOs for Africa, all over the world that is, including his Open Society Institute, which is also active in South Africa. Internationally the transparency and decision-making process of this institute is in dispute – you'll find all this on the Internet.

The Student

For those who don't know, it gives me immense pleasure to tell you that the little Famine Poster Girl is alive and well. In early 2004, Birham Woldu was a happy 22-year-old agricultural student on the brink of a bright new future.

Fantastic! But the only reason we know this is because Michael Buerk had a professional and personal interest to track her down, making it possible for reporter Angela Johnson to keep us informed.

This story of Ms Johnson has a sequel with a moral:

Despite the [Woldu] family's improved fortunes and optimistic outlook, Ethiopia is still a country that continues to hover on the brink of disaster. Even in a normal year, 6 million people would die without Western aid. This has created a cycle of dependency and hunger for a population that has doubled to 66.5 million since 1984. Half of them are malnourished.[2]

A $200 million-a-year aid programme aimed at ending hunger as a "man-made disaster" and weaning 5 million people off food aid began in January 2005. As of the end of May, only 11% of the cash and 44% of the food had reached people in need, said a government study. Beneficiaries of the programme are given food or cash in return for doing public works like building roads.[3]

Tarentaal calls some foreign NGOs the neo-colonialists of the 21st century.

---

2 *The Star*, 6 January 2004.
3 *The Citizen*, 29 July 2005.

CHAPTER 32

Red Neo-Colonialists

Creating Blue Heavens in Africa

Most NGOs are PCs. There is a non-governmental organisation, institute, heritage, foundation, or some kind of fund established for every thinkable kind of human activity. The NGOs are like the liberals: the blues and the reds. The reds are the baddies. They are zealously intent on changing society and politics to their own liking. The blues, with their love for nature and charity, are good.

Red PC NGOs and their donors believe they are saving Africa and steering it down the road to a better world. I can't stand it!

Once, I also wished I were an NGO. After the war in Iraq when that government and administration had crumbled, I had a vision. I thought it was the ideal opportunity to construct a new utopian political model from scratch – from ground level upwards. It is a proverbial grave that one digs from the top downwards, which incidentally is what the conquerors eventually did.

If one had pooled all the funds and resources, it would have been no problem to start with the villages, towns and districts and to get their civil administrations functioning to the satisfaction of the people. Then the local inhabitants could have voted for how they wanted to be grouped together in cantons, states or provinces, if at all.

Once the local and/or regional administrations were functioning well and their constitutions written and accepted by the people, then, and only then, would I have looked at establishing a central government, if there had been a need for one – or establishing a benevolent shah.

Unfortunately, or fortunately perhaps, I am not an NGO. However, an array of people – less modest than I and with the arrogance that money, ignorance and stupidity sometime bring – thought that Africa was the ideal laboratory for their lofty and impractical NGO schemes, and especially South Africa after 1994.

These people don't know us; they experiment with us and implement their controversial ideas here. They don't mind making mistakes because they won't live here long enough to suffer the outcomes of their follies.

For many decades now the European PCs have practised the most liberal policies thinkable to accommodate aliens in their countries. They have persisted with these policies in spite of protests based on sound political and social arguments. The PCs, always believing that they know better than other people, especially people in other countries, have also demanded that we follow their example. What they don't consider is that poor aliens in a rich European country is one thing, but poor aliens in a poor African country is quite another. In Africa the aliens push our informal vendors, hawkers and beggars off the streets and sidewalks. And now the PCs can't understand why we don't support their Be Kind To Aliens campaign. (I must admit though that the aliens also oust our waitrons from the restaurants because they are friendlier.)

Lately, some Europeans have made an almost complete 180-degree turn in their thinking, but regrets come too late and little can repair the harm already done in many parts of the world. As a result of skewed past thinking the *Makwere-kwere*, the alien, has become a real issue in South Africa. How many other Western PC experiments will they impose on us here, such as the post-modern outcomes-based education (OBE) system that hasn't been fully tested in their own countries? In the UK for example, it is a much-criticised topic and the debate continues.

However, there is one difference between them and me. I know that I don't know Iraq and its peoples. But at least I intended to compensate for my ignorance by imagining that I would start with the people themselves at ground level.

The international NGOs come to Africa not knowing us. That's fine, but they think they do. They come with feigned modesty veiling their arrogance. They come with a high hand and start at the top; they connive with government to thump us, on the ground, into line through legislation. This has been done so hurriedly that time and again the new laws they instigated, like the anti-gun and -smoking laws, have had to be amended before they could be implemented in practice.

These red PC NGOs are the neo-colonialists.

The old Western imperial colonialists plundered our wealth and took it back to Europe. They had their offices overseas. If any of them came to Africa they made short business visits to check their trade and industrial interests in the colonies. They didn't know Africa and its peoples; they didn't want to and they didn't have to. They didn't settle here; they were the bad guys.

The settlers who came and stayed were the good guys. They braved the new world; they made a living here, laboured and tilled the soil. Over the centuries they became one with Africa.

The international Western NGOs bring money. They educate and modernise us – and wait for applause. They don't get it. What they get is the Yankee Go Home type of reaction. But they are like ducks – these kind words flow off their backs like water.

These foreigners may not have the slightest feeling for the history and culture of the country and its peoples. If they are neutral and open-minded as a result, they could be an asset. But if they harbour a holier-than-thou and know-all attitude, supporting tendencies and causes they have picked up in Europe or elsewhere, they may be extremely dangerous.

This do-good phenomenon probably results from a guilty conscience about colonialist slavery or the *Herrenvolk* idea in a previous Germany. These people want to prove their inherent goodness by uplifting the primitive and poor people of Africa. Their business this time is to bring modernity, intellect and money... they think.

Unhappy Europeans – Happy Africans
In the meantime without any fuss the Orientals – Malaysia, Korea, Japan, and especially India and China – are making big strides into Africa and South Africa. Popular opinion is that Mugabe's "clean up of Harare" was to make room for his liberation struggle comrades, the Chinese.

But Africa is much prouder than and not quite as ignorant as these people might think. South Africa is not another Iraq. Foreign troops didn't march through our cities and streets. South Africa is not another Kosovo, Somalia, Guatemala, Sudan or Liberia. South Africa is not a banana republic or typical third-world country incapable of managing its own affairs. This is not what I say – this is what surprised foreign visitors tell me: goodwill all around, magnificent infrastructure, no signs of blood and smoke in the streets.

A major issue that concerns Africanists is that the foreign and domestic NGOs create needs on a massive scale – and these needs cannot then be satisfied!

According to a RSG early morning radio programme broadcast on 8 October 2005, the Germans have the highest per capita income, yet, according to another survey, they are the unhappiest people in the world. (Much the same goes for the English.) The happiest people in the world live in Africa, according to the same survey!

Many people in Africa earn less than a dollar a day in monetary terms, but they live happily and have a good life. Many have roofs over their heads, food to eat, clothes to wear and basic education for their children. They don't have money, but they barter.

The unhappy foreign red NGOs then come and tell them they are living below the bread line: they should have more cash, dress better and have better modes of transport – a need and a problem is created. This modus operandi now enables the NGO to register a fund, collect money, "do good" and feel good.

The government is the face, but the NGOs armed with their money keep many an African boat afloat. They govern indirectly and instigate the newest legislation models, such as those pertaining to nuclear waste, same-sex marriages, and so on.

In questioning the credentials of NGOs during the African peer review mechanism conference, our President Mbeki said there was a need to ask whether we actually have an independent African civil society, because you have civil society organisations funded by the Americans and the Swedes, and the Danes, and the Japanese and so on, who set agendas.

It is about time the taxpayers in Sweden and elsewhere came to realise that their money isn't welcomed in Africa.

However, when it comes to national NGOs subsidised by the government, it is a horse of a different colour. The ANC's obsession with racial engineering focuses on NGO staff, many of who were in the front line defending the poor and oppressed during apartheid. Gauteng's Department of Social Development has now announced that, within three years, only NGOs that serve the "historically disadvantaged" and whose staff reflects South Africa's racial demographics (quotas) will receive funding.

Apart from the fact that this department is funded by all taxpayers, there is an almost 40% shortfall of social workers in Gauteng. So who will replace the white staff shown the door? Who will care for the poor and needy, a function fulfilled by many NGOs without regard for race long before the ANC got its hands on the public purse?

This is political manipulation and social engineering of the worst kind.[1]

Jimmy: Like Al Jolson said, you ain't heard nuthin' yet.

---

1 *The Citizen*, 2 May 2005.

CHAPTER 33

Nongqawuse's Revenge

65 : 24 : 10 : 0.75

We have noted the role played by South Africa's demographics – the racial ratios of the total national population – in the government's race engineering policies. Since this subject recurs from time to time, a brief overview would be quite useful.

The official ratios required for the ethnic restructuring of human resources complements, in the public sector, published by the authorities are not always the same. The "baseline targets", given by the minister of defence in a parliamentary briefing on 9 September 2003, are: black – 65%, white – 24%, coloured – 10% and Asian – 0.75%. However, it is important to bear in mind that the national race ratios – race quotas – are based on the country's overall population figures, in spite of the fact that the composition of the population differs considerably from place to place! For example, the actual race ratios in Durban are vastly different from those in Bloemfontein and from the national ratios. The same goes for the Eastern Province and the Western Cape.

The imposition of the official macro national ratios on micro situations is a social evil. It is a source of endless misery. It necessitates the total rearrangement of personnel structures in certain localities thus affecting communities and societies, and sometimes it even means that, on a large scale, families have to move homes.

However, the human resources complement of organisations and offices of all the national departments throughout the country must change. By certain target dates each must reflect the national ratios. For example, the composition of the officials in the department of correctional services at Pollsmoor in the Western Cape and that of Leeukop in Gauteng must both reflect the same national ratios (which are different from the local and regional ratios). The same goes for the police, defence force and others.

In practice this means that blacks settled in the Eastern Cape must be moved to the Western Cape, and coloured people from the Western Cape must make way and be moved elsewhere, and so on. The problem for the people is not only changing workplace, but also changing their children's schools and the family's living accommodation – lock, stock and barrel! Every locality must ultimately reflect the official national ratios: 65 : 24 : 10 : 0.75.

While this racial manipulation is applied officially in the civil service, it is also pursued in various unfair ways and through coercion in business, sport and everyday life.

"What a mess", Jimmy observes. Ms Tarentaal sheds a tear.

* * *

With a brief but meaningful glance at Ms Tarentaal, Gnu remarks, "Everything starts with a woman: in this case it started with the adolescent Xhosa prophetess, Nongqawuse. After the British had defeated the Xhosa during the Eighth Frontier War of the mid-1850s, Nongqawuse, supported by paramount chief Sarhili and her guardian Mhlakaza, told her people to stop cultivating their crops and to begin slaughtering their cattle. She led the people to believe that on a certain day... the ancestors would escape from their graves and their warriors would drive the British and other settlers occupying their lands into the sea.

"The colonial authorities at the time believed it was a sinister plot to destroy colonial power."

"Gnu, have you been reading *The Reader's Digest* history book again?" chirps Tarentaal.

"No, I've been travelling. My cousin Inxu in the Eastern Cape told me that Nongqawuse's spirit still haunts the land, but her prophecy has not yet materialised. The Xhosas had suffered a setback from which they never recovered..."

Jimmy chips in: "Aren't Nongqawuse's revenge, and the race quotas of course, the reasons why Xhosas pop up in the Western Cape, the North-West province, well, all over the country far away from their original home turf? I'll invite them soon to my sparkling pools at Umhlanga. You know guys, the problem with humans is that their parents drilled prejudicial concepts into their heads from a young age."

"Yes," offers Tarentaal, "when a Xhosa goes for a first meeting with an unknown Zulu, he is sure the Zulu is going to be obstinate in the extreme. His Xhosa parents ingrained this idea in him."

"That's right," reacts Gnu, "and when a Zulu goes for a first meeting with an unknown Xhosa, he knows ahead of time that the Xhosa is going to toy with the truth. It became second nature, his Zulu parents taught him that."

I ask Jimmy, "Now what do your parents say about us whiteys?"

Tarentaal jumps the gun: "I was taught the English are decent and proper," she says. "They observe all the courtesies. But they don't make their intentions clear. 'Be careful!' we were taught."

Gnu concludes the discourse: "The Afrikaners are boorish. 'They have no finesse', we were told. They are backward, and are often rudely abrupt. But you know where you stand with an Afrikaner within five minutes. He is generally frank and honest, that's what we've been taught."

"Is that so?" observes Jimmy.

Gnu and Tarentaal look at each other and wink. Jimmy looks at me and smiles, impishly.

CHAPTER 34

The Politically Incorrect Ark of Prosperity

Carnival of the Animals

After our initial consideration of the forms and functions of governance, we went on a detour to look at NGOs. We are now back on track to plan a better future.

We need to create a new climate, a different socio-political culture for the people – the New Design. To function successfully within this new environment, we need a new dispensation and structures – the PI Ark. This Politically Incorrect Ark will negotiate the waters of our New Design.

However, to get to that point, we should be clear on where we are at present and what we leave behind, because that's where we begin our voyage.

To clarify our present status I arranged a people's think tank, which you might call Tarentaal and Gnu in Concert, with the ethereal presence of Professor Klrtz. Jimmy is facilitator, interpreter and trouble-shooter. Why the bird and the beast you might ask? Well, Aristotle taught about *man – a political animal*, so why can't we use *animal – a political man*? (Jimmy and our other two friends are not always clear on which is which anyway.)

Tarentaal: "Our foremothers knew the ancient Greeks and Romans well. Socrates and Galileo would be stunned to hear about our modern state-of-the-art innovations. Can you imagine Galileo's reaction if we should shuttle him to space stations and back with Mark Shuttleworth?"

Gnu: "I agree, Aristotle would be amazed to hear about us being ready to clone human beings!"

Then Jimmy comes with the fatal blow: "You guys don't know what you are talking about. They won't be impressed at all! Let me remind you about a few subjects on which Aristotle used to tutor, then I'll elaborate:

Aristotle 'talked as he walked' about logical analysis, false concepts of unity, courts of law, of plutocracies, the good citizen, government true and perverted, sovereignty of the people, kingly rule, varieties of democracy, mixed constitutions, revolutions in democracies, overthrow and preservation of monarchies, the beneficent despot and inferior kinds of democracy. He divided constitutions - forms of government - on the basis of *good* and *bad*:

> Good government by a wise individual is Monarchy.
> Bad government by a bad individual is Tyranny.
> Good government by the good few is Aristocracy.
> Bad government by the bad few is Oligarchy.
> Good government by the good many is Polity.
> Bad government by the bad many is Democracy."

Jimmy is spot on. Polity is what this book is all about. He continues: "Can you guys now see that we don't know what we are talking about. These are only a few of the subjects that the people researched and practised in Aristotle's time. What is new today? Nothing!

"If they were to know how we still struggle with the old problems of the rich and the poor, bad tyrants – Sun Kings, Papa Docs and Mugabes – and if they knew how we struggle with a decrepit non-functional voting-for-parties democracy at the expense of people's sovereignty, they would cringe! How would they react if they were to know how we still struggle to ensure a smooth transition of political power in countries all over Africa – and the world?"

In 2005 in Mauritania army officers very unsportingly seized power while their President, Maaouiya Ould Taya, was out of the country for duty and/or pleasure. What would Aristotle and colleagues say about this sort of progress?

Jimmy sighs: "There has been no improvement; all this is happening 2300 years after Aristotle! Like Klrtz, they would really be stunned to tears!"

Bird's Eye View

So, to obtain another unbiased view of our current position I refer again to the ever-reliable Professor Klrtz:

Democracy and your parliamentary system remain puzzling. What you call **politics** seems to be a time- and energy-wasting distraction ... it would seem as if the ordering of your society has mostly been based on race. Order in itself is a dangerous thing. It inherently implies restriction, and any restriction on freedom - a concept that has nothing to do with your democracy, parliaments and politicians - is a hindrance to excellence. Granted, a minimum form of order or equilibrium, harmonious or symbiotic association such as

found in nature will always remain a necessity. In nature it comes by itself. It is only when the natural course is disturbed that you have to reset the interdependent multiple balancing conglomerates.

Your race system appears to have worked quite well. In your recent past your worst violent confrontations happened within races rather than between them. People of mixed race, whom I would say are the salt of the earth, have had a hard time. They are at the receiving end of conflict of their different racial origins.

Where you have more than one race in any particular demarcated area, you maintain order through absolute domination and intolerance, which is about the worst way of handling such situations. You achieved stability for short periods only.

On the other hand, the monarchical system of **governance** has worked better than any other. Although some of your rulers have been imbeciles or juvenile kings, this evidently made little difference to the system. I suppose it may even have worked out better in the long run. Your only problems arose with the monarchs who were bad but clever enough to become rich tyrants, and with those that became self-styled kings. Except for the odd evil ruler, your monarchs seem to have reigned over happy societies. Whether by divine inspiration or some other reason, it seems they were the first to progress to gender empowerment, and at the highest level at that.

In your very recent past you tended to replace the monarchs with presidents, but this didn't change your situation noticeably. With a lot of bloodshed, some of them became self-styled kings or rulers for life anyway – without any blue blood. Having no claim to divine rights – but perhaps making the claim later – they followed the path of their evil royal predecessors, but even worse.

Finally, your real problem is religious intolerance. You experienced it not too long ago, but now it seems to be picking up a new momentum at an alarming rate. I will concede that any religion not based on a doctrine of love and goodness is wrong.

You may be making the same mistake with your concept of religion as you did with your concept of governance. In your terminology governance actually means one thing, largely good and well intended, while politics is something totally different and based on deception and cheating.

In the same way you confuse the concepts in **religious doctrines** with the matter of **church laws**. Religion is about good and evil. Church laws are something else. If you were ever to be judged, I honestly don't think that the dear Lord would mind much about what you ate and how you dressed on any particular day in the world of the living.

The battle between good and evil persists. Whatever you cherish you should guard with all your might. There is no good way of handling this conflict; the best is to avoid it. If this fails, the second best option is to engage in battle. The worst is to lose everything. With this doctrine we haven't had a war for millennia.

The essence for your world's future success is to maintain a harmonious inter-cultural relationship between peoples and nature. Good night! ¥¤§¢¿ð?φ

This story is as untrue as you want it to be.

Shipshape

Now we have a fair idea of our current situation and how to proceed to a better future. Life's like a boat: you have to brave the stormy waters and ride the gentle waves. So, we will construct a people's vessel of bliss, the PI Ark. We'll build it step by step, custom made for the new Shangri-la.

Able seaman Snooks told me you always build a ship by starting with an inverted pyramid. That's exactly what we do. This is what it looks like when we place it in the dock before we knock it into shipshape.

It consists of four strata. The pinnacle of the pyramid, now upside down, is dug in well below ground level. This is where we keep the Head of State,

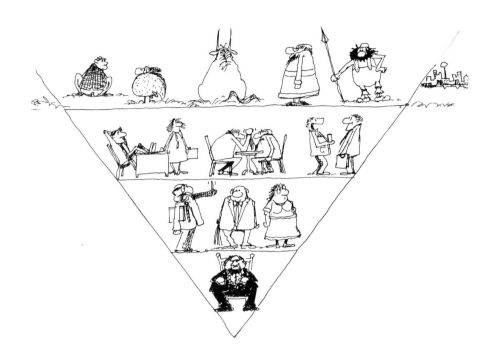

for the time being – the king or president, sultan, tyrant or dictator – safe and snug where he can do no harm.

At the other end of the pyramid, namely at the base, now at the top, we have The People with their feet firmly on the ground – the ruled, governed, regulated, oppressed, the subjects, citizens, victims and voters.

Then, below the people, and supporting them, we have what we used to call the Civil Administration. Next, adjoining the heads of state and protecting them, are the ministers and politicians. We will shortly attend to these strata one by one. For now, let's get back to the unreal world in which we live, our current environment.

Jimmy says the mistake we make when writing scenarios is that we always neglect the illogicalities, coincidences and outrageousness rampant in real life.

CHAPTER 35

The Wolf and the Lambs

"Life is infinitely stranger than anything which the mind of man could invent. We would not dare to conceive the things which are mere commonplaces of existence... the queer things which are going on, the strange coincidences, the plannings, the cross purposes, the wonderful chains of events... and leading to the most outré results, it would make all fiction with its conventionalities and foreseen conclusions most stale and unprofitable... there is nothing so unnatural as the commonplace" said Sherlock Holmes to his dear fellow, Doctor Watson – Sir Arthur Conan Doyle.

Sherlock Holmes and Fareed Zakaria

After the extraterrestrial interlude with Klrtz, we continue with our analysis of the present down-to-earth environment. The main problem that is yet to be solved is the endless conflict between bad tyrannical rulers and good innocent people.

The people are the most important. People are very complicated, as Conan Doyle points out. We are essentially and predominantly good, but it is only natural that along with our virtues we will have shortcomings. What is the African perspective? Do we really want one-party "democracies"? What about leadership by experts, in coalition with the people?

Every now and again in Africa, when there is political disagreement in a country it turns into discord, and serious or violent friction. This is followed by appeals from all around, including Western PCs, for the president and the leaders of the opposition, if any, to get together and talk, and hopefully to form a "government of national unity" – that never works.

Tarentaal chips in: "It's all your fault, Gnu, GNU – Government of National Unity."

Unperturbed, Gnu looks the other way into the serene skies of blue innocence.

Can't we understand, or is it not part of our culture to know that democracy is built on the lively expression of differing views? And different views often translate into having different parties. Governments of national unity usually mean the demise of the opposition. Can't we manage democracy – I mean our present type of democracy? Is the problem that our parties are organised on racial lines, or that they are not, or what? Are we all ready for raceless societies?

We know that dictatorships are unacceptable, and that the current form of democracy we use is highly questionable. The people should be the source of all power. As soon as they relinquish power, dictators pop up.

Democracy used to have a good reputation and governments still bask in its glory, obscuring the suffering of the people in the shadows, such as in the Zimbabwean "democracy". Autocracy has a bad name, but the system is overt in the sense that everybody knows it is autocratic and supposed to be bad. Therefore the government goes out of its way to demonstrate to all how good it is; and it may even be good, or look good – unfortunately, only for a while.

The bad thing about a voting-for-parties democracy is that it doesn't satisfy the ultimate in freedom, namely the freedom of decision-making by the people – the freedom of choice. In practice that freedom is relinquished to politicians and parties at every election.

Fareed Zakaria says, "The 20th century was marked by two broad trends: the regulation of capitalism and the deregulation of democracy. Both experiments overreached."[1]

Quoting Zakaria, Lawrence Schlemmer states, "... democracy must take on a new role in the 21st century, in practice as well as theory"[2] and points out that polls in the US, which rate the peoples' respect for organisations, structures and institutes put their Supreme Court, the armed forces, and the Federal Reserve system at the top of the list, while the US Congress comes in almost at the bottom.

Schlemmer again quotes Zakaria, who explains "how representative democracy throughout the world is being used as a screen behind which illiberal agendas are being imposed, gradually destroying the freedoms on which democracy was originally based".

When there are no effective checks and balances in the exercise of power, as in South Africa, major issues affecting society should be depoliticised.

---

1 www.fareedzakaria.com/articles/newsweek (13/9/2005)
2 *The Citizen* (quoting *Focus* published by the Helen Suzman Foundation)

Schlemmer and Zakaria agree that impartial professional commissions should prepare policies for *elected politicians* to approve or reject, thus playing a role similar to that of central banks but extended into a wider field.

This is exactly what I advocate, but solutions for the really important issues should be prepared by the experts for final acceptance or rejection *through voting by the people* – those people who are knowledgeable and who will be affected. I'm wary of so-called "elected politicians".

Bad Democracies and Peacekeeping Tyrants

The issue of the ruler vis-à-vis the ruled was often highlighted during the Iraqi war of 2003. A South African radio reporter commented from the Middle East that the friendly Iraqis in the street say they are quite sympathetic towards the Americans, but they don't like Bush whom they regard as bad. They also say Saddam was bad but they had peace and stability.

The reporter summed it all up – we must now make up our minds for the New Design:

> The Americans are good people, but they voted for the wrong man. Should we now say that the majority of Americans were wrong and therefore democracy is not a good form of government?
>
> The Iraqis are good people, but the Iraqi leader is bad. Should we now agree that undemocratic leaders are tyrants and evil, but that they are preferable because they bring peace and stability?

The conclusion is that democracy and elections don't work; voting for persons and parties instead of issues or plans don't work. War is wrong; dictators are bad but acceptable because they bring a miserable stability.

The organised international community, especially the red liberals, has sanctioned many rigged elections for the sake of peace. Africa has had a series of elections during the last decades, many of which were seriously challenged with regard to them being Free and Fair. Some were condemned outright, but their governments are still in power. The latest in this long and unfortunate list are Zimbabwe, Togo and Nigeria.

The 2005 Zimbabwean election could have been declared null and void long before the day of the election! The voter's roll was absolutely and totally inadequate – the most vital element of any fair election. The South African observers who gave it the nod made fools of themselves. Once again we must decide if we want peace, stability, democracy and misery – or what?

We, the people, have to choose between an autocracy for short-term stability on the one hand, or a different type of democracy on the other.

Jimmy interrupts. "Uncle Joe, stop your PC nonsense. The truth is, in Africa democracies are hard to find. There is very little evidence that democracy works and even less that the people of Africa want it. Democracy is a word that is used only to appease the West in order to assure continued aid. Namibia and South Africa are two of a handful of exceptions, and both would be more accurately described as one-party democracies, which are not real democracies. In practice they are much akin to old-style Greek oligarchic democracies – elitist rule. One of the reasons why such 'democracies' fail is the absence of a constitutional monarch."

If you have a constitutional monarch as the head of state – and it is absolutely necessary to have an executive head of government – your best bet could be to have a benevolent dictator like President Bongo.

"You made a mistake, Uncle Joe, or Danny Kaye did, when he sang that Bongo was from the Congo. Omar Bongo is the president of Gabon. And he is the last and longest serving of Africa's Big Men. He has been in power since 1967 and has changed the constitution to enable him to stay in power until 2012. He believes African countries need autocratic leaders to deal with ethnic tensions. Gabon's history has proved him right. He has 30 illegitimate children and is regarded as a strict but benign father of the nation – a benevolent dictator. He frequently dips into his own pockets to solve state crises. Voters turn a blind eye to his government's corruption as he is willing to spend money on the electorate and on the young."[3]

Apart from Jimmy's input, we can conclude that the best form of government for us in the New Design would be:

A constitutional monarch – as the guardian of the constitution, the sovereignty of the people, the corps of benevolent NGOs and the rule of law; and responsible to oversee the smooth handover of executive powers

An independent technocratic bureaucracy – to operate in conjunction with the peoples' experts (independent commissions, central bank, etc)

A bureaucracy and independent commissions – to prepare and conduct the regular and ad hoc elections

Elections in which the people concerned and the relevant experts vote on issues and on projects, thus restoring sovereignty – which will remain untouchable – to the people

Gnu is hesitant: "I understand, of course, but there are many people who lack perspective and who will resist change, like those who have never had

3 *Pretoria News*, 30 November 2005.

a king, queen or emperor like the Japanese have, and those like the Americans who are used to voting for parties."

"I know where to find the right perspectives," says Jimmy. "Let's see where recent history leads us."

CHAPTER 36

Royalty and Rugby

King Goodwill Zwelithini of the Zulus should be instated as King of KwaZulu-Natal, leaving the premier of the province as is – JJ Geldenhuys.[1]

Jimmy says it's a great idea, and have you ever seen a gnu smile? But Tarentaal says, "Scaly politicians have coerced our innocent king to campaign for deleting 'Natal' from the name of our province – the name of my ancestors! His uncle, Mangosutho Buthelezi, should get him back into the fold of royal decency, or the ANC should stop him before the name of the Eastern Cape is changed back to British Kaffraria."

Eastern Europe, DRC and the Great Lakes

Recent history has taught us that in the old design, if a country comprises different religious and cultural groups and if you want stability and peace, autocratic rule is the answer – for a while. However, it doesn't necessarily produce unqualified happiness and a high standard of living. As soon as rigid rule disappears in favour of democracy, instability and violence erupt.

The autocratic, multicultural Eastern European countries including Tito's Yugoslavia and the Soviet Union were stable and manageably peaceful, but had a questionable quality of life. However, when autocracy came to an end, these countries, in their new form of fragmented democracies, lived through a relatively brief, but ghastly period of friction, fighting and misery. It was only after these upheavals that they settled down to pursue a prosperous new future – after the devolution of power and decentralisation of administration.

---

1 *The Tokoloshe Times*, 24 May 2006.

In other words, if well-being, harmony and high standards of living in the long term are the main requirements, go for independent democracies or democratic federations or confederations.

The Eastern European experience, however, did not repeat itself in Africa when the vast old autocratic Zaire became the new Democratic Republic of Congo (DRC). The DRC with its continual violence is no more stable than the old Zaire. The Congolese – if there are such a people – have never settled down like the Eastern Europeans did. Why not? Because the DRC should also have been split into a number of independent democracies perhaps loosely joined in a federation, as happened in Eastern Europe and the old Soviet Union. Of course, the one spin-off of establishing more absolute independent states as they did in Eastern Europe is that it would generate more anti-American votes in the UN.

In order to achieve peace, stability and prosperity, we cannot consider the DRC in isolation. Since the African Union resolved to address the issues of international borders in Africa, we should consider the DRC in conjunction with other countries of the Great Lakes region, especially Rwanda, Burundi and so on. The fate of these people is closely interrelated and currently they find themselves in a state of shared misery – perhaps unnecessarily so.

If the African Union is really serious, but does not want fragmentation on the scale of the old Eastern Europe and Soviet Union, it may end up with one mighty United Confederated States of Central Africa. I concede that the disadvantage of such an arrangement would translate to only one anti-American vote at the UN.

However, the reason why in Central Africa we have just been going on and on and on without solving anything is because nobody cared, and everybody was scared; the real solutions are new intra-African borders and new nominal (constitutional) heads of state – solutions totally unacceptable to the PCs!

Telling the Truth Baldly

In real life it is quite often artists more than politicians and academics who show the way. In South Africa, the highly intelligent and popular superstar Nataniël has said it all. Confronted with the question, "What would you change if you could be the state president?" he said:

Everything. The state president's job is really to be a kind of top secretary to make life easier for us. Not the other way around. I don't know where the misunderstanding comes from that secretaries are not allowed to have limousines, expensive homes and private jets. Something is out of place with the job description and we fools have been brainwashed to think that we haven't got rights. The state president (just like the police and other civil servants) is here to serve us and we are not being served.

And everybody moans, but nobody does anything.

There is only one queen, Queen Elizabeth, who may sit in a palace and may drink tea from porcelain cups. Because she is a queen, not a secretary. It's her job.[2]

The best head of state would be a benevolent monarch by whatever name – queen, sultan or AN Other. The best way to make this monarch benevolent would be to strip him of power.

Why a monarch? A monarch is there primarily to protect the constitution and to ensure a smooth transition from one government to another. The Hapsburg Emperor Franz Joseph described his role as emperor as "to protect my peoples from their governments".

Why a monarch without power? Simply because we, the people, should not relinquish our sovereignty to anyone.

The people who easily relinquish their sovereignty are those who always want a "strong leader" or a "strong government", or those who have become numb, dumb and mum, or those who are illiterate or semi-literate, those who are not informed, those who feel insecure and don't want to shoulder responsibility, or those who don't care.

Monarchies are alive and well. There are 15 countries including Australia, Canada and New Zealand doing very well under their powerless sovereign Queen Elizabeth II. Other constitutional monarchies going strong, to mention a few, are Jordan under King Abdullah II, Malaysia under King Syed Sirajuddin, the Netherlands under Queen Beatrix, and Sweden under King Carl Gustav XVI.

In South Africa politicians pay lip service to African royalty and other traditional leaders, and some abuse them by playing their usual political games. Would it be very different if our royals and nobility were reinstated by a genuine South African king? Monarchs are the custodians of a nation's traditions and cultures.

Gnu cannot resist: "Jimmy, who is your favourite for King of South Africa – Nelson Mandela? He delivers magic in the field of welfare and rugby – without any executive powers."

---

2 *Finesse*, December 2003.

Jimmy gives Tarentaal a sideways glance: "Who says the monarch must be a king?"

And nodding in my direction: "I suppose, Gnu, you'll have to be patient for a few more chapters before we decide who it will be?"

Pomp and Glory

There were monarchs all over the world although they were known by different names. Africa's queens and kings were just as good or bad as those in the East, the Middle East and Europe. In Europe the royals developed over many centuries to what they are today.

The colonialists destroyed the kingdoms of Africa, thus denying our own African royalty the same process of development. Then after World War II, they suddenly got rid of their colonies as fast as they possibly could. The problem started when they did not hand over the reins to the royal African dynasties. Instead they passed power on to completely new, inexperienced and untrained politicians who couldn't combine Western democracy and African custom.

Having installed Western style political structures, the colonialists left the erstwhile socio-political systems of the Africans completely destroyed. As a result, the people's dreams were in ashes; their countries were soon reduced to rubble, and democracy became buried alive in tyrannies and one-party states. Instant ownership of Power, Wealth and Status by one person became the biggest problem that the people had faced throughout the ages.

People and their leaders should be trained to conduct themselves in a modern democratic society, and they should work at it. However, what I know now is that, anywhere in the world, if you give the unqualified vote to too many innocent illiterate, half-literate, ill-informed, ignorant and politically uprooted decent people too fast, you are bound to produce crooked politicians. Handing out the unqualified vote creates fertile soil for one-party states and tyrants – especially where you have a multicultural population dominated by one cultural group within a unitary state, with a single constitution and strong centralised governance. An upstart politician, who suddenly becomes too big for his boots, usually stumbles and causes untold misery – power gained quickly corrupts quickly.

Classic democracy with freedom in its sights could have developed into governance by the people, but then the red PCs stepped in and we ended up with the masses having a meaningless vote and being ruled by elite, untouchable, power-drunk politicians.

Capitalism with free enterprise in its sights could have developed into productivity and prosperity for the people, but then the red PCs stepped in and we ended up with non-productive, non-job-creating business moguls in cahoots with governments. As a result legislation had to be passed to protect the people against such monopolies. If these party-powered politicians and business moguls get together the people are doomed!

You may conclude that a wealthy monarch from a long line of royalty without power will be your best head of state for the New Design.

If we return to our sketch, the question now is what do we put in the strata between the people on the ground level and the monarch in his buried pinnacle?

"As little as possible," Jimmy chuckles.

Oupa Moilwa of the Bahurutse royal family and Princess Ntandoyesizwe, daughter of Zulu king Goodwill Zwelithini.

Source: S'bu Mfeka, courtesy of the *Sunday Tribune*.

* * *

P.S. In retrospect Jimmy is quite right. Those who serve the people and the country should be experts on Solving Problems and Making Decisions, and they must Deliver. But if you were to ask a panel of experts who is best qualified to meet the requirements, they would tell you that parliaments and cabinets are the worst mechanisms you can possibly think of to perform these functions.

The required expertise can, however, be found in non-governmental and non-political government organisations such as central banks, research councils and so on, and the civil service, including municipalities.

CHAPTER 37

Civil and Uncivil

We are willing to give free lessons at any school of choice on protocol on race profiling -
Mr. Panyaza Lesufi, spokesperson for the Gauteng Provincial Department of
Education[1]

Uncivil – No Knowledge, No Experience, No Accountability

We have had a good look at the stratum of the heads of state, and also at that
of the people, and the interplay between these two. We must now tackle the
remaining two strata: the one of ministers and lesser politicians, and the one
of the civil service.

Cabinets of ministers in their present form must be abolished completely. You won't miss them, I promise you. All this business of ministers makes
for a good laugh. At the highest level of solving the problems of a country,
ministers rotate from one portfolio to another to another. They voyage from
Health and Sanity to Foreign Affairs, to Correctional Services, to Sports –
now isn't that nice?

The rationale behind these musical chairs, politicians claim, is that at this
high level the top person does not need to be knowledgeable on the particular function of a department. What he needs is knowledge and experience of
leadership and management.

Politicians further argue that the minister is not the *functional* head of the
department; he is the *political* head responsible for its political management.
Now, he doesn't know the terrain of the departmental activity and is not
accountable for financial expenditure, so what politics is there to manage,
say, in the department of finance or correctional services? It's a farce.

---

1 *The Citizen*, 2 May 2005.

However, in South Africa, following the example of the political minister of sports, our political minister of correctional services may also wish to rearrange the racial composition of the inmates in his charge according to the race quota system. If so, he could plan the early release of his guests in such a manner that the remaining inhabitants of his facilities represent the officially prescribed race ratios of the country.

When we go to the polls we vote for a person or political party we think will best look after our interests. What we don't always consciously realise is that the politician probably knows far less than what we give him credit for. That is why the director-general of any particular department is much better suited to the department's function than a politician.

In post-2000 South Africa we find that the top civil servants are also deployed to rotate laterally in the same merry-go-round fashion as the ministers. The question now arises as to how far down the hierarchy we have to go before we find an incumbent who, apart from recycling, knows the job?

If we accept the status quo it means that we actually trust politicians, and that we abdicate our power in their favour for five years at a time.

Modern democracy hasn't changed with the times. There is too much emphasis on politicians governing their subjects and too little focus on the civil service facilitating living for the people. In fact, the civil service has become an instrument of the politicians. In the US, they talk about the "Clinton administration".

In South Africa it is worse: for instance, Mr Panyaza Lesufi snubbed Helen Zille of the Democratic Alliance (DA), who, on behalf of the people, queried the envisaged classification of schoolchildren by race. She said that she would submit a complaint to the South African Human Rights Commission, and also call for a parliamentary debate. This is how he responded: "... we are willing to give them [the DA] free lessons at any school of their choice on protocol on race profiling."

Lesufi is apparently only a spokesperson, an unknown spokesperson, not of the presidency, not of the government, not of the national civil service, but of a Gauteng provincial department. In any decent democracy, an upstart low-level provincial civil servant who is supposed to serve the community would never be allowed to address a legally and democratically appointed representative of the people in such a manner.

If that's the way an insignificant civil servant wants the people, his clients, to be admonished, he should get a cabinet minister or his MEC – an elected politician – to speak his vulgar language for him.

The people had valid concerns: "... this [new race] policy also throws up the terrible spectre of 'race testing' for children whose race group is not immediately apparent," Zille said.[2]

Racial classification is a violation of human dignity – let alone a child's – protected in terms of Section 10 of the constitution. The trade union Solidarity intends to take the government to the constitutional court, unless it comes to its senses. This apartheid-type race classification would probably not be opposed by the Scandinavians.

Clearly this is one of many examples of the civil service becoming integrated with the governing party – from the highest to the lowest level.

Civil Service – Foundation of the People's Well-being

We now consider the final stratum. In the inverted triangle just below The People, we find another layer supporting them – the civil service. Modern democracy must make room for a civil service with a difference – a service working in conjunction with society's own commissions in a people's bureaucracy where the people vote for plans instead of for politicians.

The bureaucracy, not the politicians, is the foundation for facilitating well-being and human endeavour. We don't want civil administrators under the command of ministers and responsible to them doing "small favours" for the people. In that sort of setup the officials try to please the ministers and to do us, the people, in.

We want an administrative service for the people and responsible to the people. In this case the administrative service wouldn't care about ministers – if there were any – and it would make sure that the people got what they needed without paying too much tax. We don't want the civil service to be called or to be something like "the Blair administration"; we want a proper Peoples' Administrative Facilitating Service – PAFS.

To achieve a harmonious society we, the people, don't need to be subjected to governance. We can achieve harmony through the constitution, laws and regulations.

All we need is a facilitative service rendering good administration. To facilitate elections its experts will join hands with the experts of society's own socio-economic organisations like unions, chambers, foundations and institutes, and will present us with identified issues to be settled. For every issue they will propose a number of alternative solutions and those of us who have an interest in any particular issue will select the option of our choice by vote.

* * *

2 *The Citizen*, 2 May 2005.

For Want of a Canton

A Civil Service – Depoliticised

The People's Administrative Facilitating Service (PAFS) will function closest to the people – at ground level where we live. It will facilitate living according to the constitution, laws, regulations and by-laws.

At grass-roots level a homogenous community, *a canton*, should have one constitution. Two or more communities of the same homogenous type, especially if adjacent to each other, could have one constitution for them all. A bigger society consisting of a number of such communities could be grouped together and be called a *province, state* or something similar, and have the same constitution.

Likewise, in an even bigger society, there could be a number of provinces, but with different cultural brands of homogeneity, yet sharing common regional interests. Then you end up with a country that needs a broadly based national constitution that will accommodate those of the provinces and cantons.

As in existing federations, you could have a national constitution that embraces common aspects such as universal human rights. However, it would not include matters such as safeguarding 11 official languages for the whole country. This is a theoretical and utterly impractical oddity and in South Africa already the cause of unnecessary friction. Every individual canton or province's constitution may provide for two or three official languages. The national constitution would acknowledge such regional official languages, and furthermore could make provision for a few national *lingua francas*.

Religion and other tricky issues such as language can be treated in the same way. If you start building your political framework from the bottom upwards, all the people's preferences can be accommodated in practice.

This model of development of political structures, from the local to the national levels, can evolve naturally over a period of time. However, if circumstances demand intervention, the development must be well planned and timely instituted. It is not a matter of "deleting" absolute monarchies and "inserting" democracies, which is unfortunately what did happen.

In the vast subcontinent of British India with different religions and languages, "partitioning" started in 1947 between India and Pakistan (leading to three wars and more than a million Hindus and Muslims killed), and eventually concluded with the independence of Bangladesh in 1971.

In Africa the colonialists indeed performed "delete and insert" operations. The large and populous Nigeria with religion, language and business issues, still struggles to come to terms with the externally imposed structure.

The remnants of the colonial delete and insert operations along the central African belt have been begging for a new dispensation to escape from the haphazard jigsaw puzzle for the last number of decades. Heads of governments not inclined to think more than five years ahead keep the mess alive.

In South Africa, with our diversity, we should have had more of a federal type of governmental structure, or even a confederated structure, which would have included kingdoms. Our provinces and districts should have had more autonomy such as the provinces or states in Canada and the US, and in many European countries like Germany and Switzerland.

In North America and Europe this has proved to be a commendable dispensation; in Africa it is probably essential. In South Africa, as a result of our national government's obsession with one-party domination and centralisation of political power at the top, our constitution does not play its rightful role in developing people-responsibility. Let's see:

Everyone at local level complains that municipalities don't deliver. Why not? Because the people at that level don't accept responsibility for their own affairs; they look to the central government to do everything for them, and they wait for the president's next visit to voice their complaints. And the ruling party machine appoints its pet candidates as municipal managers. They are only after money. They know nothing about the job. Fraud and corruption are rife, but who cares – that's politics.

Or is it? General Bantu Holomisa, leader of the United Democratic Movement, has other ideas: "Keep politics and politicians out of the civil service and corruption will stop." [1] He advises that we depoliticise the civil service completely.

---

1 *The Citizen*, 19 October 2005.

The regional and community levels of governance are paramount. This is where the civil service – PAFS – comes into its own. The people at grass-roots level want facilitation by a custom-made administrative service – not multipurpose, high-handed governance from the very top that enforces quasi-universal laws.

Article 235 of our constitution reads:
The right of the South African people as a whole to self determination, as manifested in this Constitution, does not preclude, within the framework of this right, recognition of the notion of the right of self determination of any community sharing a common cultural and language heritage, within a territorial entity in the Republic or any other way, determined by national legislation.

Big Pay, No Tax, No Vote

Even a passable but not-so-effective PAFS can probably not cause as much damage as one clever power-drunk politician. The bureaucracy can be, and often is, commendably effective.

We want an efficient skeleton civil service on all levels. It should be an elite corps with a single goal, namely to serve the people. Its formation should be based on three principles:

Officials will be highly trained and promoted according to service achievement and track record.

Officials will be paid on a par with big business and judicial functionaries.

The civil service will uphold values of excellence, honour and pride and adhere to a very strict, regulated ethical conduct.

I am not referring to the novel codes of conduct that have been made so popular by PC workshops and displayed in entrances and waiting rooms. We don't want a constitution *and* laws *and* regulations *and* codes of ethics. In the case of the civil service, codes governing its behaviour should have the same force as the law, like the military disciplinary codes of modern democratic countries.

Civil servants shouldn't have the vote. If they observe high ethical standards, and even though they are highly paid, I would also exempt them from paying personal taxes on their salaries. Yes, the right to vote is almost sacred, but to vote for people or parties means nothing. The people want to vote for the plans that will be in their best interests – for them personally, and in terms of their province and country – but the civil servants can't be partisan and vote for the plans that they themselves have helped to develop.

The most important administration takes place at the level of the towns, cities and districts. Most of the traditional civil service functions should be undertaken by independent commissions or be outsourced. Why should governments issue driving licences? With laws, regulations and procedures in place, any company can do this job.

Only those government functions that cannot be performed by independent commissions or the private sector should be retained in the People's Administrative Facilitating Service. Furthermore, the whole system should be run according to the accepted and proven methods of Management by Projects in which every project is managed on the principle of Management by Objectives.

Accounting systems should be based on productivity and formatted accordingly. There is not a single government function that cannot be monitored by using the same principles and methods as are used in the private sector.

Run affairs of state like a business. Business people are often described as *conservative*. While there is nothing wrong with that, it's not factually correct to say so. They are *realists*, for the simple reason that they work with their own money and that of their shareholders. And more often than not, shareholders have a vote on issues.

The *good* NGOs will play a vital role. They have already discreetly been doing so for a long time. Since there will be no politicians in the New Design, the NGOs can now rise from their skull-down positions. Those that are active in the terrain of charity and social welfare will perform their tasks under the auspices of the non-executive head of state.

Will the new system work? We often prefer old ways even when we are aware of their failings, because we find comfort in custom, and we shy away from novelty in spite of the benefits because the unknown creates insecurity – and worst of all we suffer from illusions of what is bad and what is good. We should rid ourselves of these human weaknesses.

CHAPTER 39

Illusions Illusions Illusions

What we see is strongly linked to our expectations, frequently to our memory, and sometimes to our emotions... – Nobel Prize winner Torsten Wiesel.[1]

Decrepit Politics and Radical Changes

Any plan, or the New Design in our case, should be assessed for feasibility. Some of you will probably not accept the ideas we have shared so far, let alone regard them as feasible. Sadly, feasibility is often all in the mind – a matter of personal opinion, of partiality and prejudice. Worse still, all of us unknowingly suffer from more illusions than we'd care to believe.

We may suffer the illusion that the political system to which we have become accustomed is good enough, or that our suggested changes to it are not feasible. The PCs won't even give our ideas a second thought.

PC minds are cluttered. If they happen to recognise a truth, they reject it out of hand if it in any way clashes with their causes and self-interests. They have unlearnt the virtue of reconsidering their views when truth and reality require it.

The normal citizen wakes up each day oblivious of the traps of political illusions. Red PCs and politicians try to make us believe that crime is not really so serious; that political power is not being centralised, and if it is that this holds no danger; and that the say of parents in their children's schooling is not being eroded. Such illusions often go hand in hand with conditioning.

The party spin doctors devise propaganda plans to demolish their opponents and to indoctrinate the electorate. In the old Soviet Union and in some places in the Orient they have political warfare schools, sometimes known by other names, run by their red PCs.

---

1 *BMW Magazine*, March 2003.

On his departure, Jimmy's guest, Gerry the Gnome von Zurich, told him, "In South Africa, apart from deceiving the people, the indoctrination seems to be aimed at eradicating all vestiges of despicable Western culture and promoting historical African grandeur."

The latest devious conspiracy is all about unity. If what the PC spin masters tell us were true, then it would mean there is no unity in most, if not all, of the real democratic countries. Germany, for instance, is divided straight down the middle as seen in the almost 50-50 split in their voting!

In South Africa, the governing party won the 2004 elections with a landslide 70% of the votes against a number of smaller parties. This reflects a united South Africa with barely a 30% dissention. The government's first announcement after the election was that it would launch a big campaign to unite all South Africans. This reminds one very much of the old Soviet Union which regarded peace and unity as meaning the absence of opposition!

Differences in political opinion do not mean *lack of national unity*. That is a PC-created illusion. But where differences do exist it is good to have national symbols of unity. The Netherlands quite often has a multitude of political parties in its parliament – one could describe it as a nation "splintered" by politics. But the Dutch never perceive themselves as a fragmented nation or lament their lot – they have symbols of unity, such as their monarch.

South African Illusions – The US

On the eve of finalising the draft for the New Design, two watershed events in the grand coliseum of politics rocked South African PC illusions – the US elections of November 2004 and the British elections of May 2005. The outcomes of the two elections destroyed South African political illusions and exposed the ridiculousness of current democracy.

The first illusion in South Africa was that Bush and his Republican Party were going to be crushed during the elections as never before. The red liberal PCs created this illusion. In the run-up to the 2004 elections, the PCs prematurely but confidently predicted not so much a Kerry and Democratic Party victory as a demolition of Bush and the Republicans. South Africans all wanted to do the "in" thing, to be "with it". You were branded as antagonistic, an outcast and ignoramus if you so much as dared to suggest any other possibility.

Of course, the people who followed the Pied Piper PCs enthusiastically thought they had good reason to believe that Bush was in for a crushing defeat. They became *illusioned*, among others by the most extensive mustering of forces against Bush and the Republicans.

Michael Moore splashed his cinematic anti-Bush film, *Fahrenheit 11*, at Cannes and won a prize. PC superstar George Soros, the founder and financier of the Open Society Institute of South Africa, tried to buy a Republican defeat with money. During May 2004 this individual pledged $10 million to Steve Rosenthal and Ellen Malcolm of the liberal activist group America Coming Together (ACT) to mobilise voters in 17 battleground states. Soros quipped, "They were ready to kiss me."

Let's hope and trust that when he takes his seat around the table of our president's advisory council he limits his advice to sound financial matters and avoids politics. With all his money can you imagine what will happen if he decides to back Eugene Terreblanche, or the minister of sports, or the South African Communist Party Youth League?

And then came the shock!

And what a shock it was! People just couldn't believe their eyes, ears and the news reports. The Americans resoundingly returned Bush to office for a second time, much more convincingly than during his first election. In the House and Senate the Republicans broke all records – their most memorable victory ever! How could it happen? Was it a miracle?

If the preconceived conviction of a Bush defeat wasn't an illusion, what was it? We simply have to admit we had fallen victim to the illusions created by deceiving red PCs. This leads to the question: How can it be that more than 90% of us, the decent people had been fooled so convincingly? And how many other political concepts in which we believe in good faith are in fact a deception and untrue?

How can we test perceptions to discover what is false and what is true? The answer is easy: introduce money into the equation and you find the truth. The only thing South Africans had to do before the elections was to consult the odds offered by the bookies! Money is the bookmakers' business; if he makes mistakes he goes bankrupt; money brings reality to the party. Bookmakers and punters have always given a better indication of the results of US presidential elections than political analysts and opinion polls, and this one was no exception.

In early 2005, the *Reader's Digest* came up with an article entitled "Why Bush Won". Anyone who keeps an open mind could have told the PC *Digest* that much more appropriate and pressing was the question "Why were there so many ignorant South Africans convinced that Bush would lose?"

UK Illusions

The second illusion involves the revered bastion of modern Western democracy, the British system. Contrary to what most believe, the British have the silliest voting system you could possibly think of – also exposed during their May 2005 elections. Mr Tony Blair also scored a record third term in office in the May 2005 elections!

I don't understand the English voting-for-parties democracy, and I'm not the only one. How did Blair win more than half the seats on offer with just over a third of the popular vote? The British "first past the post" electoral system has long been a national peculiarity, but rarely have the quirks of the voting method been more starkly highlighted.

In the May poll Blair's Labour Party won 35.2% of the vote – equal to just 21.6% of all registered electors – and yet managed to win 356 seats in the House of Commons – 55% of the total!

The main opposition Conservatives won only slightly fewer votes, 32.3% of those cast, yet ended up with 197 seats (while the smaller Liberal Democrats have 62 MPs – 9.5% of the total – with 22% of the popular vote). How confused can you get?

Andrew Kenny, arguably the second best feature writer in South Africa, calculated that the Conservatives needed over three times as many votes as Labour to get a seat.[2] This is plain unfair!

Nina Temple said: "A travesty of democracy – according to the present system a party could receive 49.9% of the vote in every constituency, yet end up with no representation in parliament." Ms Temple heads a group campaigning for a new electoral system.[3]

Are you sure that we should support such an absolutely junky political system as a voting-for-parties democracy?

Jimmy says: "Another illusion about the goodness of the blue-eyed boy, Modern Democracy, is tumbling."

Ms. Tarentaal adds: "If there is anything wrong with the British, it is definitely not the monarchy – Queen Elizabeth II with her corgis; it is the politics, the voting-for-parties system."

2 *The Citizen*, 10 May 2005.
3 *The Citizen*, 12 May 2005.

CHAPTER 40

The New Design

Those were the Days

Reflecting on our shattered illusions, we should ask ourselves how the red liberal PCs could have succeeded in conditioning us, the South African people, to accept such false persuasions. Isn't it time to close the book on our latest conviction-turned-fallacy – our obsession with parties and politicians? We have become so used to political causes, traditions, customs, conventions, routines and procedures that they have become part of our everyday lives.

Furthermore, when a new idea is proffered, we often make the mistake of trying to fit it into the prevailing scenario. During the early 1900s, when the horse-loving farmer's Ole Faithful died and people suggested he buy a motorcar, the grumpy old-timer argued that a motorcar would be too big to pass through the stable door. The mental struggle of accommodating unfamiliar scenarios is nothing new.

We have become used to shrugging our shoulders and exclaiming, "*C'est la vie* – that's life." Down here we say, "That's Africa." Let's get out of that rut!

I bounced some of the New Design ideas off friends of mine. On firing the minister and letting the director-general (DG) get on with the job, one said, "How can a director-general do the job of a minister? The minister, in spite of having very little knowledge of his portfolio, has always been a person of note and a status figure. The DG by comparison, in spite of being properly trained and actually doing the job, has always been seen to be an unobtrusive nincompoop. It can't work!"

A newspaper editor would probably say, "A world without politicians is unthinkable; I need political fraud and corruption, otherwise my paper goes down the drain."

The NGOs would be in a state of shock. Never before have they had to deal with the problem of unemployed rich ministers. However, the most important of the lot are thrilled – Jimmy the Reed, Tarentaal and Gnu, and perhaps even Professor Klrtz.

A friend suggested that we keep the old design, but do a better job when selecting persons for key jobs.

Let's have a look. If you insist on retaining an executive president, I seriously suggest you nominate your *most* intelligent and lazy candidate for the job. I would caution you though that a ruler who is intelligent and evil is bad news. Perhaps I would rather go for a stupid but decent president. That is why I maintain that a juvenile moron nominal king could be better than a manipulative fourth-term or lifelong executive president.

If you prefer to stick with the antiquated system of cabinets, I propose that you earmark those who are *not quite as* intelligent and lazy for directors-general of the most important departments.

I recommend that those whom you regard as industrious and intelligent would make good deputy presidents and deputy directors-general. Although they are not supposed to carry the responsibility, they do the work. In South Africa I would not be surprised to find them in the current Department of Finance and the Reserve Bank.

Those who are stupid and industrious and who are more likely to be the most verbose are difficult to place. I would venture to suggest that you make them ambassadors where they cannot do much harm, such as in Moscow (I am aware that a historical sage warned against overzealous diplomats, but that was in the days when they were still important), or if you must place them in South Africa, make them deputy ministers of soccer and *jukskei*.

However, if we stick to our guns and convictions, a new life awaits us in the New Design! Here it comes; Gnu and Tarentaal are on edge, Jimmy takes out his notebook.

Check against the Specs

✓ We will abolish political parties.

✓ There will be no ministers of state. Those who fail to fade can *toyi toyi*.

✓ We will replace executive presidents with non-executive heads of state. They will be rich status figures from a line of royals, but they will be powerless.

✓ We will replace the government's old-fashioned, rigid and massive civil service with a lean, custom-made People's Administrative Facilitating Service. It will work in conjunction with society's functional organisations and NGOs. Municipal PAFS will be a top priority.

✓ We will rely on nature and logic. We have accepted and lived for too long with the overused adages, "Don't look for rationale behind politics", "Politics is not logical", and "Politics is not played this way or that way."

✓ We will be realistic and practical instead of working on untested pre-sumptions. We have suffered too much for too long under politicians who say that politics is not about real issues, but about perceptions. We will base the new dispensation on an all-embracing system of what is right, fair and just.

This brings us to the commissioning of our PI Ark.

> The people are in place – as they always are.
> The People's Administrative Facilitating Service is in place – as it mostly is.
> And the head of state cannot harass the people – as it usually did.

Jimmy and Gnu (in chorus): "Where's our king?"

Now we take the two final steps.

We sanitise the Ark by removing the layer of ministers and politicians from our original pyramid. We do this by using a strong suction pump.

We gently transfer His Royal Highness from the pinnacle of our inverted triangle in the depths of the earth to his rightful place in the sun at the top. Now we launch the shipshape PI Ark to sail the waters of the New Design destined for ultimate prosperity. It looks like this:

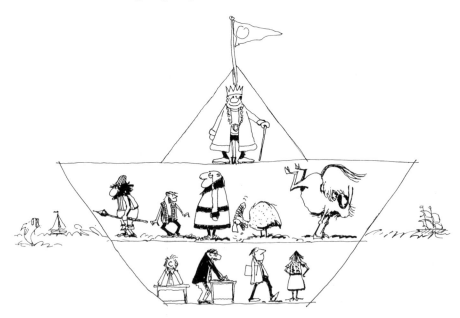

It is now time to set sail – anchors aweigh!

CHAPTER 41

Fine Tuning the PI Ark for Afrika

In zis romantic setting, we have a handsome, young man and a beautiful, sexy girl, under a full moon... n'est-ce pas! – Tertius Myburg.

Umuntu wadabuka emhlangeni – Jimmy the Reed.[1]

Afrikan Karakter – The Bigger Picture

Hurrah! We have a brand new design for a harmonious society and a spick and span people's PI Ark to sail its waters. Now we can adapt the New De-sign to the real environment – Afrika and South Afrika. The first ark did complete its successful voyage quite near to Afrika, at Mount Ararat in Armenia.

However, this situation causes me distress of the spirit and conflict of the soul. Should I express sympathy with the Afro-Arab and Afro-Indian minori-ties in some Afro-Afrikan countries, or should I demonstrate an understand-ing for disadvantaged Afro-Afrikans in Arabic Afrikan states, or show some interest in the woes of the Afro-black sheep or the Afro-white underdogs in Southern Afrika?

I usually empathise with the people, and especially the black sheep and the white underdogs. But being a blue liberal my cause is only to say so.

We all know of the ancient mess and evils preceding the mother of all floods, and that the Ark had to ship its worthy passengers to a better life. Now we have to look at the present mess, the new evils and threatening tem-pests that we will have to brave once again for a better future.

(You will have noticed that I am not overly fond of the spelling A-F-R-I-C-A. It is too Anglo centric for my liking. So, to give these Afrikan chapters

1 *The Tokoloshe Times*, 29 February 2004.

a true Afrikan karakter, I will continue in my best Afrikaans English. Incidentally, our government has already minted its blessing on my language initiatives with the inception of a five rand coin featuring Mr Gnu and stamped *Afrika Dzonga* and *Ningizimu Afrika*.)

Let's look at the entire Afrikan environment. The world has become so small that nowadays we can hardly analyse anything, be it politics or business, without also considering the bigger picture. The first step is an entertaining exercise. Let's be realistic. It's all about dynamic retrogression for a prosperous future.

Top scientist Sagan once postulated, "If time will one day flow backward and effects precede causes..."[2] Turning the clock backwards and forwards is rampant in contemporary sci-fi stories, and the sci-fi of yesterday is the reality of today and the history of tomorrow.

Sagan's children asked, "... how it is, if there was chaos early, that there is, apparently, order today."[3] This question may be quite valid regarding the cosmos, but regarding life on planet Earth it may well be the reverse. It could be that society was much happier and more peaceful in the past compared to the present. If so, why? Perhaps we can learn from that past.

If we could turn the clock back to a certain time in the past, we could determine what the mistakes were that turned a harmonious society into one that became progressively discordant. Then we could restart from that point and take care not to repeat the same mistakes.

The first question that comes to mind is to what point in the history of human society do we turn back the clock? The obvious answer is to restart at the beginning – Adam and Eve.

Afrikan Genesis

There was an enormous big bang 15 thousand million years ago, followed soon after by the age of the sun and earth in 4.6 thousand million BC. The first life appeared in 4 thousand million BC; vegetation and the first land animals colonised the earth in 425 million BC, and the dinosaurs emerged in 230 million BC. The earth's surface drifted into a number of continents separated by oceans in 200 million BC.

Human life started in Afrika after the continents had formed. What we do not know, for the racially, ethnic, tribal and nationality minded, is what Adam and Eve's cultural affiliations were.

2 Hawking, 1989.
3 Hawking, 1989.

Jimmy claims, "*Umuntu wadabuka emhlangeni*" (The first people came out of a reed-bed). They were Zulus.[4]

There are other opinions on this matter dating to the Cold War era that may still throw some light on this burning issue. It was Tertius Myburgh who personally exposed this thesis to me. He was then editor of the *Sunday Times*, so it must be true. Here goes:

The English largely ignore issues about race, and about which is superior – they know.

So, when Lady Ponsonby heard the story of Adam and Eve she responded: "There is no question! Here we have a lady and gentleman in dire need of sustenance with only one measly apple between them, and what do they do? They share it! That's fair play, that's cricket, British justice – Adam and Eve were English, what!"

The French more often than not, and by sheer coincidence, do things just the opposite way to the British. Mademoiselle Celine's reaction was: "In zis romantic setting, we have a handsome, young man and a sexy girl, in a beautiful garden, under a full moon, beside a tinkling stream, eating fruit togezer, both naked – but of course, zey were French, n'est-ce pas!"

The Soviets are always more Russian. Former Commissar Sternovsky had his own opinion: "Nyet, you are all wrong. They were Russian. Here we have two brave comrades, shivering in the open with no clothes to wear, starving and with almost nothing to eat – and they think they are in paradise!"

In a whisper between friends through the reeds Jimmy confidentially tells me this is not the complete story. Whatever the name of the first human clan, it grew in numbers and split up into groups.

Afrika was peaceful and quiet. Then two things happened. The first was that many of the Afrikans decided to abscond. How did this come about?

Out of Afrika

The human race was living in the second paradise after that of Adam and Eve – in Utopia. All their leaders were happy and peaceful. Admittedly they fought for land and honour as all respectable rulers do, but they lived close to nature and maintained a modus vivendi for all their people.

Alas, bliss did not last forever, and some of the leaders started to challenge those in positions of supreme authority. Some of the stronger contenders left to form new regimes in foreign lands. A number of the overlords

---

4 *Country Life*, September 2004.

remained with those too weak to travel. During 100,000 BC, the first wave of enterprising modern men left Afrika, going first to the Levant and central Asia, and thereafter to Eurasia.

Now, unfortunately, I have to remind you once again of Dystopia. This exodus was the start of the monarchical dystopias, autocratic dystopias, totalitarian and later, unfortunately, voting-for-persons democratic dystopias, followed by the fatal hegemonies caused by voting-for-party democratic dystopias, and all the other -cracy dystopias – all equally bad. Those who left Afrika founded new immoral paradises in which the strong ruled successfully by oppressing their people with impunity, and in which the weak were slain rather than protected – gods and their slaves.

Perhaps this unwise exodus was the first mistake in our history. The clansmen could have stayed happily in their comfortable Afrikan niche, doing their thing – or nothing. Why didn't they leave the rest of Afrika to its other worthy inhabitants, the plants and the animals, to do their thing – under the caring eye of his majesty, their beloved, benevolent and culling King Lion?

Had the original inhabitants of Afrika stayed put, another advantage would have been that there would have been only one race on the planet. But this would not have been a guarantee to no conflict and strife – quite the opposite. And it would certainly have caused extinction by boredom.

Was it a mistake for them to leave Afrika for other less hospitable continents, or was it not? Those who relocated to chilly Europe turned sickly shades of pinkish white; those exposed to the hues of the rising sun of the East turned yellow, and those elsewhere tanned to shades of bronze. Those who remained became black.

As they migrated, they increased their populations and, vegetarians apart, slaughtered more and more animals for food. Ultimately this meant fierce competition for survival and they had to fight with other clans to secure their interests.

However, the good guys stayed put in Afrika, side by side with the plants and animals, as I would have done. If this had been the end of the story we would have lived happily ever after as in the fairy tales. But this was not to be.

After some time, unfortunately, some of the expats started to revisit Afrika – chasing their roots. That's when the trouble started. We track their spoors in the next chapter. Have you spotted the mistakes we made so far?

CHAPTER 42

What If

No Interest — The Chinese Experience

We are reconnoitering the past for a starting point to mankind's renaissance. We want to establish what we can repeat because it was good, and what we shouldn't because it was bad. We now continue our time travels in Afrika, circa 5000 BC – the return of the expatriates.

The first émigrés to come back to Mother Afrika conquered Upper and Lower Egypt. Among the invaders were Afro-Libyans, descendants of the early emigrants to Europe, and Afro-Semites who came back from the Middle East and Central Asia. The nobles of the new master race governed these two realms; they introduced us to the art of a well-developed written language and construction techniques of monumental dimensions. Arts and industry advanced in leaps and bounds.

The rest of Afrika did not experience such dramatic progress. In many parts of the continent the inhabitants still followed the ways of the docile berry and fruit gatherer and the crafty and brave stone-age hunter and nomad.

I have developed the "what if" technique – nowadays called uchronian – to consider hypothetical concepts that may have practical application.

What if? I wonder what would have happened in Afrika if these waves of returnees had also included expats such as the Afro-Hindus. The Hindus (Indians) also started writing their language circa 2500 BC and they built their cities on a grid system – with drainage and central heating. If you don't like Indian writing, think what it might have been like had the Afro-Chinese come back? They could have taught us their writing and familiarised us with their first calendar that they started under the Hsia dynasty around 2200 BC.

What if, a little later, we had welcomed back some Afrikan expatriates from the civilisation of the Andes? They too developed community settlements, building programmes and pictographic writing. Or what if we had invited the Afro-Hittites to come home from Asia Minor? They were clever with iron.

During this period, circa 1900 BC, Afro-Semites lead by Father Abraham moved from Ur to Canaan and he transformed history. In time he became the patriarch of the three monotheistic faiths of Judaism, Christianity and Islam. Immediately after Canaan – 200 years later – the Afro-Hyksos, who in the meantime had conquered Egypt, welcomed the Afro-Israelis home to Afrikan soil.

Some of the ancient Afro-Semites came back to the benefit of northernmost Afrika. They had a good family tree comprising all the descendants of Shem, son of Noah – the Jews, Arabs, Syrians and Phoenicians.

The Greeks will tell you that few others could match the Semites' contributions to the progress of mankind. In recent times, according to the historian Herodotus, the Phoenician branch had already sailed around the Cape by 600 BC. In South Afrika we stand accused of having been incapable of luring them onto Afrikan terra firma for permanent settlement.

Wu Done It

What if the Afro-Chinese, now yellow, had become homesick and returned?

They had made huge strides in the terrain of warfare: Afro-Taoist alchemists had developed gunpowder under emperor Wu Di (156– 87 BC). It completely transformed the ways of warfare – all because Wu done it.

The Chinese produced the first cannon around 1127 – a full 150 years before the West. The Song Dynasty made flame-throwers, anti-personnel mines and many other gunpowder weapons. By the close of the Song dynasty the Chinese had invented multiple-stage rockets.

The Afro-Chinese used true rockets in 1232 to repel the Afro-Mongol invaders with their "arrows of flying fire", a simple form of the solid-propellant

rocket. With some Afro-Sino expats we would have chased the Afro-Portuguese, Dutch and English back home northwards with rockets up their behinds when they rounded the Cape during the middle of the previous millennium.

The Afro-Chinese Song Dynasty's ceramics were the first commercialised industry in the world. And that magnificent shrub, tea, began to conquer the planet with its cult status.

The Afro-Chinese eunuch Zeng He led seven expeditions into the Indian Ocean basin and reached Madagaskar, the east coast of Afrika, the Persian Gulf and the Red Sea between 1405 and 1433.[1] However, our public relations was not good enough to lure the Chinese back to Afrika. They never showed any affinity for our continent. But we can still ask whether we wouldn't have been better off if the Chinese had occupied Afrika instead of Afro-Europeans, then we would be eating noodles instead of pap.

Alternatively, if we could start our renaissance afresh, it might have a positive effect if we could involve the Sumerians and the Semitic Phoenicians to a greater extent in Afrikan affairs.

The Arab branch of the Afro-Semites conquered the defenceless North Afrika and still permanently occupies it today. If we could start all over from the time before that happened, we would be forewarned and could take care knowing that only to be good doesn't mean much; you have to keep abreast with science and technology, and defend what you have.

This history exercise taught me a lesson. I started to write Afrika's story; I wrote about Afrika itself as well as the way the continent was influenced by the world around it. But it was only as I reached the end that I realised I had written only about northernmost Afrika! I searched for the reason and found a simple answer. Southern Afrika had little recorded history of significance.

While Egypt was overrun by various different peoples one after the other, and just about the whole of North Afrika was conquered by the Arabs and their allies, the history of Afrika south of the Sahara up to this point is virtually non-existent. Nothing happened in the region. We were just good and going along nicely.

Another thing I have learnt from this exercise is that the past may be interesting, and it can teach us a few lessons, but it is better to live in the present. There is life beyond history – this side of history, that is.

1 *The Citizen*, 31 May 2003.

We can go on with these time travels and "what if?" exercises, and doing so will probably become more interesting, but we have to watch out – matters become more complicated as we go along!

So much for the past; I think there are other important matters we have to sort out.

"I still say gnus were first," says Gnu in his best Gnuese, and gives a snort.

Tarentaal in her best Trantralese responds: "You are a scruffy beast, and unbecoming as a gentleman. If you want a woman you need to bath and shave properly. I've had gnough of gnus."

"Don't get personal, woman, you don't even have chicks..."

"'Lady' to you."

"Don't think you're beautiful just because you're a bird. You don't look like a peacock and you can't sing like a nightingale, and you have only one horn."

"It's not a horn, it's a glengarry africanus ..."

Jimmy shuts them up in his best Jimminese Esperanto. "C'mon guys! Gnu, you are the First Lord of the Highveld, and Ms Tarentaal, you are the Grand Lady of the Green Green Grass of Eden; we must be more mutually sensitive – all for one, and one for all!"

CHAPTER 43

Rapid Strides Forward to the Past – Stepping Stones

These days, there are far bigger, more powerful forces in control than a quaint sense of national identity.[1]

Global and Afrikan Villages

Let's continue to analyse Afrika's past and present with a view to tuning our New Design and launching the PI Ark.

Afrika is a great continent. It is also large. It covers about 30,000,000 square kilometres and is nearly three times the size of Europe; it makes up nearly a quarter of the world's land mass. It is smaller than it used to be, but it is more in touch with the rest of the world than ever before. We are becoming globalised.

Through scientific and technological development, every individual in reach of a telephone, TV or computer is instantly in touch with people and events throughout the world. You can watch international sporting events, conclude business transactions or hold personal conversations from almost anywhere. Those who can afford it can travel by road, rail, sea and air to any destination on earth – with the same effort and in the same time as if they were travelling locally. Space travel for fun has already begun and we even have cyber space travel for more excitement.

Can you blame a person from Afrika for claiming to be completely confused? Such a person may tell you that where he grew up he never saw skyscrapers and congested highways, but now watches BBC, CNN, or Pirates against Sundowns on the TV and then walks back home through an alley of satellite dishes to the informal settlement – with no running water.

---

1 *Fair Lady*, October 2004.

With trade and commercial progress, followed by political development, countries started to form coalitions or blocs such as the European Union. Call this phenomenon *continentalisation*. These coalitions became stepping stones to the global stage. However, it is not imperative to follow the European model; there are many ways in which a person or country can become globalised without this type of stepping stone.

However, anyone who has any ideas about the composition of Afrika's future socio-economic-political ocean and the PI Ark will have to consider the almost unavoidable bloc formation and globalisation processes. We will have to think very carefully about the steps towards our new dispensation. We could follow the path of continentalisation, or another route, or a combination of possibilities. Let's consider Afrika's options.

Afrika does not Exist

Anyone who tries to deal with Afrika as a homogenous concept must surely have his head read! One can consider Afrika in various ways, such as Afrika north of the Sahara and Afrika south of the Sahara; littoral Mediterranean, Atlantic, Indian Ocean, and interior Afrika; Islamic, Kristian and traditional Afrika; or one can think of the Gadaffi and the Mugabe-type Afrika, or the Mali type. However, one can never consider Afrika per se – it doesn't exist! (Incidentally I forgot to mention that Mali was named after the ancient West Afrikan Kingdom of Mali).

Unfortunately, Southern Afrika doesn't exist either! The author of a book that I consulted, HJ van Aswegen, deals with Southern Afrika under the heading of "Central Afrika" – no Afrika South![2] However, Afrika is characterised by its diversity and consists of two distinct regions physically divided by the Sahara Desert. We'll first deal with Afrika in terms of Afrika north of the Sahara and then Afrika south of the Sahara; thereafter we will look at South Afrika, which is completely unique.

Even if, with the best intentions, we want to steer the PI Ark for Afrika in the best possible way along the continentalisation route, we can't! We have missed the boat. We are too late. We'll have to take the second best course. We – you and I – had to accept that the whole of Afrika should form only one bloc, the AU – the Afrikan Union! That was a mistake. We had no say in the matter. No longer can we start from a sound continentalised basis because this AU's foundation is flawed; it is not sound – it is a conglomerate

2 Van Aswegen, 1982.

of disparates, a mixed bag! In time the imperfections will inevitably cause stresses and strains in the Afrikan political superstructure that is being erected upon it.

If it should ever occur that countries take sides in terms of Islam versus the rest – or the Arab world versus any other international bloc, we might run into problems. It could be argued that through the AU, Afrika has already committed itself to side with the Arabs and Islam. There is an often-quoted adage in politics: My enemy's friend is my enemy.

The other glaring defect is that the architects and building contractors have left the proverbial holy cow intact!

Holy Cow of Misery

Throughout the last half century, all interested parties and especially the post-colonial governments were unanimous on two counts. The first was that the intra-Afrikan borders were wrong: the European colonial powers had drawn lines on a map regardless of geography, culture and business. This had caused endless violent conflicts, death and poverty. The second, inexplicably, was that any review of the international boundaries inside Afrika would be absolutely Politically Incorrect. Even the slightest hint of a border change was "not on, not in, absolutely out, not with it, not PC!"

It is beyond comprehension that the 21st century Afrikan statesmen would make exactly the same mistake as the one for which they blame the colonialists. But clearly, up to now, while continuing to blame the colonialists, the Afrikan statesmen indeed keep the borders intact.

If the new Afrikan statesmen are bold and courageous, they will come up with a more sensible intra-Afrikan border dispensation. And there are encouraging signs. During 2004, I read that our leaders were at the forefront and were looking beyond the borders of political correctness. In discussions on the future of the Afrikan Union, these leaders asserted that the matter of intra-continental borders would soon come under review!

I am convinced that the modern Afrikan statesmen will be wise and bold enough to pull it through. When the pale European colonialists were in control they didn't consult the people; they thought they could decide better for us dark Afrikans. Surely the modern Afrikan statesmen won't think they can decide better for us, deeming us politically klumsy Afrikans? Of course, the issue will probably cause more dissent than consensus, not among the people, but among the rowdy lesser politicians. That's politics, but that's not Afrika.

I was greatly encouraged by the news that the Sudan would be allowed to split into two, thus ending a north-south war in Afrika's largest country. Sudanese leaders signed a peace deal on 9 January 2005 that was to end Afrika's longest-running conflict after 40 years of misery. It was agreed that southerners would have the right to vote for secession at the end of a six-year interim period – a new era of Afrikan politics has dawned!

I sincerely hope that the panel of Afrikan peers monitor the agreement's progress so that it does not dwindle into oblivion. If this deal works, it will probably be the most lasting solution to problems of this kind to date. Sudan is the first visible case of the root cause of a problem eventually being addressed, and of Afrikan leaders amply illustrating their conviction and intention of reshaping Afrika's borders according to common sense.

Intra-borders aside, why didn't we, the citizens, have a vote on issues concerning the formation of the AU, or AUs? Did the politicians really apply their minds to the size, shape and composition of the AUs-to-be, or did they merely take the line of least resistance, the lazy and easy way out – together with the signatures, champagne, floodlights, and TV?

* * *

Jimmy elaborates: "You get the impression that they looked at the world map and liked the sexy shape of the land mass that is Afrika. They then assumed that taking the whole of Afrika *voetstoots*, as is, would be the obvious route to follow. Or they copied the first available model that came to

mind, a questionable example for Afrika set by the European experiment –
the European Union.

"However, the European people are still voting on it. Have we already
accepted our Union, without a single citizen's vote?

"Are we convinced that we should follow the continentalisation route?
How and where do we want to end up in the global village? Do we have to
continentalise to achieve our aims?

"The Sahara Desert forms a cultural bridge between north and south. If
Afrika did need a stepping stone, what would you say to her having two different blocs instead of only one – the Northern Afrikan Union (NAU) and
the Southern Afrikan Union (SAU)?"

CHAPTER 44

More Stepping Stones

☪ The PI Ark sailing the Seas of Afrika North of the Sahara

A few days later I prod Jimmy about where he has been.

"Looking," he says.

"Looking? For what?"

"For Tarentaal and Gnu."

I also want to know where Ms Tarentaal has been for so long.

"Big news, Uncle Joe! She's back from maternity leave..."

"Twelve chicks, after all these years!" adds an excited Gnu.

"And you, Gnu?" I enquire.

"I entered the annual jumbo cross-country marathon in Serengeti, Tanzania, with some relatives and very old friends, the Zebras."

Then I ask Jimmy about their ideas on bloc formation.

"We have no ideas; there isn't a choice, there's only one acceptable solution – a Northern Afrikan Union and a Southern Afrikan Union, take it or leave it."

Tarentaal stares into the skies, Gnu whistles and says, "And if you don't believe us, go ask the Lion King yourself."

* * *

North Afrika, historically, culturally, geographically and in terms of religious affiliation, has much more in common with the Arab world, the Middle East, Mediterranean Europe, Asia Minor and the Near East, than with Afrika south of the Sahara.

In fact, the North Afrikan Arab countries, together with other Arab countries in the Middle East, long ago put in place their stepping stone towards globalisation with the formation of their own bloc – the Arab League.

Furthermore, North Afrikan countries are members of myriad overlapping multinational organisations together with European and Middle Eastern countries. The question arises, with the AU as it is, are the Afrikan Arab states now going to secede from the Arab bloc because they have joined us, or are they going to become "multiple continental passport holders"? Would that be a satisfactory system?

If my suggestion of two stepping stones carries your approval, this problem can be eliminated. The Northern Afrikan Union can be a group embracing all the countries north of the Sahara Desert. They are all, incidentally, Arab and/or Muslim. So they could join the Arab League if they wished to do so, en bloc or individually; or they could form one mighty state under the leadership and watchful eye of Libya's Muhamar Gadhaffi.

However, when the United States of America compete in sports internationally they are allowed only one team. And with our obsession with quotas, how are we going to represent over 50 countries in one united states of Afrika soccer team?

Despite the achievements of the biggest empire of all times, that of Queen Victoria, the Semites in general, and more specifically the Arabs of old, were much more successful conquerors of Afrika than anyone else. All that Victoria's granddaughter, Queen Elizabeth II, can show for her erstwhile empire in Afrika are those former colonies that are still members of the British Commonwealth.

By contrast, the Arabs have invaded, conquered and retained all of Afrika north of the Sahara, complete with their culture, language, religion *et al*. The last brave Afrikans still resisting and fighting without arms are the ones in the Sudan in the South; they need South Afrika's support and alms more than Haiti does.

Even with improved, superb international communications, Algeria in North Afrika has still very little in common with Swaziland in Southern Afrika, or Tunisia with Botswana, Ethiopia with Namibia, and Egypt with Sierra Leone. It is true that there are Arabs and Muslims in countries south of the Sahara. But it is also true that there are Indians in Afrikan countries, which doesn't mean that the subcontinent of India should form a bloc with Afrikan countries.

We should also consider political culture. Let's use only one of democracy's criteria, namely Freedom of the Press. It appears that sub-Saharan Afrika scores fantastically according to the 2004 rankings by Freedom House: a whopping 15% of the countries (7 out of 48) got a rating of *a free press*. Thirty-five per cent (35%) got a rating of *partly free*; and a mere 50% are *not free*. If you think I'm being sarcastic, please continue reading.

In sharp contrast the Middle East and North Afrika scored as follows: *Free press*: one whole country – Israel, 5% (not one in North Afrika); *Not free*: 17 countries, only 90%.

I am being sarcastic, but it is because I want to make a very important and practical point. In a sub-Saharan grouping, such as the SADC, on a one-country-one-vote basis we have a 50% chance of obtaining democratic decisions. If sub-Sahara combines with Afrika north of the Sahara, the totally overwhelming majority of voting states are non-democratic in their own countries! Jimmy will remind you about this very important matter when we review the Pan Afrikan Parliament.

Our PI Ark must also negotiate these waters.

Besides the Northern Afrikan Union, the other bloc would be the Southern Afrikan Union. This brings me to the last, but most important argument in favour of two blocs. If it should ever happen that voting in the international community of states takes a one-bloc-one-vote form, there would be an incidental, but meaningful spin-off for Afrika. A north and south grouping would give us more bloc votes against the Americans and Europeans. Could we afford to let this golden opportunity pass us by?

Bad Fellows – Nam is a Scam

We also have to consider that there are Afrikan countries that are already part of another long-existing group, namely NAM, the Non-Aligned Movement. This is a problem that should be solved in the ongoing process from national states to blocs to globalisation.

NAM originated during a meeting of 29 Asian and Afrikan countries in 1955. According to criteria set in 1961, only countries that were not involved in alliances or defence pacts with the main world powers could become members. The first summit meeting took place in Belgrade, the capital city of Marshall Tito's Yugoslavia – then one of the closest allies of the communist Soviet Union.

One of NAM's commitments is to restructure the world economic order. Now isn't that nice? The last meeting of the heads of states took place in Kuala Lumpur in 2003 where our president, Mr Thabo Mbeki, called on his colleagues to take a stronger stand regarding issues of concern. Cuba assumed the chair at the summit in 2006.

Of course, the non-aligned movement is a scam. Any honest composite international organisation in the sane world will only be formed on the basis of common interests, more or less.

What was the interest shared by the NAM countries? It certainly wasn't that they were all "non-aligned". Granted, some of them were more non-aligned than others, and others were less non-aligned than some, but there was still a considerable gap between those who were more less non-aligned and those who were less more non-aligned – like India and Pakistan.

The common cause among them – a tightly kept secret for decades – was that they were all mostly anti-American or anti-West, and either pro-Soviet Union or Red China, or both. Anti-West schemers who started the movement recruited members such as Yugoslavia, Cuba and Libya. Incidentally Yugoslavia and Cuba are neither Afrikan nor Asian.

The name "non-aligned states" is typical of the cloak of Cold War propaganda – playing with words to create smokescreens and cheaply camouflaging deceptive activities behind them. During the Cold War the Soviet-trained or -dominated countries were unashamed masters of the use of the talking tactic, "Don't judge me on what I *do*; be politically correct and check the record with regard to what I have *said*."

It was well known that in spite of what Fidel Castro said, he had an agreement with the Soviet Union allowing it to have long-range missile bases on his island right next to the Soviet Union's prime Cold War target – the US. But Cuba became one of the most prominent members of the non-aligned states. How non-aligned can't you get?

These countries should cease their transparent double play and disband with honour. I am not just picking on the friends of the now defunct Marxist Soviet Union; the British Commonwealth should also come under severe scrutiny. It is no more or less of a sham than the non-aligned states.

The countries of the Commonwealth have no common interest but one. All of them (but the UK) were colonies and peoples suppressed by the greatest colonial oppressor of all times, Her Imperial Highness, Queen Victoria.

To correct this injustice of the past, the UK should forthwith dishonourably be expelled from the British Commonwealth. But the British should not become over-enthusiastic at the prospect!

To conclude this dissertation about international political groupings, I suggest we give serious consideration to establishing another bloc embracing certain countries with substantial and long-standing common interests – the sound basis of group formation. The common interest is sharing the same bed. The bedfellows are: South Afrika, Libya, Kuba, Zimbabwe, Palestine, Red China, Syria, Haiti and North Korea, and a few others who asked me not to mention them by name.

"Crazy world created by crazy politicians, but Uncle Joe, you don't say anything about rich blocs and poor blocs," Jimmy rumbles.

CHAPTER 45

Think Tank by the Reeds

Là Bas

On my way to Jimmy at the bulrushes, I bumped into a cute little guy sporting a red bowler hat and walking in the opposite direction. I said hello and
asked him who he was. He told me he was Mr Ťröll, an envoy of the Queen
of Ťröllandia, above Norway...

"*North* of Norway, you mean," I corrected.

"*Above* Norway, I mean. I reported for Jimmy's think tank, but was chased
away by the bird and the beast, even before he turned up."

I persuaded him to change his mind and to accompany me. When we
arrived at the think tank, Jimmy was facilitating a discussion on "PCs Blur
Perspective" with Gnu, Ms Tarentaal and some others – including two representatives from Pauritania!

This is my own version of what Jimmy was telling them:

This is not just another prata-prata; it is a serious discussion on affairs of
state. A very important PC trick concerns the classification of countries.
Once upon a time when Europeans inhabited Northern America they called
it the *new* world. Dvorak composed the *New* World Symphony.

Colonialists also tried to settle in newly discovered South American,
Afrikan and Asian lands. With the exception of some South American countries, and the islands of Australia and New Zealand, the Europeans never established themselves there in the same way as they did in North America.

These faraway lands were shrouded in mystery and romanticism, and the
Frenchman Georges Guetary, in his best French English sang *Là Bas* – the air
is so sweet, it tastes like wine, *là-bas*, yonder. Then, quite recently the wine
turned sour; the PCs made the incredible discovery that these countries
were not romantic, but, in their eyes, primitive, uncivilised, backward and
poor.

To camouflage their shameful findings and minimise their own feelings of guilt, they changed the whole world order. They named the European countries the *Old* World. It had a delightfully sentimental ring about it – smelly and musty. But merely calling Europe old and America new didn't work out for them; it didn't make the poor romantic countries sound any better. So they came up with another idea: the European countries would be called the *first world*; the North American countries, the new, would be known as the *second world*, and those countries formerly called poor would be referred to as the *third world*.

Third Out of Three

Jimmy continued: Of course, this is a lot of hogwash. Even Gnu knows that Afrika was the first world, the Levant and central Asia the second, and China and Europe the third. I prefer to call Europe the rich countries, North America the super-rich countries, and the rest the average, and poor to not-so-poor countries.

Then in stepped the red PCs once more! The PCs said third out of three means last, and how on earth can anything be last – it's an insult! So they transformed "third world" into "developing countries". Consequently, the rest became known as the *developed countries*.

Of course, the negative connotations accorded the third world countries existed only in the evil minds of the PCs, but that's beside the point. The point is, during the renaming process the PCs have done the poor, third world countries, in dire need of development aid, a huge disfavour by calling them developing countries.

"Developed" means something has already happened, without any indication of what followed. For all intents and purposes the developed countries have developed and then stagnated. "Developing", on the other hand, means they haven't stopped developing.

By their definition the PCs have clearly indicated that Ivory Coast, Zimbabwe, Liberia, Sudan, Pauritania and Burkina Faso are all actually developing progressively and are therefore in no need of aid whatsoever. By contrast, the countries that had already developed in the past may well need assistance in order to get them going again.

Jimmy adopted his mean look: So if the PCs want to reverse the situation for the sake of global well-being, let's propose that the developed and stagnant Norway forfeits its right to vote at the UN, while the developing and progressive Pauritania, which can make a difference, get two votes.

One of the Pauritanian representatives interrupted: It's the PCs' fault. We are realists, but the rest of the world became illusioned. They have got so used to hearing of the developing countries that they have become oblivious of the fact that we are regressing. PC-illusions create the feeling that we are on the up and on the move.

Jimmy resumed: The PCs created a halo around the heads of the poor countries, an image that boomeranged on them.

Now it was Mr Ťröll's turn (and I relate their exchanges): As a final thought, we Scandinavians should be called developing countries instead of developed, because we are in fact continuing to develop progressively; but with the likes of Pauritania it would be in your favour if you were called T&M countries instead of developing countries, then you would stand a much better chance of launching fund-raising campaigns. Why T&M? Because nobody sympathises with those who prosper, but the honest, struggling Toil and Moil countries are a different matter!

Jimmy was very impressed with Mr. Ťröll, so he allowed him to present his paper as originally intended: *To Struggle or Not To Struggle.*

Ťröll kicked off with his gaze fixed on the representatives from Pauritania:

The developing countries fail to develop. They would do better if they were struggling. They should struggle with all the means at their disposal, determined to make a success. If they demonstrated that they were *working hard* at educating the young to appreciate that they are poor at present, but at the same time instilling the sense that there is no shame in poverty, and that there is pride and honour in *hard work*, and if they demonstrated with dignity that they respect donors for helping them to help themselves, then they would be on the way to success.

Ťröll is not so bad after all, but he has a lot to learn, thought Jimmy.

With his tongue in his cheek he wrapped up: Well said, Mr Ťröll, but take care not to go overboard with goodness and industry. If we don't watch out, we run the risk of launching the world into a new wave of wickedness and misery. Investigating the galaxies like Hesiod and Ovid did, we find that our Golden Age was when Saturn reigned; a world of innocence and happiness. *Work* changed it all.

It started to go bad with the Silver Age of Jupiter, a world of godlessness and trouble. It progressively became more evil through the Brazen, Heroic and Iron Ages of Neptune and Pluto - that is when the word "work" entered the scene for the first time! It proliferated through successive ages. In the second millennium English speakers became obsessed with work. "Work" is the 16th most used common noun, while the words "rest" and "play" are not listed in the top 100. And look at the calamities in the US and the UK!

* * *

As much as Jimmy's expressed aversion to labour appeals to me, I have to qualify his statement. He got his cause-and-effect mixed up. Adam and Eve did not sin because they had worked; they had to work because they sinned.

Tarentaal asks: "How would you like to visit Rudolph in Scandinavia, Gnu?"

Frostily Gnu replies: "Red-nosed reindeers are not my type, Madam."

* * *

While we are shaping the New Design amid globalisation with its leagues and blocs, and knocking the PI Ark into shipshape to sail its seas, we can't afford to become blinded by continents, blocs, leagues, nams and scams. What about oceans and islands?

218

CHAPTER 46

Islands in the Sun

The West is and will remain for some years to come the most powerful civilisation ... non-Western societies confront a choice. Some attempt to emulate the West and to join or to "bandwagon" with the West. Other Confucian and Islamic societies attempt to expand their own economic and military power to resist and to "balance" against the West – Huntingdon.[1]

Continentalisation – Home-made

We will make silly mistakes if we model ourselves on European transformation. We can look at it a decade or two from now, but not just yet. They are still experimenting with continentalisation and are bound to make mistakes from which we can learn – later.

The forming of groups, such as continentalisation, requires planning for the long term. Many experts believe that the national state will remain the basic building block. There is also much talk of the world moving towards a division between the rich and the poor countries; towards forming a Western bloc versus an Eastern one; to Islam versus others, and to democratic versus non-democratic countries. And what about the Defenders and Demanders?

Many studies have already been done and the most logical finding is that the future groupings of the world are going to be based on business in the short term and kultures in the long term.

The biggest mistake regarding all these proposed groupings is the use of the word "versus". It creates entirely the wrong climate for reaching sound and workable solutions. Plan with a view to creating harmony instead of

---

1 Huntingdon, 1997.

forecasting conflict. Although I support the principle of "Believe in peace but keep your gunpowder dry", I propose that we base our planning on *apposition* instead of *opposition* – placing countries side by side rather than in confrontation.

The important point is that different national kultures could be subkultures of a certain international grouping of states, with countries having common business interests.

What is the kulture of sub-Saharan Afrika? The time has come to examine the land of the Southern Cross – Afrika south of the Sahara, and our country, South Afrika.

† Afrika South of the Sahara

Naturally, the primary element of the kulture of Afrika south of the Sahara is our Afrikan kulture. But Afrikan kulture is not a single concept. Every individual country in sub-Saharan Afrika has its own subkultures and its national kulture – a subkulture of the region.

The secondary element of the kulture of the global village of austral Afrika is more an Afrikan-Western kulture than anything else.

If I am wrong, then how would you classify our Southern Afrikan kulture: Afrikan-English, Afrikan-European, Afrikan-Arab, Afrikan-Indian, Afrikan-Oriental, Afrikan-Russian or Afrikan-Amerikan? And would you like to combine any one of these with one of the following: Afrikan-Kristian, Afrikan-Muslim, Afrikan-Buddhist, Afrikan-Ancestric, Afrikan-Afrikan, Afrikan-Hindu or Afrikan-Voodoo? Where do we fit in?

The languages of the sub-Saharan countries are Afrikan, and include Afrikaans. There are many official national languages, but international languages such as English, French, Portuguese and Spanish are also used regionally and for business.

In Southern Afrika we inherited Dutch. The Dutch *burghers*, the French Huguenots, the English and German settlers, the Portuguese Malay, and the Khoisan concocted it into Afrikaans. Our government is trying to wipe Afrikaans from the face of Afrika, but it won't succeed. The Afrikaners will preempt it by Anglo-Americanising the language first. The new wave of pseudo Afrikaans intellectuals, yuppie performers, arrogant neo-language PCs, and public TV and radio announcers are turning Afrikaans into an American English pidgin/Creole/Esperanto/*fanagalo* – an alternative language for standard Afrikaans with their generous use of *Hi – great – amazing – stunning – cool – shit – so what – anyway – oh my god – show – beautiful – either way – fine – cheers – awesome*.

On the other hand, the Afrikaans language has become greater than the people who speak it. There are people who definitely do not regard themselves as Afrikaners, but whose first language is proudly Afrikaans. Afrikaans is also the *lingua franca* of Namibia. The most spoken languages in South Afrika are IsiZulu, IsiXhosa, IsiAfrikaans, SeSesotho, SeEnglish and SePrata-prata. The greater majority of all our people in Southern Afrika are Kristians of sorts. The people of Southern Afrika have become used to a way of life that combines traditional Afrikan kulture and its Afrikan know-how, and Western kulture, with its scientific and technological inventions, and other shenanigans.

I don't have to tell you that kultures and subkultures are not confined by borders. But if, on a map of the world, you colour in the Afro-Western and all the other broadly Western countries, on the basis of language, religion and kulture, you would find that the colour stretches all the way across South and North America, Europe, Australasia and Afrika south of the Sahara.

However, if we do not want to position ourselves as a subkulture of the West – an Afro-Western kulture – then we should place ourselves in the Eastern bloc. I rather like Japan.

RDP

Or why don't we form a totally separate Afrikan kultural blok? I like that too. If we look at planet Earth, Afrika is geographically well poised between the East and the West with lots of water between them and us. We can easily walk a tightrope between the other main kultural groups. They certainly do exist, and they ooze strong influence, whether we like it or not.

It is unlikely that our government will recommend that we, the Republic of South Afrika, see ourselves as a subkulture of the Afro-Western kulture. But if it does, we should reap the full benefit of such a stance. We must then change our anti-Western posture and show more goodwill towards the Americans and Europeans. It is not enough merely to commute en masse to and from Europe and the US, and it would not mean that we thumb our noses to Afrika north of the Sahara, Scandinavia and the rest of the world.

Jimmy's ears prick up as I relate what my other uncle told me:

"Geldenhuys, you have no vision, no perspective. You must decide whom you want as Southern Afrika's kultural conquistadores. But before you do that, you have to answer Liberman's question, 'Does Conquest Pay?'[2] Now

2 Liberman, 1996.

let me tell you, the only way everlasting conquest can succeed is through RDP – the combined application of Religion, Democracy and Proliferation. If you claim that your motive for everything you do is your god, that is, your Religion, then you can get away with anything; if you claim freedom as a civil right, that is, you back Democracy, then you can get away with anything; and if you produce the numbers through vibrant intercourse, that is, you promote Proliferation, then you gain the power through elections. That's exactly what is happening. Therefore you should seek your future in conjunction with the Indians and Chinese, or the Muslims. Long before the end of the century Europe will be Muslim."

Jimmy responds, "If that's what we want, that's what we'll get." He continues with a twinkle in his eye: "Or perhaps there's another option. When we search for kultural companionship and business partners there is another possibility. When we consider globalisation, we can't look at continents only; we should also consider going with the islands. Islanders are great achievers. They play a very important role in the international society of states.

The British, Irish and Japanese are top performers in the world. The English have spread their language across the globe, the Japanese their motorcars, and the Irish their seed. The Taiwanese Republic of China is a business and financial miracle that has shown the world how to develop an economy to benefit the man in the street and on the job.

The French sent their prisoners to the West Indian island of Haiti and Napoleon was retired to the island of Elba. The British sent their prisoners of crime to Australia and dispatched their prisoners of war to Bermuda, the Bahamas or Ceylon – and Napoleon to St Helena.

The South Afrikans in turn sent their prisoners of politics to Robben Island.

Islands are important. Corsica gave us Napoleon; and Malta gave us the world's guru on thinking science, Dr Edward de Bono, the Maltese Cross, and poodles.

And Robben Island gave us Nelson Mandela."

* * *

"Cultural diversity is a funny thing," observes Gnu. "The Indians are very practical; they eat with their hands."

"Yes," says Tarentaal, "the Americans and South Afrikans are innovative – they brandish warlike accoutrements like knives and forks to devour huge slabs of steak."

222

Jimmy adds: "The Chinese are highly civilised. From tiny porcelain bowls, with dainty little sticks, they savour delicate cubes of snake and dog meat."

Then he rambles on about various Afro-, Euro- and ethnocentrisms and ruminates aloud on the diaspora sentiments that brought Haiti's Aristide back into the fold.

Gnu whispers in Tarentaal's ear: "Can you explain this to me later in private?"

"Yes, but how's Daisy?"

"Mind your own business."

* * *

Let us prepare to secure pole position so that we start on the right track for our new destination.

CHAPTER 47

Southern Afrika's Future Past

For life goes not backward nor tarries with yesterday – Kahlil Gibran.

Then Something Happens

There is more to Afrika south of the Sahara than globalisation and continentalisation. However, we cannot evaluate it properly if we do not put it into perspective in the same way as we did Afrika north of the Sahara. So, we board the time-travel machine once again to collect more tips for fine-tuning the PI Ark for Afrika,

We know the history of many parts of the world from whence knowledge and innovations developed, but that of Central and Southern Afrika is shrouded in mystery. It is scanty legend based on archaeological findings and traditional beliefs handed down to posterity by word of mouth through countless generations – the worst way of formulating history.

Languages of Southern Afrika were not written and we had to rely on the writings of Herodotus and other such historians who recorded man's activities since before Christ. Cunning spin doctors, in their feeble endeavours to crush "malicious colonial myths", point out that evidence of *early southern Afrikan* written records was found at Timbuktu in Mali. This southernmost site of early Afrikan writing was a hub on the old Arabic caravan routes between Algeria, Morocco and Tuab during the 12th to 15th centuries.

However, Mali is not in southern Afrika. It is in another world. While South Afrika is located on the southernmost tip of the Afrikan continent, Algeria, Mali and Morocco are situated in northernmost Afrika. Timbuktu is three times as far from Cape Town as Mexico is from Canada!

Long ago, there was a remarkable quest for knowledge and development in Europe. However, as the era of the ancient Greek civilisation and the Roman Empire drew to a close, the sun also set on the search for knowledge and scientific know-how. The PCs reigned during the obscure centuries that followed – the Middle or Dark Ages.

Fortunately, the gloom of ignorance eventually gave way to a new dawn of scientific discovery and invention that spread light over the European continent – the Renaissance. The quest for knowledge was reborn. In spite of PC resistance, Europe soon began to experience significant changes in about the 1400s.

As we scrutinise the past, we are going to have to deal with the PCs again. Even if we use time travel to help our creative analysis, we must still consider all the relevant and legitimate information, and draw valid conclusions while observing the rules of logic. This is precisely what PCs with causes don't do!

While we delve into the past to plan a better future, the PCs dig up history to concoct a better past. They don't allow us to liberate ourselves from the past, and the past still to come.

What ploys do they use to create their illusions? Their theme is that Afrika and Afro-Afrikans were at the forefront of modernity. Every splinter chiselled off the Afrikan prehistoric block becomes an illustrious civilisation.

The relentless pursuit of a new, glorious, ancient Southern Afrikan civilisation is futile. We are either painting ourselves into a dark corner or we are digging our own grave – for an imploded corpse. It will be a real catastrophe if we don't find such a civilisation after the expectations the PCs have created! If we do find it, what are we going to do with it? How are we going to reconcile the glories of a past era with the lacklustre results? That will be an even greater catastrophe.

These cheap propaganda tricks are an embarrassment. They force people to ask the awkward question of what happened to us here in Afrika after our glorious past when we were at the forefront of modern civilisation? What did we eventually achieve?

I am proud of our Afrikan heritage, proud of the fact that modern man emerged in Southern Afrika in about 300 000 BC. We are all proud that South Afrika is the Kradle of Mankind. What worries my uncle is that "people are kute when they are babies, then something happens". What happened to the babies after they climbed out of the kradle? Where are the towns built on a grid system, the written languages, and the kalendars?

It doesn't worry me. I am tuned into the future.

Chinese Occupation of Southern Afrika and Black Holes

Ancient history now produces exciting news headline topics and one is hard-pressed to keep up with the latest in the history of Southern Afrika.

PCs not only play around with history, they use it as a tool. They are constantly looking for exciting new Afrikan histories more to their liking.

Very early in the 2000s the red PCs and politicians, notably the Madam Speaker, became extremely excited when a chip of an antique object, believed to be of Chinese origin, was discovered in South Afrika. The PCs were quick to remind us also of evidence of early iron smelters in Southern Afrika. And so I could go on.

Perhaps we are on the brink of discovering that the Chinese play such an important role in our fortunes that it will change the course of China's future and South Afrika's past. Finding an antique Chinese object or iron items merely leads us to ask again why the Chinese decided to stay away from Southern Afrika for ever after their brief visit, and why the iron smelters did not lead to further technological advancement?

Oriental artefacts and rubies have never lost their mysticism and their links with bad omens – the Madame Speaker got the sack.

We have become addicted to looking at yesterday. However, just mention Red PCs and Archaeology and Jimmy sees red. Towards the end of 2004 he told me of exciting discoveries in Indonesia, where toddler-sized adults, only three feet tall, with human faces and called hominins had been found. They had walked the sands of these eastern islands more than 18 000 years ago, long before we started to record human history.

He quoted the scientists:

"...the remains of a new species of human have been discovered on a remote Indonesian island – a spectacular find that could rewrite the history of human evolution... This questions current ideas about intelligence, further undermines traditional ideas about modern humans being unique, and even hints that other species of Homo may have survived into recorded history... (They) crafted stone tools, roasted elephant, built rafts and probably used language... The find represents a new and surprising twig on mankind's family tree. It is often claimed that new fossils rewrite the textbooks, but in 'this case it is no exaggeration' said Prof Chris Stringer of the Natural History Museum, London... and may overturn understanding of intelligence.

Until they found this creature, they would have dismissed them as tales of leprechauns, but no longer." [stated] Dr Henry Gee, the senior editor of the journal Nature."[1]

I recorded the story in this manuscript with great anticipation, but before we went to press a distressed and furious Jimmy came and told me

1 The Weekly Telegraph, 3 November 2004.

"something happened" – his hominins were ordinary human juveniles! It had been a false finding!

With due respect to my friend Jimmy, the disadvantage of looking back is that it prevents us from developing an eye for opportunities ahead: everyone is constantly searching for an exciting new history while a begging better future passes us by. It seems as if the PCs have got us stuck looking vertically downwards into a black hole of archaeological strata in search of a new history.

Politicians also use history as a tool; they believe in the adage "Who controls history shapes the future" – only for history to repeat itself.

Furthermore, the use of alternative history is of extreme concern to some of the more acceptable red liberals, and quite understandably so:

...it may be the start of a dangerous development – the beginning of an insidious process of rewriting history that will eventually seep into official history textbooks and lead to future generations who will know nothing of Helen Suzman (veteran liberal South African anti-apartheid activist and member of parliament) or, for that matter honourable liberals of the calibre of Alan Paton, Peter Brown, Margaret Ballinger and Edgar Brooks.[2]

In the use of this alternative history it is apposite to recall George Orwell's warning in *1984*: "... who controls the past controls the future: who controls the present controls the past."

I share Lawrence Schlemmer's warning. Psycho-political rewriting of history is evil and fatally dangerous. In the meantime, PCs with their eyes firmly fixed on the past are blind to the future, and stumble over the present.

* * *

Jimmy: "Uncle Joe, as you know Tarentaal, Gnu and I are going on a short holiday to watch the whales at Hermanus. We'll catch up with you at White, Yellow and Grey."

2 *The Citizen*, (article from Focus 30 by Lawrence Schlemmer)

CHAPTER 48

Which Way to run from the Future

It is a fickle thing history. More often than not it records events but not the deep backdrop and all its mystery. Sometimes it is for the good. – Pat Symcox, popular, wise and wily Springbok cricketer.[1]

Baby Jake and the Rose of Soweto

We designed the PI Ark for moving forwards, not backwards. We are critical and positive, so who would we like to board our vessel? What about those who don't look back, but rather get on with their lives?

Charlize Theron of Benoni didn't care who invented cinematography, but she was the first Afrikan to win an Oscar – she qualifies.

Also from Benoni, the little Lebanese South Afrikan, Viccie Toweel, won the world boxing bantamweight title in 1950. Since then we have produced, among others, three multiple world title holders: Brian Mitchell, 1986–1991; my hero, the charismatic Rose of Soweto, Dingaan Thobela, 1990–2000; and national hero and SA sports ambassador, Jacob "Baby Jake" Matlala, the only SA boxer to have won four world titles in three different divisions, 1990–2001. Not one of these astute men invented the square ring! And they didn't care – they qualify.

Mark Shuttleworth demonstrated what happens if you look at the future and work in the present. You land up among the stars – the first Afrikan in space. Josia Thugwani was blasé about the escapades of the ancient Greeks and Persians – he just went along like KK McArthur at the 1912 Stockholm Olympic Games and won the marathon for South Afrika again at the 1996 Atlanta Games. All these South Afrikans excelled. If modern man was born

---

1 *The Citizen*, Spinning Tales.

in Afrika, raised in Central Asia and matured in Europe, so what? Nobody cares that the Chinese invented ice cream, but we all eat it, as did the Venetian, Marco Polo.

How is any knowledge about the beginnings of the modern human – whether in Europe, Asia or Afrika – over 100,000 years ago – going to help us shape a better future and win the World Cup, save the gnu and solve poverty?

New discoveries of the past are not always good; they may well reveal that in Southern Afrika our Afro-San were made to work as slaves for our Afro-Afrikans; and further north, that Afrikan chieftains sold Afrikans as slaves to the Arabs, the master slave traders, and that we had habitual cannibals in our midst.

Although this book is from the man in the street to the man in the street, you can get excellent food for thought from women's magazines. In an article published in *Fair Lady*,[2] Mike Behr quotes a man as saying, "If you tell someone a truth that they don't like, they say you haven't got good people skills." This man was that successful Springbok rugby coach Nick Mallett.

Four pages further on, the editor of the UK fashion bible, *Viewpoint*, Martin Raymond, proceeded to burst our new South African bubble with a very pertinent observation: "It is clear that this country is re-inventing its past quite successfully, but have you given much thought to the future? If your aesthetic is defined by your heritage alone how do you hope to move forward?"

The author of the article, Adam Levin, concluded: "Our future lies in our innate ability to define and design an African aesthetic for tomorrow."[3]

The rewriting of history-with-a-political-cause evokes reaction, and reaction upon reaction, upon reaction...

On rewriting history and tradition, RW Johnson states:

"... the new elite, to prove its Africanness delighted in dressing up in garb loosely borrowed from West Africa – which had no history or tradition of any kind in South Africa where, alas, it belonged to the realms of pantomime fancy dress. Similarly, the Africanist government of Thabo Mbeki had within it several women who retained their maiden names in double-barrelled form – though, of course, this ran clean contrary to patriarchal African tradition. Seldom has the invention of tradition been a busier occupation than in post-1994 South Africa. Before one's very eyes many

2 *Fair Lady*, May 2005.
3 *Fair Lady*, May 2005.

assertive individuals – a whole new elite – reinvented themselves, proudly parading in new dress and new names. The historian, regarding this spectacle, may blush but may also safely ignore it."[4]

What I am happy about is that the foreign name of Afrika has remained unchanged; it is only the Anglo spelling I didn't like.

Since times long forgotten, people have bragged about being victors while others have sought to be recognised as victims. The usual pattern of overrunning and running away yesterday, of overpowering and succumbing today, and vice versa tomorrow, changed very slowly over the centuries:

> Sidon and Tyre, the two coastal cities of southern Lebanon, were once the principal towns of ancient Phoenicia and spawned a mercantile empire from Turkey to Spain... Lebanon has been overrun in turn by Canaanites, Egyptians, Assyrians, Babylonians, Persians, Greeks, Romans, Arabs, Crusaders, Arabs again, Turks, French, more Arabs, Israelis and occasional US Marines. Perhaps by means of the past one can begin to comprehend the present or learn which way to run from the future.[5]

Present-day Europe only really started to resemble its present form in the 1800s after clans, societies, dynasties and the like, over a period, united to form nations. Even since that time alterations have occurred and borders have shifted and only now seem finally to have been sorted out.

However, it is time to draw closer to Southern Afrika once again, and to those people who invaded us. Who were they, where did they come from?

In Splendid Isolation

The Afro-Europeans also had their fair share of the normal cycle of invade, settle, defend, retreat, regroup, advance and invade, settle, defend...

The Roman province of Iberia, which included present-day Portugal, was overrun from the 4th century by hordes of Alani, Germanic people, Visigoths, Saracens and Arabs or Moors in succession. The Moors, who were Muslim and came from North Afrika, took control of Iberia in 711 and it remained in their hands for the next seven centuries.

Then in the 16th century the Spanish and Portuguese took their chances and grabbed most of South America. Later, the Portuguese also snatched Goa on the Indian subcontinent, and Macao and Timor in the East. They suf-

4 Johnson, 2004.
5 O'Rourke, 2002.

fered misfortune in South Afrika and therefore avoided it, preferring to take charge of Portuguese Guinea, Angola and Mozambique. Incidentally, I forgot to tell you that Angola got its name from the king of the Quimbundu called "Ngola".

In the meantime, Central Europe descended into ferment. The Prussians (today's Germans) established themselves as a force in Europe and flexed their muscles against the mighty Austrians. All of Europe, including Russia, had to contend with Napoleon and his French armies. They looted Egypt and many other countries in Europe and abroad, and occupied thrones as diverse as those of Mexico and Sweden. Many of the stronger European powers occupied less strong countries in Europe and grabbed colonies in newly discovered territories.

Even on the peripheries of Europe people like the Finns had their fair share of fighting for existence against the Swedes in the west and the Russians in the east. Sweden eventually ceded Finland to Russia. The Russians ruled over the Finns until 1917 when Finland became independent. Soon after independence, Finland slid into the civil war of 1918–1919. When tyrannical rule ends, faction fighting begins.

During all these upheavals, nations formed, national states came into being and borders were established – the borders of the Arab world were only finalised after World War I and II.

On the other hand, the modern borders of Afrika haven't yet been drawn. How many more wars must we have in the DRC, West and East Afrika, and the Great Lakes region before we can settle down in the New Design? Or do we think we are going to escape history, or the future, or both?

World War I was from 1914 to 1918, and World War II from 1939 to 1945. I don't know if World War I solved any disputes: nobody can tell me what it was all about and what the problem was that had to be sorted out. Who knows?

For a long time before the start of the ferment in Europe, life moved at a much slower pace than in the present era. Southern Afrika had proceeded in splendid isolation for centuries, completely untouched by invasions and other civilisations and cultures that came and went in the rest of the known world – Europe and Northern Afrika, and the East. Then for a fleeting moment in the lifetime of the planet the Afro-Europeans visited Southern Afrika, some to stay, others just to visit and move on. In South Afrika this rush happened roughly from 1650 to 1960.

The main similarity between the permanent occupation of Afrikan countries by the Arabs and the later, brief sojourn of the Europeans in Afrikan countries was that the Arabs converted the Afrikans to Islam or Afro-Islam, while the Europeans converted them to Christianity or Afro-Christianity.

The Arabs came, they stayed, and they remain firmly in command. In the Sudan, Afrikans are the disadvantaged majority and they continue to fight a lone battle for their right to survive. Millions of men, women and babies have been displaced, robbed, maimed and killed in the Sudan for years. In mid-July 2004, the United Nations belatedly condemned the government of the Sudan for not lifting a finger to protect the oppressed, terrorised and abused people whom the UN claimed were being victimised on a massive scale. And what do the PCs do? They focus on Palestine and Israel – to hell with the real problems of Afrika. Why?

Afrika's modern history starts in about 5000 BC with the return of the Afro-Libyans. Apart from the odd reference in the writings of historians such as Herodotus, records of human life in Afrika south of the Sahara really only start with the coming back of the Afro-Europeans to Afrika in about 1400 AD – over 6000 years later. Let's take it from there.

CHAPTER 49

Tormentas e Esperanças

One day, I hope the natives will understand what we Romans have done for them. But by then, I shall no doubt be dead and buried – Julia Marciana.

Port and Gin

AD 1652. The Afro-Swedes erect a fort near Accra, Ghana, to trade in slaves; the Dutch East India Company opens a replenishment station at the Cape to produce fresh produce for mariners sailing around Southern Afrika. (incidentally, I forgot to tell you that Ghana is named after the ancient West Afrikan Kingdom of Ghana); and the Afro-Brits make a terrible but useful mess in Afrika from which we still benefit today. Let's get to know them better:

AD100. The land is the Roman province of Britannia; its capital is Londinium. The main player is Julia Marciana, the wife of a wealthy civil servant, Gaius Antonious Faustinus, on the staff of the top Roman administrator governing Britannia. She writes a letter to Rome describing their way of life in the province. She mentions her children, her German slaves, her eating and dressing habits, and continues:

"Compared with Rome, it's terribly uncivilised. Before we arrived, the natives were illiterate and lived in small tribes at subsistence level. Most can now speak a few words of Latin, but they are so primitive they haven't yet learned how to think and behave like us. They're also incredibly ungrateful. Sometimes I wonder why we bother trying to educate these people. Without us, they would still be living in mud-hut villages, dying of starvation and cold in winter. They'd have no running water, no drainage, no roads, no arithmetic or culture, and a limited diet."[1]

---

1 *Fair Lady*. January 2001.

That was 100 AD. Let's see how the natives lived in 18th century England. Here is Robert Ergang's account:

> ... beneath its surface refinement, was still an age of ignorance, brutality and drunkenness. The masses of the population were largely illiterate. The poverty of the poorer classes in the cities – particularly London – cannot be exaggerated. Higher education reached only a few. Women were too often illiterate and they had few rights before the law. The brutality of the age is seen in the popular amusements, such as bear-baiting, bull-baiting, and cock-fighting... Executions became occasions for merriment. The insane were chained, beaten, and generally mistreated. Londoners went to see them for amusement, much as one goes to see the animals in a zoo today.

Ergang contends that drunkenness had become the national vice:

> No section of society was free from it. It was a habit among men occupying the highest positions in the state, among fine gentlemen, and among the lowest classes. Prodigious quantities of port and 'carnivoracity' made gout a common ailment among the upper classes. If the upper classes suffered much from port, the lower classes suffered more from the gin.[2]

In the meantime our own forefathers were going about their daily lives doing what people did in Afrika. Then in 1795 the British took the Cape; in 1803 the Cape returned to the Dutch, and in 1806 the British retook the Cape; in 1807 the slave trade was abolished and in 1833 slavery was abolished.

The British performed unrivalled feats. Already during the 16th century Sir Francis Drake had been the most successful pirate that ever sailed the high seas. He looted, raided, murdered and smuggled his way right around the world – and said the Cape was the fairest of them all. He was the first to circumnavigate the world in one voyage.

The Dutch were also one of the biggest European seafaring nations. They grabbed territories from Suriname (Dutch Guiana) in South America right around the world to Indonesia in South East Asia. Southern Afrika was no big deal for them.

The British had chalk and the Dutch had cheese. The Orient had spices and exotic merchandise, and to get there the Europeans had to sail around Afrika, or to be specific – South Afrika.

It was the Afro-Dutch and Afro-British that eventually became involved with South Afrika.

---

2 Ergang, 1967.

South Afrika is Fantastik

"South Africa... It is a land of great danger... it is, and always was, a varied place that defies easy classification" states David Mason.[3]

We can be proud of our fellow South Afrikans and our place in the international community of nations, but we can't be smug about it. We perform better than some arrogant Europeans such as the Finns, Belgians and Irish. On the other hand, we can learn a lot from some modest Afrikans who are better achievers than us, such as the Kenyans, Moroccans and Ethiopians. Look at the scoreboard – the 2004 Athens Olympics medals table!

South Afrika is fantastik! But it is not the most beautiful country in the world. We don't have something like the Namib Desert of Namibia. We don't have anything that approaches the Kalundula Falls of Angola. We have no rivers like the Congo or the Nile. We have no great lakes, no snows of Kilimanjaro, or fjords of Norway.

What do we have? We have us. South Afrika is not a country because we are a nation; we are a nation because South Afrika is our country – we are good.

I don't love our country because of its natural splendour. I am passionate about South Afrika because of us – the country is ours, it's mine, it is yours. It is the best and I am one with it. It is the land of our past, our present and our future – of our fathers and our ancestors for ages and generations. I love South Afrika because it is my *patria*, my country, my people, my harmony and my rhythm. It owns me, body and soul. South Afrika is my blood, breath and spirit.

South Afrika is my rhapsody and my song. Like Al Jolson I sing:

The sun shines east, the sun shines west,
I know where the sun shines best.

South Afrika is where we belong.
If you have left, I don't blame you
I wish you success.
If you want to come back home, I won't say
I told you so.
I'll welcome you back with open arms
But I can't guarantee you'll have a fair chance.
I'll wish you success.

You have to consider South Afrikans in the context of their time and space. This goes back some centuries.

---

3 Mason, 2003.

235

White Afrikans – The Whole Bloody Lot

We pick up again with the Afro-European colonialists who brought the developments in other parts of the modern world to Afrika. We will start with the bitter-sweet story of our Afro-European settlers and migrants to South Afrika.

Afrika and Southern Afrika were sparsely and intermittently inhabited and there were no borders to speak of – just as it was in most of the world centuries before nation states came into being.

Southern Afrika's past is all about Afrikan royalty and plebs, rich and poor people, migrants, nomads, invaders and settlers, scramblers, strugglers, trekkers, traders, missionaries and settlers, fortune seekers, farmers, hunters, hard workers, layabouts, colonialists and settlers, deceivers and crooks, honest people, smugglers, comers and goers, strugglers again and neo-Afro-Afrikan settlers – the whole bloody lot!

The first invaders, migrants, nomads and settlers were Bushmen – Afro-San and Afro-Khoi (Khoisan). They were the first to meander the lands of the Cape. The first prominent farmers were the Khoi, Afro-Afrikans and Afro-Afrikaners. The first hunters were the San. The first missionaries in Southern Afrika were Christians: Catholic and Protestant. The San were and are South Afrika's First Nation; the Nigerians are the last, for now. The second lot of migrants was the Afro-Afrikans who followed the Khoisan trail.

In southernmost Afrika, the Afro-Afrikan and the organised Afro-Europeans were the first invaders, settlers and migrants. The first Afro-European invaders and settlers in the Cape were the Afro-Dutch in 1652, followed soon – one and a half centuries later – by the Afro-British colonialists at the turn of the 19th century.

The Khoi and the Afro-Dutch were also the first main traders in modern South Afrikan times. All this happened when European trading in human resources was prolific in Western Afrika, and when the British had not yet reached their peak of inebriety.

The replenishment station that the Dutch trading company established at the Cape of Good Hope (*Boa Esperança*) – also called the Cape of Storms (*Tormentas*) – was to provide fresh produce and facilitate maritime movement around Southern Afrika.

Then in 1657 some company employees took their leave to become farmers as "free citizens" of Afrika. Others followed to swell their numbers, and they became known as citizens or *burghers*.

In March 1707, the burghers received the news that they had won a petition against the governor of the Dutch East India Company, WA van der

Stel. This was an occasion for jollification and some probably imbibed more than was necessary. On Sunday 7 March, four young scallywags galloped through the streets of Stellenbosch in cowboy fashion and caused a little consternation at the mill. The miller apparently supported the governor. Magistrate Starrenburg investigated the fracas. He tried to silence them and chased them away with a rattan cane, threatening them with imprisonment.

One of the rascals, Hendrik Bibault, then screamed at the top of his voice: "I am an Africaander; I will not shut up, and I will not go away, even if the magistrate beats me to death or slams me in jail." He was the first South Afrikan activist.

After recuperating from the *babelas* and fulfilling their self-inflicted transformation, the burghers adopted the name of the continent, becoming "Afri-
caanders" and eventually "Afrikaners".

Intermittently from 1688 onwards, Afro-French immigrants settled at the
Cape. They were Protestants, called Huguenots, who had fled France to escape religious persecution. Marrying into the Cape Dutch community, they
easily adapted to a new language and culture.

The first trekkers and strugglers for independence of note were the
Afrikaners – first independence from the Dutch trading company, then from
British rule, then from Dutch rule, and then from British rule again. To
escape colonial rule, many of them kept trekking further and further east,
and later further and further north, eventually becoming stateless.

"In a sense the trekboers were southern Africa's first white Africans..."[4]

Thus the Afrikaners became permanent inhabitants of Afrika. Their story
is one of struggling, of trekking, of poverty, plagues and epidemics, and of
war and misery, the story of winning and losing. The vast majority of them
were farmers, *Boers* as they were called.

That's how the Afro-Dutch ended up in South Afrika – for a while.

---

4 Oakes, 1989.

CHAPTER 50

Cape to Cairo

General Louis Botha and General Jannie Smuts would probably have called Churchill's son-in-law a racist – Uncle Joe.

Naked and Wicked

Having started in the British era of gin and port, we continue our story of Southern Afrika with special reference to South Afrika and Zimbabwe.

"At the end of the 18th century, and again at the beginning of the 19th, a new element was added to an already complex mix of people at the Cape: the British. Motivated by imperialism, deceit, greed, prejudice and humanitarianism, the colony's new rulers would play a leading role in constructing one of the world's most troubled societies."[1]

The British were among the prime "scramblers" so well described in *The Scramble for Africa* by Thomas Pakenham.

The story of the early British in South Afrika is the story of imperial governance, colonial administration and business, a story of trade, commerce and mining, of diamonds and gold, of rugby and cricket, of coming and going – and of coming and staying.

Rule Britannia, Britannia rules the waves; There will always be an England; Land of Hope and Glory; God save the King/Queen. And so Tommy Atkins came to the Western Province waving the Union Jack.

The Pommies were very serious about establishing and expanding permanent colonial rule in Afrika.

"'Stay... so long as a kaffir remains alive.' ...Lieutenant-Colonel Graham was determined that his war against the Xhosa would teach them a lesson

---

1 Oakes, 1989.

they would never forget – and he set about his task with a ruthless efficiency..."[2]

That was 1812. In the early 1830s Sir Harry Smith, who was very "with it" and politically correct in terms of British imperialism, introduced his policies of integrating the locals into the colony of British Kaffraria. He explained to the chiefs that Kaffraria would be divided into counties, towns and villages with English names, and that "...you may no longer be naked and wicked barbarians, which you will ever be unless you labour and become industrious... you must learn that it is money that makes people rich by work".[3]

Smith probably got his ideas from the letters of Julia Marciana and the Roman colonialists of 100 AD.

Now in the 1800s in Southern Afrika, the new colonial power settled British and German immigrants in the Cape border region to protect the eastern boundary of the British Empire.

Later, in 1845, the British annexed Natal as a district of the Cape Colony and continued with the same policies of racial segregation. Theophilus Shepstone was appointed as diplomatic agent to the "Native Tribes" and the task of the new administration was to divide the territory between the blacks and the whites.

Some decades later, within a few years of his arrival in Natal in 1893, Gandhi became very disillusioned. He had been a firm believer in British justice, but the ill treatment and the racial discrimination he encountered changed his mind.

A Mixed Bag

More than a century of British colonial rule bore witness to a mixed bag of events, both inside and outside the borders of the colony, including a variety of battles between black and black involving a great number of tribes, sometimes with black or white allies on one or both sides – the white allies being Boers or British. There were also battles between black and white, again with or without cross-colour allies on one or both sides, and battles between white and white with or without the same assortment of alliances.

One of the historic black versus black campaigns was the Mfecane, which started in 1818 with the great Zulu chief Shaka seeking more *lebensraum*. This had extremely far-reaching results for Southern Afrika as a whole. It set in motion a colossal chain reaction of migrations and fighting that spread to

2 Oakes, 1989.
3 Oakes, 1989.

such an extent that it brought about changes in political and social structures not only in the present South Afrika, Lesotho and Swaziland, but also in Central Afrika, notably Zambia, Zimbabwe and Mozambique.

One of the most significant battles of black against white was the disastrous defeat of the Zulu warriors when they attacked the Boers during the Battle of Blood River in 1838. Much later there were also the battles of the Anglo-Zulu War of 1879.

In the meantime, in 1858 in the Cape, the British finally broke the Xhosa resistance when, in a strange form of retaliation initiated by the young prophetess Nongqawuse, the Xhosa people slaughtered their cattle and purposely ceased all agricultural cultivation.

The century of British dominance of the Cape, and later also of Southern Afrika during the 1800s, during which Britain occupied various Afrikan territories in fulfilment of the imperial vision of Afrika being British from the Cape to Cairo (and for the benefit of imperialist pockets such as those of Cecil John Rhodes) – eventually culminated in the white versus white Anglo-Boer War, 1899–1902.

In 1903, the British searched for a political system suitable for a reconstructed Southern Afrika. Although the British High Commissioner, Alfred Milner, despised the defeated Afrikaner communities, Boer and Briton agreed to maintain white domination at all costs.

Thus the British handed on their policies practised in the Cape Colony to the Eastern Cape and to Natal, and later to the Union of South Afrika. "Although total separation on every level between black and white became official policy only after the National Party election victory in 1948, its foundation had been laid nearly half a century previously in a policy then known as segregation – not by Afrikaners but by British Government officials."[4]

Peace after the bitter fighting of the Anglo-Boer War led to the birth of the independent Union of South Afrika in 1910. Thus the Union of South Afrika, which became the Republic of South Afrika in 1961, was launched into the future with a policy of segregation.

This new era was characterised by another form of friction – that between the British and Afrikaners of the white population. Early in the 20th century Milner implemented a vast and dynamic policy to anglicise the two former Boer republics. This made the Afrikaners hate Milner as much as he hated them. His Reconstruction and Development Plan entailed importing Britons to settle on the destroyed and vacant former Boer farms, and he

---

4 Oakes, 1989.

241

employed these immigrants as teachers and preachers to reshape the depleted Afrikaner communities.

In his book, *A Traveller's History of South Africa*,[5] David Mason calls the first prime minister of the Union of South Afrika, General Louis Botha, and Field Marshall General Jan Smuts "Two segregationists".

Jan Smuts has been internationally acclaimed for his role in Churchill's war cabinet against arch-villain Adolf Hitler, and for his contribution to international peace institutions like the League of Nations and the United Nations. Mason's depiction of Smuts, however, characterises him as a villain of the highest order in present-day terms.

Those British colonialists who exploited South Afrika, those who came and went – they were the bad guys; and the others, such as businessmen, miners, farmers, professionals and technicians, who came and stayed – they were the good guys.

In the end, as in other parts of the European colonial world of that time, it was mobility and power – the horse and the wheel, and firearms – which reigned supreme on the field of battle.

Epilogue

With the different paths to independence of South Afrika and of Zimbabwe came different endings, illustrating perhaps what might have been, "what if..." At the height of Western colonialism, British rule in South Afrika came to an end as early as 1910. At the height of the East–West Cold War, British colonialism in Afrika came to an end in Rhodesia as late as 18 April 1980. (This was preceded by a brief interlude of unilaterally declared independence under Ian Smith from November 1965.) *British style* and *colonial characterisation of Afrika* prevailed for a further 70 years.

With regard to *British style*, Lord Soames was the last governor of the British Dependency of Southern Rhodesia. His wife, Lady Soames, was the daughter of Sir Winston Churchill. His ADC was Colonel Parker-Bowles. Government House in Salisbury was decorated and furnished in a manner that made Versailles seem middle class. The magnificence was obviously meant to demonstrate the sheer power and awesome prestige of colonial Britain.[6]

When it comes to the *British characterisation* of the Southern Afrikan scene, 150 years after Harry Smith preached to the "naked and wicked barbarians",

---

5 Mason, 2003.
6 www.guardian.co.uk/zimbabwe

Lord Soames echoed similar sentiments: "You must remember, this is Africa. They think nothing of doing filthy, beastly things to each other."[7]

Today – or in 1980 – Jan Smuts and Louis Botha would probably have called Soames a racist.

Of course, we all know that Soames' sweeping statement is flawed, but unfortunately in this case it turned out to be true. In the new Zimbabwe – one president later – the babies of democracy and prosperity have been thrown out with the colonial bathwater. In a country previously known as the Bread Basket of Afrika, hundreds of thousands of people have no bread, and thousands have been killed!

In conclusion, in South Afrika, Nelson Mandela became president and by 2005 Makhaya Ntini was the best ever South Afrikan fast bowler; in Zimbabwe, Robert Mugabe became president and by 2005 his League of Gentlemen had reduced cricket to rubble.

That's how the Afro-English ended up in Southern Afrika – for some time.

7 McAleese Bles, 1993.

CHAPTER 51

White, Yellow and Grey

Not Orange, Not Free and No State

To determine the feasibility of the PI Ark to float the Southern Afrikan New Design we need to know more about the real environment and its peoples. The permanent settlement of Afro-Europeans and the evolution of the Afrikaners caused different outcomes than in other Afrikan countries in terms of timescale and independence, but more importantly with regard to the aftermath.

It was mainly due to the Afrikaners that South Afrika was one of the first Afrikan countries to escape from colonial rule to become an independent state with its present-day borders. This is how it happened:

The Afro-Afrikaners settled in the Cape. Many stayed there, while others migrated to the Eastern Cape. In turn, many stayed there, while others embarked on the Great Trek northwards into the vast unknown – to escape British colonial rule. They were the *Voortrekkers* – the pioneers.

Having wandered beyond the umbrella of the Dutch East India Company, and subsequently also of the British colonial authority, they were simply "citizens of Afrika" – stateless Boers. During their peregrinations in uncharted territories, by necessity they established a number of independent republics, including Natalia. It was here where King Shaka founded the Zulu nation.

The British showed little regard for both the Zulu and the Afrikaners and most unsportingly annexed Natal in 1843. Thus a pattern was established: the stateless *trekboers* would pave the way to the unknown hinterland and create settlements. The British would follow, annex the territory and consolidate their colonial interests.

Once again, some of the Afrikaners stayed in Natalia, while others crossed the Drakensberg Mountains into the country north of the Orange and Vaal Rivers. They joined up with some of their kin who had taken a direct route from the Eastern Cape. North of the Orange they established the Republic of the Orange Free State (OFS), and north of the Vaal the Zuid-Afrikaansche Republiek (ZAR), also called the Transvaal – one of the first states on the continent with the word "Afrika" in its name. The Free State's capital was Bloemfontein and the ZAR's Pretoria.

South Afrika is very colour conscious. The *Orange* Free State stretched from the majestic *green* Drakensberg with its dragon-like silhouette against the *azure* sky in the east to the confluence of the *Orange* and *Vaal* (grey) Rivers in the *sepia* west.

When *white* diamonds were discovered in the triangle between the Orange and the Vaal with their murky *grey* waters, the English took action. To save the backward locals, Afrikaners and Griquas, from the dangers of the decadence that diamonds would bring, they annexed the territory to the British Cape Colony.

When *yellow* gold was discovered in the Transvaal, the British were itching to come to the rescue again. However, the Afrikaners didn't get the message of goodwill, especially not after the botched Rhodes-inspired Jameson Raid that was aimed at overthrowing the Pretoria government.

The British didn't react to a final ultimatum that expired on 11 October 1899 to withdraw their troops from the ZAR borders – and the war was on. So Queen Victoria deployed British *khakis* to subjugate the Boers and to expand the colonial empire. It became the biggest war that Britain had ever fought at that stage.

Ultimately the *red* necks, the English, won the war on account of their Scorched Earth and Concentration Camp Strategy. Farms far away from the battlefields were burnt to the ground and ransacked. And 26 000 women and children died in the British camps – a devastating number for that *black* period in Afrikaner history. If that had not happened, the first *white* Afrikans would have been the biggest tribe on the *Dark Continent*.

Politically the war led to a new dispensation called the Union of South Afrika – the unification of the two Boer republics, the ZAR and OFS, with the two British colonies, the Cape and Natal. That is how South Afrika's present international borders came into being. If it had not been for Pretoria and Bloemfontein, the story would have been different.

The Afrikaners and others persisted with their struggle and eventually in 1961 South Afrika gained full independence and became a republic with a non-executive president. Comprehensive democracy came some 30 years later. In 1994, struggler, prisoner, Noble Prize laureate and superstar

Nelson Mandela took over as executive president of the Republic of South Afrika.

On the other hand, from 1914 onwards, apart from a few Jews, English-speaking South Afrikans did not participate very actively in local politics. They generally conducted their politics through the press, big business and clubs. After the formation of the Union of South Afrika they mostly supported the liberal (for their time) Afrikaner leaders – General Louis Botha and Field Marshall General Jan Smuts, and their successors Mr JGN Strauss, Sir de Villiers-Graaf, and eventually Dr Frederik van Zyl Slabbert, one-time leader of the Progressive Federal Party (PFP). In the 1980s people used to say that the affluent English-speaking community of Johannesburg's northern suburbs voted for the PFP, while secretly hoping that the National Party, the main political home of Afrikaners, would make it.

What started causing a wobble in the New Design in 2005 is that our government is hell bent on changing the name of Pretoria to Tshwane. Pretoria was the bastion of the Boers who fought the colonial forces. If the government goes through with its idea, it will never again be able to claim with honesty that it "fought the hated colonialists". The name "Pretoria" wasn't a spontaneous people's itch that needed scratching. The place never had a name before it became the town of Pretoria. It was only a place. The secretly concocted history of an idolised chief Tshwane is an unworthy propaganda trick.[1]

Very South Afrikan

The Afrikaners are South Afrikans like everyone else. The extremist Afrikaners are South Afrikans like everyone else, only exclusively more so. The Afrikaners have produced top statesmen and politicians. Abram Fischer and President Marthinus T Steyn were esteemed statesmen of the internationally acclaimed model republic of its day, the Orange Free State. President Paul Kruger of the ZAR was internationally renowned, and the Field Marshall, General Jan Smuts, was the only foreigner to serve on Churchill's war cabinet. Another top statesman is Nobel Prize laureate FW de Klerk.

They also excelled in the military. In distant Europe people revered General Christiaan de Wet of the Anglo-Boer War. Jan Blaauw was a fighter pilot hero of World War II and the Korean War. He was one of only two South Afrikans ever decorated with the American Silver Star for bravery and leadership; the other pilot was awarded it posthumously. And today South

---

1 Prof L J Louwrens, Department of African Languages, University of South Africa.

Afrikans still sing the praise of General Koos de la Rey, another Boer war hero and a protégé of Jan Smuts.

You will also find the Afrikaners tops in the medical world and the world of science and in sport – FW de Klerk was also once a minister of sports.

Afrikaners have also been tops in religion – sometimes in combination with politics. Dr Daniel (DF) Malan, former National Party prime minister of South Afrika, had a main highway in Johannesburg named after him until the 1994 government renamed it after another Afrikaner cleric and key ANC political leader, Beyers Naudé.

You can find them in the churches and in the prisons; they are top crooks and fraudsters. Stander was the (Bonnie and) Clyde of South Afrika.

They have also been top strugglers: Afrikaner Bram Fischer, grandson of the first prime minister of the Orange River Colony, was the most wanted, on-the-run, underground communist top gun in South Afrika.

Andrew Kenny says:

> Whatever you might think of certain Afrikaner governments and policies in our history, you have to accept that the Afrikaners have fundamentally shaped our country and produced more than their share of her statesmen, builders and thinkers. Thanks in large part to Afrikaners, SA is now the most developed economy in Africa.[2]

The English-speaking South Afrikan is very English if you are a South Afrikan, and very South Afrikan if you are English. Nevertheless, the English speakers in the country are as much South Afrikan as the English speakers in Australia are Australian.

Jimmy, just back from Hermanus and quick to express his opinion, sympathises with the English: "During the 1800s they had to contend with black barbarians as Sir Harry Smith called the Kaffrarians of the Eastern Cape; during the 1900s they had to face the white kaffers of Afrika, as singer Anton Goosen hailed the Afrikaners; and in the 2000s they have to put up with a black Englishman, as Van Zyl Slabbert described our President Mbeki."

The Zulus are South Afrikans like everyone else. They are proud to be Zulus, and they show it. This makes other people jealous, but they don't show it because they are respectful or scared.

The Basutos inhabit the mountain kingdom of Lesotho on the roof of Afrika from where they overflow into, among others, the Free State, where I come from. These Basutos are South Afrikans like everyone else; they are proud to be Basutos but for tactical reasons don't show it, and they don't have to.

---

2 *The Citizen*, 22 November 2005.

The coloured people, by whatever name or no name, are the most underrated. The Xhosas have given us Mandela and Mbeki and one party. They rule the roost.

Without foreign capital and the enterprise of Jews, the English and others, South Afrika would not have become what it is. Those who became native South Afrikans – the Brits, Afrikaners, Jews, Portuguese, Lebanese, Greeks, Italians and so on who settled here – have all made and are still making a monumental contribution to our South Afrika of today. There is no substitute for enterprise, aptitude and hard work.

At the end of the day, all South Afrikans have made their contribution. Without them in the past, the present and the future, South Afrika would not be what it is and will be.

If the Afrikan émigrés who became Afro-Europeans made a big mistake in leaving Afrika, perhaps an even bigger mistake was to come back. However, maybe we are being unfair to the Afrikans-turned-Europeans returning to Afrika and turning from Afro-Europeans into Euro-Afrikans. This is all very confusing. I am South Afrikan, without hyphens, and you can classify me as you like.

Staging the 2010 Soccer World Cup

What if Southern Afrika had been completely inaccessible to any potential visitors during the years 1600 to 1900 – no Afro-Europeans whatsoever, no expatriates at all! This is not entirely hypothetical. There are people in parts of South Amerika and the East and its islands who have been left alone in splendid isolation for centuries and centuries up to the present.

If nobody had ever come to harass and plague us where would we have stood today? Well, for a start we would probably have missed staging the 2010 Soccer World Cup.

Is it a miracle, in spite of our own problems, that we seem generally so much better off than many other Afrikan countries? Why do people from all corners of Afrika flock to South Afrika, not only now, but for the last number of decades? If you don't believe me, enquire after the nationality of any Afrikan waitron, legal immigrant or otherwise, at any restaurant in town. He or she will bear me out.

We are not better off because of South Afrika's gold and diamonds. Many other Afrikan countries also have these in greater quantities and of better quality – and cheaper labour. Some of them have assets of greater value than a few gold and diamond mines, such as oil, or *pula* – rain, water, large rivers and lakes. Nevertheless, South Afrika, classified as having poor agricultural potential, until recently had a quantum edge over most other Afrikan countries in food production. Why? And so I could go on.

Failing to acknowledge what our forefathers have left us, in spite of all the pros and cons, would be wrong and a denial of the truth.

* * *

We have seen how the Afrikaners and Afro-European South Afrikans came to be in South Afrika, for ever more – on the launching pad of the New Design.

CHAPTER 52

To Kill a Farmer

South Afrika and PC Scands

We have analysed Southern Afrika's modern past: how Europeans became permanent inhabitants – South Afrikans – and how the Afrikaners originated. What now are the realities at the dawn of the South Afrikan New Design?

The opportunist fly-by-night colonialists were the bad guys and the struggling settlers the good guys. However, these days a settler-turned-South Afrikan with his roots in Afrika is an evil person. Hate speech such as "Kill a farmer, kill a Boer" and "One settler one bullet" is officially accepted. Western PCs, including Scandinavians – Scands – also accommodate these sentiments.

Do they know that South Afrika is not really farming country? Of its approximately 1.27 million square kilometres only 17% is arable. In international terms only 1% of all the land is classified as "good" for agriculture. However, owing to the acumen and expert management of our farmers, we put that figure of "good land" at 3%.

Do the Scands know that for sustained living we need 0.4 hectares per person, based on optimal commercial production (that is for all categories: livestock rearing and soil cultivation, irrigated and non-irrigated land)? According to the above figures, we should be able to produce food for 34 million people. However, if we take the illegal immigrants in the country into account, it means that we have to cater for another 10 million.

In 1995 there were 63 000 commercial farmers, but by mid-2005, after land reform, there were approximately only 44 000. With a population of 44 million, one farmer should put food on the table for 1000 people. Theoretically, if one farmer goes out of business, 1000 people go without food.

By August 2005, 90% of the farmland transfers had resulted in a breakdown of commercial farming in favour of subsistence farming. Clearly it is not easy to merge the notion of the traditional communal possession of land for food with the modern Western practice of business-oriented private land ownership. As you can see, it's not about race; it's about survival in the New Design.[1]

Can Queen Margrethe of Denmark not persuade our government to set a prerequisite for such transfers – a guarantee that commercial farming will continue after every transfer, irrespective of race? We cannot afford to import food. Or do we have to wait for crown princess Victoria of Sweden?

However, unfortunately, our government gives no credible indication that Zimbabwe-type land grabs will not be copied in South Afrika. Ironically, in 2006 Zimbabwean ministers said that those blacks who took over white farms had been apathetic and were responsible for the serious food crisis – an accusation they had earlier denied. Those now pointing a finger are precisely those who were responsible for the catastrophe. Is that awaiting us in the New Design?

The decline has already started. During October 2005 our own minister of agriculture, Thoko Didiza, announced that the greater majority of the 70 farms given to black farmers in the Limpopo province had collapsed. The first step towards the expropriation of farms in South Afrika began in mid-October 2005 when a Notice of Intent was served on Hannes Visser of the farm Leewspruit in the Lichtenburg area.

Israelis and Cubans in Cohoots

Tarentaal in critical mood: "For the government it is not about black empowerment, production of food, land for homes, or about providing jobs. It is about crushing commercial white farmers. The astonishing fact is that 90% of the 3% of arable land in South Afrika lies in the former Bantu homelands. It is completely underutilised, used only for subsistence farming to support only the farmers' households directly and does not produce anything for trade."

That was quite a mouthful for a Trantraal lady!

Jimmy, in a positive frame: "Tarentaal is right. Let's devise a scheme for the transformation of *subsistence* farming into *commercial* farming – in the old homelands! It would make money for the incumbent farmers, feed the nation, and provide work for the jobless. Let's find people who will invest in this sensational long-term, multibillion, agricultural project. How about the King of Saudi Arabia, the Sultan of Brunei, Queens Beatrix and Elizabeth II?

1 Adapted from *Omgewingspraatjie*, RSG, SABC radio station, 10 September 2005.

Approach President Fidel Castro for experts and training, and of course, the kibbutzing Israelis are very good at collective commercial farming, as are the Russians. They will operate under the watchful eye of Trevor Manuel, our minister of finance, and the guiding hand of Dingaan Thobela, our Rose of Soweto. All this will happen in the northern and eastern region of South Afrika, under the auspices of a royal senate chaired by King Goodwill Zweli-thini."

I agree with Jimmy. Our New Design cannot tolerate injustices in the same way as the Scands do by turning a blind eye to them.

Martin of the *Mafikeng Mail* crosses swords with the Scands. He threatens to sue them, the PC Vikings – Norwegians, Swedes and Danes. They raped, looted and plundered their way through the dirt tracks and dongas that were the Carnaby and Oxford Streets of Londinium. And he insists that the West Afrikan governments should be sued for selling their own people into slavery, and then 300-odd years later blaming it on the dreadful colonialists.[2]

James, these events happened a long time ago; the PC Scands are the neo-culprits. I'm joining Martin to sue the Norwegians, Danes and Swedes who are all sponsors of IDASA, but who do not lift a finger to bring an end to in-stitutionalised racial discrimination.

And, if we compare the Scands with the Germans we can prove the point: currently in the 21st century German companies are being prosecuted for their activities in the colonial Deutsch Südwest Afrika of the 19th century – activities which were commonplace at that time. And legal proceedings have also been instituted in the US against other international companies that did business with the South Afrika of the 20th century – not as commonplace – but not unique.

However, times have radically changed from the 19th and 20th centuries to the 21st century. Equal Opportunities, Fair Practice and Universal Human Rights have become universally ensconced in international agreements, national constitutions and codes of conduct. They are the "in" things, and if you are not "with it", you are wrong and evil.

Being blamed for something that happened long ago which was then locus communis, common place, but is now regarded as wrong, is one thing, but being accused of wrongdoing now which is regarded as wrong now, is quite another.

Now in the 21st century in South Afrika, some parties, such as Scandi-navians, are quite aware of ongoing practices branded as wrong now, to

---

2 *The Citizen*, 7 February 2004.

which they turn a blind eye now – such as the violation of equal opportunities and fair practice on the basis of institutionalised racism. They are hypocrites expediently hiding behind the present-day and highly questionable Political Correctness. Do their majesties King Carl XVI Gustaf of Sweden and King Harald V of Norway know that Politically Correct and Legally Correct are different concepts?

Jimmy speaks up on behalf of the three musketeers and other music lovers: "What we need in South Afrika is an Ovlov – a Volvo going backwards. We'll invite the Scands to return once they change their stance and also care for Gnu and Tarentaal, and support racial minorities. In the meantime, we should not forget the Saab, but it should not go backwards since it will be politically incorrect. Between the Ovlov and the Baas the best by far is ABBA, coming or going."

And I would also like to join Martin "in suing Nelson Mandela, all-round nice guy and reconciliator par excellence – for making the rest of us look like bloody fools."

The UK and Us

Our final exercise is to see what tips we can get from our peers and contemporaries by comparing ourselves with other real-time set-ups, places and peoples. Namibia or Botswana may not be a bad idea. They live and let live. But that's Afrika. Let's look north.

More recently, some European countries have begun to experience similar concerns to those that plagued South Afrika since many years ago: they too now have serious legal/illegal aliens/immigrants/refugee problems. As early as the late 1970s, the influx of illegal aliens into South Afrika, seeking and finding a better life, was horrendous. Now, 30+ years later, the offspring of those aliens have more than a 70% chance of getting a job, while my grandchildren have less than 5% chance – without even considering the more recent influx of about 5 million Zimbabweans. Why? It is because of unequal opportunities and unfair business practices.

Perhaps I should be a little bit more carelessnessful – live and let live, be more lackadaisical like the Brits. The UK is one united monarchy, but when England, Scotland, Wales and Ireland take on each other at rugby, they call those matches "internationals". When it is England versus Wales, they sing different anthems before the game: "Land of our Fathers" for the Welsh and "God save the Queen" for the English. Likewise the Scots sing "Flower of Scotland", and they all wave different flags. Unlike white South Afrikans, the Irish can also sing.

253

Do you remember the outrage over what became known as the Zulu Hate Song directed against the South Afrikan Indians? It goes like this:

> Oh brothers, Oh my fellow brothers. We need strong and brave men to confront Indians. This situation is very difficult, Indians do not want to change, whites were far better than Indians. Even Mandela has failed to convince them to change... we struggle so much here in Durban, as we have been dispossessed by Indians;... I have never seen Dlamini emigrating to Bombay, India. Yet, Indians arrive everyday in Durban...

In analysing the South Afrikan realities at the dawn of our New Design we have briefly compared ourselves with others. So, what are we going to do to shape the PI Ark for South Afrika and Afrika? Are we going to stick to the outdated and overrated modern democracy? President Mahmoud Ahmadinejad told President George Bush: liberalism and Western style democracy have not been able to realise the ideals of humanity...

Jimmy interjects: "Don't bite his finger, look where it's pointing. Constitutions and governance are not supposed to run the business of a country, to provide employment and solve poverty. They should only facilitate for society to do these things, and what brings prosperity is freedom, not democracy.

"By the way Uncle Joe, how many more times must I beg you to give me a chance to start a chapter; you always give me a say only at the end... if you have space."

So I tell him, "You're on, but I don't want the sort of stuff you dish up in your 'Jimmy's Corner' of the *Tokoloshe Times*."

CHAPTER 53

Jimmy the Reed de Umhlanga on PAP and Scrabble

Afrikan Divide – Prata-prata

On the eve of the New Design, we focus on the South Afrikan realities. Jimmy is at the lectern:

"I noted with interest how Ms Maria Matembe, chairperson of the 2006–2010 Pan-Afrikan Parliament (PAP), outlined the strategic route PAP will follow for the next five years. She did not say where the route would lead, but PAP also now has a Vision, Mission, Goals, Objectives and miscellaneous fieterjasies.

Speaking from the PAP headquarters at Midrand, near one of my favourite splashing spots on the Jukskei River, she said that PAP lacks human and financial resources. 'Most important of all,' she said, 'is that we are to transform PAP from a consultative advisory body into a fully-fledged legislative organ.'

The question is how and for whom do they want to legislate – for Tarentaals, Gnus, Uncle Joes or for us Tokoloshes? Are they going to pre-empt the AU? Whether there is an AU or a PAP, are they going to vote on a one-state-one-vote basis with the majority of the undemocratic countries sweeping the floor every time?!

The Big Ones (humans) don't understand that minimal laws are indicative of maximal civility and civilisation, and it's the optimal in freedom. What Afrika needs is an independent Afrikan Bank, Afrikan Monetary Fund, Afrikan Court, Afrikan Trade Organisation, Afrikan Health Organisation, and the Afrikan Association for the Preservation of Tokoloshes. What we don't need is another parliament and more prata-prata. During 2006 South Afrika chaired the G-77 with the aim of promoting North-South relations for more prata-prata! Personally I prefer Miriam Makeba's *Pata Pata* anyday.

The Big Ones should understand: Uncle Joe's 'Defenders', namely the democratic Afrikan countries, which are in the minority in PAP, will suffer under the laws made for them by his 'Demanders', the undemocratic states, which are in the majority. There is hardly a democratic country in the true sense of the word in Afrika north of the Big Desert.

Instead of a PAP, let's institute a VAC, Voice of Afrika Commission, reserved for the representatives of all the opposition parties of the continent – where they do exist and even where they don't. That's the only way the voice of the Afrikan majority will be heard. With less PAP and less prata-prata and more productivity, we'll have more energy, water and sanitation in the townships – and more pap."

Political Scrabble

Jimmy continues: "On a different tack, I trust that most of us are already convinced that in the neo-new South Afrika there will be no place for conventional political parties, parliaments and governments. South Afrika is very poor with regard to political parties anyway. We have a multitude of insignificant parties and really only one of any consequence – for the time being.

Once upon a time, at a Scrabble Party, politicians gathered and drew letters from a hat. One party got four letters: ACDP – the African Christian Democratic Party. Others got three letters: IFP – the Inkatha Freedom Party; NNP – the New National Party; UDM – the United Democratic Movement, and PAC – the Pan-Africanist Congress.

Three parties wanted only two letters. The one is called the DA – the Democratic Alliance, and the identity of the second is the ID – the Independent Democrats. The third one wanted a little more, but got only two of the same: FF+, the Freedom Front Plus. The rest are Minus parties.

The IFP is more or less strong in the province of KwaZulu-Natal. The PAC is more or less. The FF+ is popular among many Afrikaners even at second- and third-tier levels. The DA is the official opposition in parliament with some support countrywide.

All these parties and other smaller ones combined take up less than one-third of the seats in parliament. This is less than the number of seats that are vacant at any given time during normal parliamentary sessions!

The only party of real consequence is the one that declined the invitation to the Scrabble Party – the African National Congress or ANC. It already existed before the other parties got their names. It is the ruling party. It has little regard for the legislature. South Afrika has effectively become a one-party state since any party like the ANC with a two-thirds majority can amend the constitution at will, and probably will."

Thus spake James. Thanks, James.

The Arrogance of Power – Quotas remain in Force

It is not only Jimmy and I who have problems with politics. "While political parties were established to perform an aggregative function in the political system, in reality they became tools to manipulate the citizenry for the benefit of the party elite," says Xolela Mangcu, Executive Director of the Steve Biko Foundation.[1]

We are seldom sure whether we are dealing with the government or the ANC. The party is full of ploys: it deploys and redeploys ministers and civil servants more than the government and official structures do. When it comes to matters of misdemeanour, the ANC often applies its own party disciplinary measures instead of allowing departmental disciplinary and/or the judiciary system to deal with the issues.

The following illustrates the dominance of the party over the government and the civil administration:

Our minister of defence, Mr Terror Lekota, appealed to South Afrikans to ask themselves this question: "When will we cease to be Africans, coloureds, Indians and whites, and [be] merely South Africans?" The new minister of sport, Mr Stofile, agreed: "I'm tired of the artificial use of sport quotas as mere window dressing... We want our teams to be representative, but artificial quotas are not the answer."

But they are only ministers of state; the party secretary-general, Mr Kgalema Motlanthe, was quick to tighten the reins on them: "There is no change, policy remains the same, quotas remain in force and affirmative action will be in place for as long as it takes." He told the public that the ministers had been "misunderstood".[2]

The ANC is very conscious of its position of absolute power and exhibits all the symptoms of being power drunk. Xolela Mangcu continues, "...citizens could formally have the right to vote without any authority over those whom they voted into office. To paraphrase Mahmood Mamdani, we became loud citizens because of the vote – but pretty ineffective subjects because of this lack of political authority..."[3]

1 *Business Day*, 20 August 2003.
2 *The Star*, 7 July 2004.
3 *Business Day*, 20 August 2003.

Mangcu claims that the incentive for the party managers is the patronage they receive through jobs and contracts, and that party managers in turn deprive communities of services if they do not vote for the party. He says violence has become a tool for ensuring voter cooperation, and corruption has become the informal means of ensuring political survival for the party elite:

"This led to... corruption that springs from the arrogance of power, from a sense of unassailability and invincibility, from the knowledge that 'you can see me but you can't touch me'... we have become what the Indian scholar Partha Chatterjee would call 'empirical objects of empowerment policy, not citizens who participate in the sovereignty of the state.'"[4]

The next question is whether we would lose anything if we had no parliament. That grand lady of South Afrikan parliamentary politics and tenacious anti-apartheid campaigner, Helen Suzman, stated in a TV discussion programme that the apartheid government had more respect for parliament and the opposition than the ANC ruling party.

What the top leadership of the ANC says at its annual national executive conference is more important than its speeches for the press gallery in parliament. The regular Internet newsletter of the leader of the ANC to his party is much more important than any occasional statement that the president makes to the public. And this party leader and state president is the same person.

Don't be alarmed. One-party states are neither un-Afrikan nor unusual; they abound in the UN. The red PCs called Allende's regime in Chile a Marxist communist democracy. Zimbabwe, Iraq and the Soviet Union also claim or claimed to be democracies.

However, the ANC government under Nelson Mandela and his successor, Thabo Mbeki, should be complimented for what it has achieved in South Afrika. The macroeconomics is in place, and state and country prosper dynamically. Unfortunately the man in the street doesn't really know about this.

The micro situation is horrendous – the suburbs, townships, informal settlements, and the villages and towns in the rural areas where the people live all beg attention. South Afrika has become a friendly country – farmer killing and violence friendly, and a haven for asylum seekers, refugees and illegal immigrants. It has also become crime, fraud and corruption friendly. There is a lack of employment-generating growth, and poverty is on the increase.

---

4 *Business Day*, 20 August 2003.

The government has much to explain. Instead of challenging Christian education, minority rights and languages, it should have embarked on a nation-building programme. To create the right climate for such a plan it should observe the following tips:

Avoid harnessing diversity with the straightjacket of sameness.
Cultural diversity is good; what we need is harmony.
We don't all have to be, and think, alike; what we need is synergy.
Freedom and democracy have their price; they come not only with rights, but also with responsibilities, duties and obligations.

It is good to have a number of strong political parties. Critical reasoning, quality problem solving and sound decision making should precede legislation. Strong opposition makes a strong democracy.

Your country is one thing; your government is another. You are not unpatriotic if you criticise the ministers and the president, especially if you have a one-party government and an executive president. In five or ten years' time they will be gone – replaced hopefully. The country goes on, definitely and indefinitely.

These are the current realities in South Afrika during the first decade of the third millennium – on the eve of the National Divide.

CHAPTER 54

The National Divide

The End of the Beginning – The Miracle is Over

We are at D-Day for the New Design. How do we respond?

We should be a country of achievers. Minister Balfour can't say we should be less white, lose against Australia and be proudly South Afrikan! On the other hand, Jimmy says he proudly flies British Airways because they are Rugby South Afrika's official carrier. So, what are we?

The government is for the ANC party; it has no choice. In the meantime the elite get richer and the poor get poorer. Those who care for Jimmy, Tarentaal, Gnu and all of us are Cosatu, Solidarity, the good national NGOs and some others. Bad foreign red PC NGOs are against us.

Cosatu or its member unions could mean much if they shed the ANC cloak and operated as independent trade unions.

The South Afrikan Communist Party (SACP) could be even more useful if it decided to come out into the open. It could play a meaningful role as an independent political party, not in spite of the drain it would cause on the ANC, but it would be a welcome bonus.

If Solidarity were a political party it would pass with distinction. It supports the workers, cares for the people, displays quality of leadership, decency and integrity; it subscribes to the concept of live and let live; it is not arrogant but determined, not boastful but confident, reasonable but firm; it is focused; it is devoted and faithful to its members.

At the moment the ANC keeps Cosatu out of politics, and the SACP uses the ANC to get its members into legislatures and governments.

Jimmy interrupts: "You are scratching the surface, Uncle Joe; if you dig deeper as your Pat Symcox hinted you could, you'll find that government means nothing. South Afrika's future is being determined by the ANC. With a Xhosa strong arm, and imbued with passion, they steer the country towards exclusive black Afro-centrism."

Jimmy continues: "Together with Cosatu and the SACP the ANC has marginalised the other parties into a position of oblivion, but not for long. The tripartite alliance faces a fissure down the middle with the intellectual, rich black elite on the one side and the poor, semi-literate populists, who have already demonstrated early signs of taking the law into their own hands, on the other. And the Zulus adopt a new role. Now you can see why political parties are for the birds – begging your pardon Ms Tarentaal. We don't need them; the only thing we will lose is elitist party autocracy, and I don't mind that. We don't even need a parliament in its present form, and the desirability of having an executive president is highly arguable to say the least. The future will be decided by powerful black business leaders – not politicians, except where they are one and the same – the Tokyo Sexwales, Cyril Ramaphosas and a host of others. Coloureds, Asians and whites, to use the official nomenclature, won't play a political role except for convenience, or by accident or incident, or if they are business leaders – the Oppenheimers, Kebbles, financial institutions, banks and others."

The Sweet Years are Over

"Uncle Joe, you described the dilemma so well; you exposed the International Divide at the top – the UN – and you revealed the Continental Divide one tier lower in the Afrikan Union. I can't understand how you fail to see that lower down we are stumbling over the first steps of a National Divide – the false equilibrium of the South Afrikan socio-economic-political dispensation. I take a leaf from your Chapter 5:

In South Afrika the Defenders are the minority. They are those who possess the most know-how required by modern society. They are largely adult and experienced, the most literate, and the most educated and trained (and I don't mean in political science only), stinking rich and wasteful. Apart from business leaders, the Defenders consist mostly of the upper echelons of the ANC; the dominant elements of the Exiles such as Mbeki; the Inziles such as the UDF, Terror Lekota and Trevor Manuel; and the fading Robben Islanders, Mandela and friends. And for good luck there are also many of the DA, a few PACs, IFPs and so on.

The Demanders and their supporters are in the majority. They are those who lack the know-how and skills required by today's world. By comparison they are young and inexperienced; they are also largely illiterate, uneducated and untrained (especially in science and technology), and too many of them are extremely poor. Most of them are jobless, or industrial and commercial workers, and those located in the rural areas flock to the townships

261

and shantytowns. They demand to be employed and to receive basic governmental and municipal services or they threaten to take the law into their own hands. These people include most of the SACP and all of its youth league members, the overwhelming majority of COSATU members, all but the upper crust of the PAC, the entire ANC youth league, and much of the ANC's women's organisation, and so on. Their spokespeople are often suave, erudite and rich, but this doesn't reflect the real status of the people they are supposed to serve or represent.

The Power of Black Business versus the Champions of the Poor – that's what it will all boil down to, you'll see.

The point is this, the threatening Divide is not a rearrangement of political parties and alliances; the Divide cuts through parties and partnerships. It is a spontaneous arrangement of hungry and frustrated populists and 'jungle justlers' leading frenzied rabble rousers against the rest. It's a class thing, no longer a race thing.

What is the solution? Victory by the minority (the Defenders), through appeasement over the majority (the Demanders), will serve only to prolong the status quo and will not provide a sustainable solution. A takeover by the Demanders through populist violence will lead to a showdown, the unmanageable collapse of the system and misery for all. We should shed antiquated concepts and develop an entirely new dispensation."

Jimmy is right. What Marcello in Puccini's *Boheme* called "... the sweet years of illusion and utopias of hope, faith and trust" are over. We have reached the end of the beginning, the miracle is over.

Jimmy resumes: "There is a solution – a new beginning. The main obstacles to making it work are the Political Correctivists and the outdated, unqualified and unmonitored concept of modern representative democracy. We will never succeed unless we liberate ourselves from the shackles of political correctness.

The Defenders who are in power should initiate a new system of meeting the needs of the people – an honourable, fair and effective scheme for the benefit of all of us. For a start, ponder the question of whether we need the parliament.

Our constitution and democracy are not supposed to eradicate poverty, nor will they do so. We don't need hundreds (or is it thousands?) of politicians busying themselves with prata-prata – talking at assemblies, conferences, seminars, congresses and the like. Government overrules parliament in any case – such as giving the Gautrain project the green light contrary to parliamentary advice.

Government forced the people of the Khutsong township in Gauteng province to fall under the administrative jurisdiction of the North-West province against their will. It led to clashes with the police, death and bloodshed in the streets, and arson. It was shocking that the provincial premier advised the angry residents to sacrifice their personal well-being in the interest of the greater South Afrika – for the sake of a municipal border! The government does not serve the people.

Why can't other bodies - with the necessary adaptations - perform the governmental functions in the same way as the following bodies perform theirs: the Reserve Bank, the Human Rights Commission (HRC), the Council for Scientific and Industrial Research (CSIR), the Human Sciences Research Council (HSRC) and the justice system?

The threat of a National Divide between the Defenders and the Demanders should be defused to avoid disaster. A solution is in the offing, but it won't work without a monarch."

Now Gnu chips in: "Where do the Afrikaans South Afrikans fit into the Divide? Whom do they support? I have an idea for them; they must do what they do best – fight on the side of the underdog, the poor, the Demanders.

If their role had been reversed during the pre 1994 era, most of them would probably have been freedom fighters anyway. And many of them have told me they have been betrayed by the likes of Volkskas/ABSA and Santam, those institutions which got where they are on poor Afrikaners' pennies, so what have they got to lose?

I suggest they become the political wing of Solidarity and join the SACP. Voting en masse, by sheer weight of numbers they replace the incumbent office bearers of the SACP and take over lock, stock and barrel – and fight the good cause for the people! Back to you, James," Gnu ends.

All of us, including Jimmy, are dumbstruck.

I gather myself and address Jimmy: "I give you half a chance and then you and Gnu take over the whole bloody book!"

* * *

There are two major challenges we have to face: we must ensure that we don't pursue change simply for the sake of change and we must remove the impediment of political correctness.

Doing away with conventional political systems in favour of a New Design will be as nerve racking as graduating from fiddle sticks to test cricket, but well worth our while.

CHAPTER 55

UBF

Most institutions demand unqualified Political Correctness; but the institution of science makes scepticism a virtue – based on a saying by Robert K Merton.[1]

Three Envelopes

One doesn't just change something because it was the "in" thing at the latest NGO workshop jolly. But the one thing that I do concede is that the time is overdue for a change in the state of affairs of the state. It is now the UBF – the Ultimate Bloody Final – chance to make up our minds.

Let's consider the aspects influencing "To Change or Not To Change."

Many organisations merely revise and update their long-term plans on an annual cyclical basis. However, as time goes by the quality of any long-term plan progressively diminishes. One should therefore, periodically initiate a new planning programme right from scratch and produce an entirely new long-term plan. Changes will follow.

Changes are also bound to happen when a new executive chairperson takes the chair, or when there are a meaningful number of replacements of other senior executives. New bosses usually have different perspectives. So, kick-start a fresh planning process and develop a new plan.

Furthermore, occasions may arise when failure has to be turned into success before it is too late. It is better to bring about change on your own initiative than to have it forced upon you, especially when desired results are not achieved. In politics, when the government's promises do not materialise, and departmental target dates are repeatedly not met, then get a new government or start devising a new plan. A good example is: between the government and its parastatal Eskom post 1994, they failed to execute the

---

1 Mackay, 1977.

long term plan's maintenance programs, as well as the planned future construction of additional power stations – with serious repercussions. In 2007, it will now take eight years to catch up again, and the people will suffer.

Also, when the original circumstances which determined the formulation of the existing plan change in an unforeseen manner, one has to adapt. Such changes are often brought about by scientific and technological developments, as well as international trends such as continentalisation and globalisation. Alternatively, they could be related to threatening collapses of infrastructures, or social phenomena such as HIV/Aids, excessive violence and poverty. Initiate a new planning process from scratch, find new solutions, formulate a new plan, and change things.

And then you could start anew when you have fallen victim to the Dutton Syndrome.

Korean veteran General Jack Dutton familiarised me with this very important truth of management science. He illustrated the thesis by way of a parable:

An outgoing commanding general handed over his responsibilities to the incoming general, giving him three envelopes with an operating guide. When the new incumbent encountered his first real serious problem and was at a loss for a solution, he was instructed to open envelope 1 and follow the enclosed instructions. He was told to treat subsequent serious problems that may arise in the same manner, acting on the instructions contained in envelopes 2 and 3 consecutively.

After a while the incoming general encountered his first real problem for which he had no answer and opened envelope 1. He found a slip of paper that read "Blame your predecessor."

He blamed his predecessor and got away with it. It diverted attention away from him and everything ran smoothly for a while. Then, after a breather he once again experienced serious unmanageable trouble. He opened envelope 2. It read "Reorganise."

He reorganised. Restructuring proved to be a complicated and time-consuming process that overshadowed every other problem. All interim problems had to wait until after the reorganisation. Then came the third big problem. He opened envelope 3 and read the instructions: "Prepare three envelopes."

If Dutton's story of the generals was applied to politicians and the person in a fix was an incoming president or minister of state, how do you think the typical instruction in envelope 1 would read instead of "Blame your predecessor."?

Gnu chips in, "Take a trip overseas, minister."

Tarentaal disagrees and opts for "Appoint a commission of investigation, Mr President."

In politics, after a period of ten years or so, if heads of government and majority parties have fallen into the well-known pattern of one-party rule and dictatorship, then radical change becomes essential for survival. The Afrikan peer review system failed to initiate change in Zimbabwe, with disastrous results for the people and the reputation of the continent.

In the 1980s a political analyst told me that a new democratic government (such as we later acquired in 1994) would probably go slowly for the first four years, finding its feet and learning about governance. However, during the second four, it would become more confident and arrogant. Incumbents start to make laws. They realise that they actually have power and begin exercising it, and enjoy doing so – and become immune to criticism. This is the situation we face in South Afrika. A one-party state is bad, bad news. Fortunately, it may well be on its way out.

The problem our government faces in South Afrika is that we are not all international squatters or rootless Pan-Afrikan dwellers – just numbers in a global mass. No, we are proud nationals of South Afrika, and fortunately we are not all identical.

The only way to avoid becoming an absolute one-party state is to shed the un-Afrikan and Western party-driven representative democracy. Let the people vote for issues instead of voting for parties; free them from political party intimidation and tricks.

Irritating adjustments to democracy such as allowing politicians to cross the floor mean nothing. Updating election speeches every five years means nothing. Sovereignty must be restored to the people. Voting for politicians and parties must end. Deceiving and arrogant politicians must make way for a proud, apolitical, elite – not elitist – ethical and effective people's bureaucracy.

Nothing changed after the 2004 elections. Nor did anything change after the previous elections. Nor will the high rate of unemployment and poverty change after the next elections because the government isn't willing to release its strong legislative grip on business and labour.

And no change for the good will happen as long as we cling to the posts of political correctness.

How Not to be Politically Incorrect

"Politicians use political correctness as a drunken man uses lampposts – for support rather than illumination" – based on a saying by Andrew Lang.[2]

---

2 Mackay, 1977.

Jimmy says Gnu finds the double negative on the front cover of our book confusing, *Everyone's Guide How Not To Be Politically Incorrect*. Allow me to explain:

It is quite clear to all of us at this stage that to be politically correct is to be wrong. For the good of our country and mankind we now know that we should go all out to be right, and therefore politically incorrect. There is nothing double or confusing about that.

What may need an explanation is the question of *how* should we be politically incorrect? There are two ways, a right one and a wrong one. Up to now I have guided you according to the wrong one: I didn't set a good example. I was too considerate towards the PCs and I achieved nothing, perhaps because I'm a blue liberal. I am now going to put you on the right track, *how* to be politically incorrect the *right* way. Let's proceed. Let's be practical. If you believe you can make a difference, and you want to rid us of the fraudulent political correctivists –

Be bold about it.
Be assertive.
Ask your question, say your say.
Don't be bashful.
Don't be inhibited.
You have rights – speak your mind.
Have fun.

Be like the policeman. In Warsaw during the Soviet occupation, a poor, oppressed Pole went to a police charge office and mumbled: "A Swiss stole my Soviet watch." The courteous police officer corrected him: "You mean a Soviet stole your Swiss watch."

"You said it, not I," said the Polish victim.

Maintain your good manners, but don't shut your mouth just for the sake of being nice. Win friends and influence people, but you'll never make friends with the good if you are not prepared to make enemies with the bad.

People who don't want to be open to my sound ideas will be those red PCs who won't bother or dare to read them anyway – scared of becoming contaminated, or being ostracised.

You shouldn't call other people racists if you condone the application of legalised reservation of jobs for people on the basis of race, without a sunset clause. If you do, you're a racist yourself. If legalised discrimination was wrong in the past, it is also wrong in the present, and it will be wrong in the future.

If you don't agree with this, you are a racist; if you live in a country where the constitution allows the rules of fair practice and equal opportunities to be ignored, that country does not uphold the universal principles of human rights.

Jimmy: "Don't despair, follow the Leading Star."

CHAPTER 56

Stella

It is only now in the early 2000s that we see a glimmer of the real dawning of the new age of love, peace and brotherhood. Something remarkable is under way – Marilyn Ferguson.[1]

Phantom of the Opera

Fortunately for us we have our own guiding star to follow into the New Age. Her name is Stella Aquarius de Navio Fantasy Mahlangu. She is loving, lovable and resolute.

Stella is the one we were waiting for.

She formed her own loosely federated movement for the people called the Abolish Political Parties Party – the A Triple P.

I took her CV to socio-astrological scientist, Marilyn Ferguson, who was introduced to me by Ms Muqita. They confirmed my hopes. What they told me correlated so precisely with what I have been telling you, and with what Stella has in mind, that I have highlighted parts of what they said:

The arena of politics and power in the past was based on a solely masculine, rational-orientation and linear model. Everything followed the mechanistic view of Newton's universe. **Governments were monolithic, centralised institutions.**

The New Age favours **decentralised government**, subject to flux and change and accommodating both **rational and intuitive principles** with appreciation of non-linear interaction.

The accent is on foresight, ethics, flexibility, resistance to rigid programmes **and a partnership with nature.** Mutual help and self-help networks are encouraged.

---

1 *The Citizen*, 2004.

The new paradigm sees education as a lifelong process, striving for whole-brain education (as opposed to only left-brain thinking) and helping the learner to transcend his or her perceived limitations within a relatively flexible structure. The accent is on **learning how to learn, how to ask good questions** and access information rather than accumulating book knowledge.[2]

Gnu has been nodding in agreement all the way through.

At a key meeting, Stella with her followers formulated their mission statement, having taken tips from Ross Perot and his Reform Party:

We, the members of the A Triple P, commit ourselves to abolishing our present political system. We will re-establish trust in our ethical officials dedicated to fiscal responsibility and social accountability to the people.

Their constitutional principles are as follows:

We shall seek to reform our administrative practices to ensure that our officials owe their allegiance and remain accountable to the people whom they serve.

We shall require ethical conduct of all our officials.

Our party will be positioned in accordance with the best interests of our country and its people, without regard for partisan or personal advantage.

2 *The Citizen*, 2004.

The foundation of our people's well-being is the activity of grass-roots officials.

We celebrate our individual liberty, recognising that one of our greatest strengths is our diversity; and we will foster tolerance of the customs, beliefs and private actions of all persons and cultural groups as long as they do not infringe upon the rights of others.

Moreover, we strive to unite all South Afrikans in spirit and in purpose.

The founding principles also set the highest disciplinary standards for the administration:

No more gifts
No more jollies
No more free meals

The A Triple P offers all South Afrikan people the only real prospect of a vessel to pursue their hopes. The present policies of our politicians and political parties are determined by a powerful elite. The voice of the people is not heard.

We will show the South Afrikan people that we will establish a fair system and not simply another partisan group seeking power for its own rewards. We will ensure that our administrative processes remain responsive to all our people, who are our main resource.

Only by ensuring that the procedures of our people's facilitative administration are both democratic and inclusive can we preserve growth and well-being.

Stella wins the first up-coming election, if there is one, establishes a new dispensation, then disbands the movement and bails out.

Bail out? No, not just yet. Before she does so she disbands government and the civil service in its present form, and outlaws political parties in the same way that King Mswati III of Swaziland and President Museveni of Uganda did. Stella becomes the darling of Southern Afrika. She does her own thing and leaves us with the new People's Administrative Facilitating Service – PAFS.

Porcelain Cups

The whole system will work as follows:

At the national level the Monarch will host the high-ranking foreign official visitors and they will drink tea from porcelain cups.

The directors-general, under the chairmanship of one of them, will form the Advisory Council to the People for the Affairs of State (in lieu of the defunct cabinet). Chairmanship will rotate every three months. Since the DGs will be promoted on merit, they will automatically be the intelligent and lazy ones.

The deputy directors-general will do the day-to-day running of the downsized departments of PAFS (the upper tier of the downsized elite civil service). These experts will be the intelligent and industrious ones.

The people's organisations – unions, cultural institutions, heritages and foundations, independent commissions and agencies, the good national NGOs and subcontracted private sector companies – will do the job for the people (in lieu of the remainder of the defunct state departments). They will function under the protection of the Monarch and, with PAFS, will prepare the I-BPs and the P-BPs – the Issue Ballot Papers and the Policy Ballot Papers – for voting purposes.

The same format will apply to the PAFS of the second and third tiers. Princesses and Duchesses will be the Premiers; Earls and Countesses will be the Mayors.

Long live our stately royals and popular icons – let's find them!

CHAPTER 57

Lesson of St Helena

Afrikan leaders must correct their unjust behaviour – Tröll.

Now was 1964

We need a constitutional monarchy that includes royals and nobles without any powers. It is appalling that the colonials almost completely destroyed our Afrikan royalty. As a result it left us with upstarts such as Idi Amin, Jean Bédel Bokassa, Charles Taylor and Menghistu – and their ministers of sports.

The first generation of post-colonial Afrikan leaders battled to reconcile Western culture with Afrikan structures, and with themselves. With few exceptions, they were all like Jean Bédel, His Imperial Majesty, Emperor Bokassa I of the Central Afrikan Empire.

Bokassa had himself crowned emperor in 1972 with much pomp and in the style of the Sun King, Louis XIV. It cost the impoverished country almost £10 000 000. He was also known as the Butcher of Bangui where 200 children were massacred. That's what you get if you turn a stupid blind eye to Afrikan reality and royalty and just bungle on.

On this subject of Afrikan structures, various PC spokespersons for Afrikan countries have called tribes a curse. Even our own regime is antagonistic towards South Afrikan royalty and nobility, although former president Nelson Mandela was a little more conciliatory. He urged traditional leaders not to join political parties but to stay mum when they did join the ANC. The leader of Contralesa – Congress of Traditional Leaders of South Afrika – said the traditional leaders were not in favour of being placed on the lists of political parties since it compromised their role – and he was right.

Eastern Cape premier, Makhenkesi Stofile, told traditional leaders that their structures were the creation of colonial rulers. This is blatantly untrue and he was severely criticised by the outraged leaders. No wonder after the 2004 elections he succeeded Mr Balfour as the minister of sports. The UDM has accused the ANC of having an agenda to sweep the traditional leaders into the sea.

Chief Mwelo Nonkonyana said the true history of the indigenous people clearly teaches that traditional leaders owe their legitimacy to no authority other than the masses themselves; the institution was in the minds and hearts of the toiling masses and no government would ever destroy it. Traditional leadership and governance was in place long before the arrival of the colonialists in South Afrika. "As a matter of fact, history teaches us that all traditional leaders fought against colonialism..."[1]

St Helena and Robben Island tell us the historical facts. Besides Emperor Napoleon Bonaparte, Chief Dinizulu and more than 6000 Boers from the Anglo-Boer War were also exiled to St Helena.

Why the British dethroned the Zulu and Xhosa kings, I cannot tell. To me their actions are little different from the communist revolution that deposed Emperor Haile Selasse of Ethiopia, or the murder of King Faisal II of Iraq and his family in 1958, or the ousting of King Idris of Libya in a *coup* led by Qaddafi in 1969.

I have often wondered whether the kings were always so bad and the communist rulers always so good. Strangely, all over the world the communist rulers are disappearing and leaving their countries in ruins, while the royals are making a comeback. King Juan Carlos of Spain was restored to the throne after 44 years in 1975. King Sihanouk of Cambodia, who had previously reigned from 1941–1945, was restored to his throne in 1993, and King Letsie III of Lesotho was returned to the throne in 1996.

It saddens me to see the present regime following the example set by the colonialists and the former South Afrikan government. Why do they continue to denigrate the Afrikan royalty and nobles by calling them traditional leaders, chiefs and headmen? Why don't we call our own nobles Dukes and Duchesses, Earls and Countesses, Viceroys and Baronets? Or do you want us to call our president "Big Chief Mbeki"?

You can do whatever you like about clans and nations, but you make a fatal mistake if you try to

fight them and kill them politically;
legislate them out of society;
wish them away or close your eyes to them;
arrogantly patronise them;
paternalistically provide them with toys and token appreciation; and
blame them – for being the curse of Afrika.

---

1 *Anonymous.*

Granddaughter of King Norodom Sihanouk, HRH Princess
Norodom Rattana-Dévi, attired in traditional gold and silver.
Source: *Deborah Groves Photography* (www.grovesphotography.com)

The upstart Afrikan politicians, who gained power, wealth and status in a
sudden manner through the flawed and un-Afrikan system of the modern
voting-for-politicians democracy, or through a *coup d'état*, did all these
things. That is why we have bloodshed and misery.

We cannot forever ignore royal demands. While then deputy president
Jacob Zuma was courting a Swazi princess, he allegedly neglected to deal
with a claim by Swazi royalty in South Afrika who wanted their land to be
incorporated into Swaziland...

Pallo Jordan, chairman of parliament's foreign affairs committee, said the
issue was dismissed on the basis of a 1964 OAU resolution that stated "to revise the borders now could be a recipe for disaster".[2]

Since "now" was 1964 – already more than 40 years ago – and since the
modern Afrikan Union has stated its intention to revise intra-Afrikan borders, there is new hope for the Swazi royalty.

2 *Daily News*, 18 September 2003.

King Kgosi Leruo Molotlegi

Instead of wishing the system of clans and nationalities away, the politicians should just modernise it like modern Afrikans should. While the homeland leaders of the miserable past were one thing, a traditional prince in a modern democracy of the prosperous present is another. King Kgosi Leruo Molotlegi of the Bafokeng in North West said the tension between traditional and democratic leadership is unnecessary.[3] According to him, democracy is deemed to be progressive, modern and Western, while some (shrewd) people claim that traditional leadership represents all that is old, uneducated, backward and elitist.

He refutes these notions: "Much of the Bafokeng system is democratic; mechanisms exist to ensure the king carries out 'the will of the people'. Councillors are democratically elected. More women are involved than ever before...and 'the people can overturn my decision'."

He believes that tradition and values are part and parcel of the system of governance they embrace: respect, a sense of community, and a sense of commitment to one's neighbour and oneself. Consensus is sought, rather than strong-arming by individuals.

The king then asks the most important, if embarrassing, question in this book: "In the context of Afrika, has democracy lived up to its promise?"

You know the answer. It hasn't.

It is a pertinent irony that while a leader has to defend the "curse of traditional leadership" democracy fails all around him in Afrika. Nor does the king stand alone: traditional leaders headed by Mpiyezintombi Mzimela accused the South Afrikan government of betraying them by reneging on a promise not to diminish or obliterate their (few) powers and those of their institutions:

> Unfortunately, as African majority governments have been voted into power using Eurocentric democratic constitutions, they [have] generally refused to give recognition to their own traditional systems. The tragic consequences can be seen in the wars and strife that are pervasive throughout the continent.

Mzimela continues:

> ...(the rural communities') wishes must not be ignored in what appears to be a determined effort to impose foreign systems of governance at any cost in South Africa.[4]

---

3 *Sapa*, 10 September 2003.
4 Mzimela, Mpiyezintombi. Internet.

He further states that President Mbeki had given an undertaking that it was not government's intention to diminish or obliterate any powers exercised by the traditional institutions, but would instead grant more powers and functions to them.

Jimmy becomes animated, "This is highly encouraging news."

"Yes," says Ťröll, donning a new blue bowler hat, "it is high time your Afrikan leaders drastically correct their unjust behaviour of the recent past. They must immediately have your traditional leaders Affirmative-Actioned, Fast-tracked and Enabled. They must become powerless mayors of cities and towns, princes of states and provinces, and monarchs of countries. My queen will never invite Afrikans to Ťröllandia without a royal envoy."

"A bit cheeky for a blue liberal," remarks a surprised Jimmy triumphant-ly, giving Gnu a smile.

* * *

Tarentaal comes running, flapping her wings, "Gnu, Gnu! Farmer van der Merwe is looking for you!"

"What does he want?"

"It's Daisy! Daisy has a bonny baby. He wants to invite you to the chris-tening!"

277

CHAPTER 58

For Want of a King

The Majestic Chain

We are now at H-Hour.

I am sure Stella is going to guide us into the New Design. I happen to know she is in favour of a monarchy and believes in icons. I agree. People need icons. Icons must have lots of spare time, wealth and status – with no power.

When I was 12 years old, I had the privilege of seeing King George VI. He was dressed in mufti and accompanied by Queen Elizabeth, and Princesses Elizabeth and Margaret. Escorted by the local mayor, they attended a ceremony at the Goble Park recreation grounds. All this happened in my hometown of Bethlehem.

Once we were back at home, my mother asked our casual domestic worker Emily, who had also witnessed the event, what her impressions were of the king. She raved about him, his black and red robes and especially the majestic chain around his neck!

That was my standard four schoolteacher, Mr Schalk van Niekerk, His Worship the Mayor!

This event proved to me that a monarch could be humble. It also illustrates that people want icons, substitutes for idolised but menacing rulers with power. Monarchs don't have to have power, and they shouldn't! They represent a nation's heritage and its royal lineage.

Mayors are not executives; they don't govern cities and towns. They party; they are the good guys. In South Afrika the town clerks or municipal managers, by whatever title, are in charge of the third tier of civil administration throughout the country.

In the PI Ark we now restore the Afrikan royal families and nobility. The local and regional aristocratic leaders become the powerless mayors of cantons and provinces or states. Members of the lofty royal families are also in line for heading up the provinces as well as the national state.

Political heads of state are too keen to prove themselves and to demonstrate their elevated status. Afrikan royalty won't bother to do this – like the English, they know.

Heads of state must make way for decent people, and since royalty fits this bill better than anyone else, we now *enwealth* and *enstatus* our sadly neglected monarchs. Please note I don't say *"empower"*.

Rectifying Wrongs of the Past

Mr. Mbeki, in one of his weekly party Internet newsletters, explained that in 1910 in Southern Afrika Britain formed a government that combined the (defeated and destroyed) ex-Republics of the Transvaal (ZAR) and the Orange Free State (OFS) with the two British colonies of Natal and the Cape. This, he said, represented the political consolidation of the military defeat and destruction of the indigenous Afrikan kingdoms. He lamented their sorrowful demolition by Queen Victoria.

Surely, we are all highly encouraged by our president's firm stance on this wrong of the past. Southern Afrika is blessed with a vast array of nobility. There are monarchs for Afrika: kings, queens, princes, princesses per se and by other names. In the envisaged New Design of the Union of Confederated Monarchies of Southern Afrika some of them are already properly instated, such as Their Majesties King Letsie III in Lesotho and King Mswati III in Swaziland. In South Afrika they need to be reinstated as soon as possible.

So, since there will be more than one monarch, there should be a Doyen or Doyenne of the Royal League – the First Among Equals. This supreme throne will be occupied on a *rotating* basis. Who will the first one be? I am sure the members of the royal league will sort it out amicably. Whoever they choose, I would dearly like them to consider the following:

A number of our kings and queens have demonstrated to the world that they have what the people so dearly love – the common touch. They have all demonstrated their love and aptitude for excellent cuisine on television – BBC Food.[1] They were King Letsie III, King Goodwill Zwelithini, King Kgosi Leruo, Kings Makhosonke II and Mayitjha of the Ndebele kingdom, Queen Regent Ndamase and Queen Sigcau of the Xhosas.

---

1 *Croxon*, BBC Television.

It is not incidental that it was the BBC that hijacked our South Afrikan royalty to entertain the English and the world. The Europeans know that monarchs and palaces, pomp and ceremony fascinate the entire world. The
Americans, who profess to disapprove of royalty, flock to Europe for a
glimpse of a royal gesture every year. Perhaps Queen Beatrix will graciously
oblige tourists with a wave from the balcony of the Royal Palace in Amster-
dam, or Queen Elizabeth II will acknowledge their admiration as she passes
by in a black limousine on her way to the annual Royal Chelsea Flower
Show. Or if you like music, you can go to Buckingham Palace and join the
crowds at one of the stately ceremonies and listen to a royal regimental band
playing delightful, swingy German marches.

In South Afrika, at least we have an annual gathering at the Enyokeni
Royal Palace for the Umkhosi woMhlanga festival. Up to 15 000 bare-breast-
ed maidens perform the reed dance. With eyes bulging, an excited Jimmy explains that it is the only forum where King Goodwill Zwelithini showcases
the beauty and purity of young Zulu girls. The dance is very popular with
tourists and the foreign media. This event again supports the statement that
royalty is royalty and will capture the imagination anywhere in the world.[2]

HRH King Goodwill Zwelithini kaBhekhuzulu's annual royal uMkhosi woMhlanga – reed
ceremony 2003 – led by Princess Sinethemba
Source: Fanile Mkhize

2 *Daily News*, 19 September 2003.

However, we must return to our search for a monarch. Wouldn't it have been wonderful if Nelson Mandela had been a king and our first doyen of all the monarchs? A retired and powerless Madiba has possibly achieved more for South Afrika than when he was our president for five years. But some South Afrikans might feel neglected should the first doyen be a Xhosa, the prime minister a Xhosa, and then there is still the minister of sports.

If Mr Mandela were not available, then for the first reinstated doyen I would prefer a doyenne. Queens are good at giving parties. They are good at achieving a country's goals through diplomacy and means other than power. More than men they exude regal mystique – the Queens of Sheba and the Cleopatras.

In cavemen days the goddess was revered above all, and women, who brought life into the world, controlled the world. Furthermore, Pythagoras was taught all he knew by Aristoclea, a woman. Another, Diotima, taught Socrates.

On a mountainside a wealthy Meccan businesswoman watched a lonely shepherd. Her name was Khadijah. She invited the epileptic Muhammed in and taught him to read and write.[3]

The First Farewell

Having requested an audience to apply for leave of absence to go on an overseas jolly, Jimmy turns up in *bonne humeur*. He is accompanied by a radiant Gnu and a bubbling Ms Tarentaal, and guess who else – the Lion King in full regalia! Jimmy wears a tuxedo and orange bow tie. Gnu sports a laurel wreath around his horns. Ms Tarentaal is wrapped in a Hermès cashmere scarf.

And then comes the big surprise! Tarentaal and Gnu produce a regal headgear made of fine, crystalline, royal blue peacock plumage, which they ask me to present to the Lion King. He is to crown our friend Jimmy the Reed as the First Prince of the principality of Umhlanga – which he promptly does and disappears.

Tröll then appears on the scene, swaggering under his blue bowler. He is taking the three of them to Tröllandia, above Norway, by invitation of his queen. Gnu is going to meet Rudolph to find out more about intercontinental airborne sleighs. Tarentaal is going to lecture on "Family Planning in a Hostile Environment".

---

3 *The Citizen*, 31 May 2003

Jimmy enquires about our progress with the book. We have only another chapter or two to go, I tell him.

He looks me in the eye and whispers, "There is a solution – you'll find it in Monomotapa."

So, Prince Jimmy, with a twinkle in his eye, Madame Tarentaal, with a tear in hers, and Mr Gnu, with a silly grin on his dial, all give me a huge, affectionate hug and Ťröll says, "Thank you."

The three musketeers are on their way, "All for one and one for all."

"... And all for love!" Ťröll echoes.

CHAPTER 59

Monomotapa

The Rumble of Thunder

The day Queen Modjadji V passed away the rain stopped.
Three years went by.

The day Queen Modjadji VI was crowned the rains came.

Modjadjis reign.

Like all genuine idols, our Queen Modjadji is shrouded in hazy legends.
The royal Modjadjis come a long misty way.

In the absence of proper early written records, the history of the Modjadjis is as intriguing as the fable of the mysterious Christian empire of Priest John. European kings commissioned their seafaring captains to find him – somewhere in the East, Abyssinia or elsewhere in Afrika.

But there is a difference. Priest John and his empire were never found. He remains a mythical tale. However, the ancient Portuguese did eventually locate King Monomotapa, and records, however scanty, do exist, and so do the Modjadjis.

Queen Modjadji V, who died in June 2001, was a direct descendant of the once powerful royal house of Monomotapa. It ruled over the Karanga people during the 15th and 16th centuries. The wealthy kingdom oversaw the construction of places of worship today known as the Zimbabwe Ruins.

The world-renowned author Rider Haggard's classical novels, *King Solomon's Mines* and *She*, published in the 1880s, drew the world's attention to the legendary Rain Queen of the Lobedo peoples.

The first signs of development towards anything resembling the concept of statehood in central Afrika came in the 14th Century when the Rozwis started to inhabit the Zimbabwe region. Many claim they came from the Karanga dynasty. It was under King Mambo Mwene Mutapa that the great empire of Monomotapa came into being after 1420.

He launched one military campaign after another. His subjects named him Mwene Mutapa – the great plunderer. His armies were called *korekore* meaning locusts because they swarmed and devoured everything in their way. When he died in 1480, his empire stretched from the Zambezi to the Limpopo Rivers, and from the Kalahari Desert to the Indian Ocean.

It was during 1514–1515 that the Portuguese eventually traced Monomotapa. Antonio Fernandes visited Monomotapa and also the goldfields. This was no big deal for Fernandes. His mission was to strengthen the Portuguese Indian Ocean trade against the Arabic threat.

In 1560 the Jesuit priest Gonçalo da Silveira visited King Monomotapa, who was subsequently converted and christened. The Portuguese had good relations with Monomotapa, but did not exercise any authority in the region.

During the latter part of the 1580s the old king gave his daughter Dzugundini a magic horn and medicines for making rain. She and her child fled to establish a new kingdom further south.

For the next 200 years the Dzugundinis built a substantial territory and increased their power among the other tribes. During the 1800s the then chief, Mugodo, was warned by the ancestral spirits of a plot by his sons to overthrow him. In accordance with the wishes of the spirits he had all his sons killed and married his daughter in his attempt to ensure that the new heir to his throne would be a queen and that a new female dynasty would be founded.

Mugodo's daughter's first child, a son, was strangled at birth. Her second child, however, was a girl, and she signalled the start of the female dynasty. She was the first Modjadji, and ever since the queen has lived in complete seclusion, deep in the forest, where she practises the age-old secret rituals of making rain.

In the world of Modjadji the largest cycad trees on earth grow in profusion amid uncharacteristic swirling mist and rain. The land encompasses virgin Afrikan bushveld, awe-inspiring valleys, spectacular mountains and enormous baobab trees. It hosts the majestic giant Afrikan elephant and an untold variety of birds. This is a wonderland of fascinating kultures and legends shrouded in a mythic haze.

Politically, Afrikan leaders have always accorded the Rain Queen special respect. More than a century ago these leaders included the great King Shaka, who sought her help to alleviate a severe drought in Zululand, as well as King Moshoeshoe.

"In fact, Shaka used to send black cattle to pay tribute to Modjadji I, and he called her the Rainmaker of Rainmakers. Not only Shaka... the Swazis, all of the kingdoms in southern Afrika paid tribute to her," said Modjadji royal family spokesman Dr Mathole Motshekga.

Modjadji V is thought to have been the only person apart from the late, volatile President Laurent Kabila of the Congo to have kept Nelson Mandela waiting for a meeting. (Incidentally I forgot to tell you that the Kongo is named after the 15th Kingdom of Kongo that thrived on both banks of the River Congo.)

During 1994, when the meeting took place, Mr Mandela could and did speak to her only when spoken to, and then only through an intermediary. Mr Mandela told reporters that just like Queen Elizabeth II, Queen Modjadji does not answer questions. Queen Modjadji did not welcome the prospect of an ANC government. Its campaign of mobilising the youth against traditional leaders in the 1980s had diluted her authority.

The Rain Queen's 25-year-old granddaughter, Caroline Makobo, succeeded the late Queen Modjadji V and ascended to the throne in 2003. Twenty-eight cows were slaughtered for the occasion.

So now in the 21st century it is once again the Rain Queen, Queen Modjadji VI, who is held in affection and respected by our former president Nelson Mandela. Such a royal shall also have my respect and support. What is good for Madiba is good enough for me.

She was introduced to the world and crowned by King Mphephu of the neighbouring kingdom of Venda: "May you enjoy good relationships with your people, and that of (sic) South Africa at large... You have a woman dynasty that was established during wars between blacks themselves, and Europeans and blacks. And they held the kingdom together. When others collapsed, this one survived, and is still going on. So that says a lot about the capacity of women to rule. And it also explodes the myth of inequality between men and women," the king explained.

On a continent where rulers run around beating their breasts in authority, you'd be hard-pressed to name a leader who doesn't command from a position of splendour. The Rain Queen is an exception. She's closely guarded by a bevy of "wives", the daughters of headmen sent to live with her in the royal kraal. She doesn't get out much, except to attend a computer course, and she spends most of her time being a mystery to her people, who speak guardedly about her.

It started to rain as the coronation began; this was considered an excellent omen for the new queen. The rain was also welcomed by many in South Afrika's Limpopo province, and by all who had been suffering under the drought conditions that had beset most of Southern Afrika over the preceding two years. Queen Modjadji's devout followers pointed out that the drought had started around the time of the previous queen's death.

At that time we were desperate. We needed rain – Pula.
Now, again we need a new Queen – Queen Modjadji.
A Rain Queen for the Rainbow Nation.
Our Doyenne – Long Live Modjadji.[1]

---

1 Information of the Modjadjis obtained from: Du Plessis, P. 2003. *South African Balobedu people crown 'Rain Queen'*. Internet 13 April 2003. Van Aswegen, 1982. *Getaway Magazine*, October 2003.

CHAPTER 60

Epilogue

News Headlines

At the end of my story, on 14 June 2005, news of watershed proportions hit the headlines:

- *Swazi constitution upholds absolute monarchy*
- *President tells Deputy Zuma to step down*

And then:

- *Rain Queen dies*

Obituaries

The Modjadji kingdom is in mourning. Her Royal Highness, Rain Queen Modjadji the sixth passed away on Sunday, 13 June, 2005 – The Regency, The Modjadji Royal Council, Reuters.

Queen Makobo Modjadji [was] descended from the only dynasty in Africa with a matriarchal monarch.

The rain queen is an agent of God and the gods are our supreme rulers and her rain charms work in conjunction with their will, a will she cannot override – Royal spokesman, Dr Mathole Motshega, Reuters.

She was 27 years old... the youngest queen in the history of the Balobedu people whose reign was the shortest and also the most controversial...a mistake of not knowing how to reconcile tradition and modernity – *Point De Vue*, Paris13–19 July 2005.

The ANC-controlled provincial government was sympathetic and supportive of the Modjadji royal household – *The Daily Telegraph*, 15 July 2005.

We all know the Modjadjis have no end.

* * *

Life and Death – The Last Farewell with Professor Klrtz

Dougie prompted the professor. He responded:

"Unfortunately you people only believe in what you understand. You miss a lot that way because you understand so little. You are not yet developed enough to grasp what I have to tell you. I'll try my best.

Death happens, but there is life after death. Death does not mean the end of consciousness. As the body dies, your consciousness enters into a different phase of aliveness.

Even living beings such as you humans can be knocked out leaving you unconscious for a while, after which consciousness returns. But for the time that the person is unconscious, for all intents and purposes he might just as well be fast asleep or 'dead'. He comes alive again when consciousness returns.

In your terms, when a person dies, his now de-blemished consciousness instantly or soon starts another phase of its being. This is a very blissful, ethereal existence as opposed to the drag of planetary life. Without a body of flesh and bones, you live by ultra-developed thoughts and visions, and communicate with others in the same way.

So to answer your question, it is only the body that withers away."

Dougie thanked him and said, "It is not in the least that I don't believe you, but I find your thesis very strange."

Klrtz continued:

"You should rather say, 'I find it very strange, but I believe you.' Allow me to explain; I speak from personal experience.

I came here to study primitive civilisations. I came from the future. In my planet's time as it is now, I'm not sure if your planet still exists, or if it does, whether human beings still exist. They might have destroyed life on earth. But don't be upset, let me quickly add that if your planet does not exist in my planet's time, it may mean that you still have millions of years to go.

What made it possible for me to visit you was that I could travel faster than light. Permit me to clarify.

The fastest that you can communicate on your planet is by the various methods of telecommunication and line of sight, but you still struggle to master the speed of light. However, anything that can travel faster than the speed of light can move back into the past. One thing that is faster is instantaneous telepathy, or even faster are things like omens. Once you have harnessed that, you can go into the past. We have succeeded in making it work for us. Nevertheless, to communicate is one thing, but to travel is another, and to travel at the speed of thought and vision – with luggage – is a complicated affair even for us.

When I tell you about life beyond your body, please believe me even if you don't understand. I know what I am talking about; I speak from experience. I came here without luggage; I travelled here only in my conscious form."

Then pointing with his hands to his body, he said:

"This is not me; I've adopted it for practical purposes on planet Earth. In your terms – I am dead."

Cast

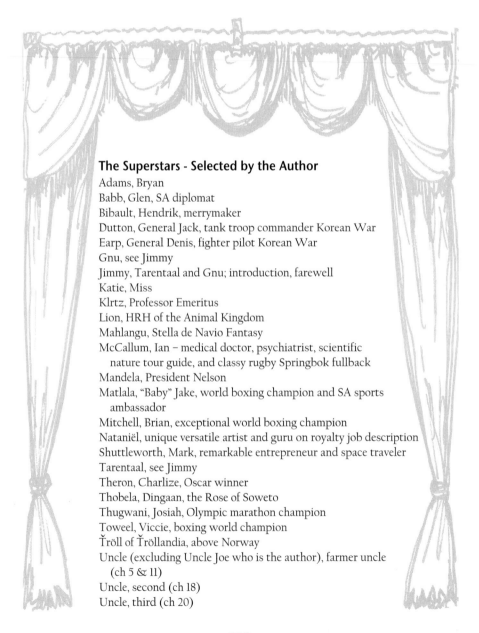

The Superstars - Selected by the Author

Adams, Bryan
Babb, Glen, SA diplomat
Bibault, Hendrik, merrymaker
Dutton, General Jack, tank troop commander Korean War
Earp, General Denis, fighter pilot Korean War
Gnu, see Jimmy
Jimmy, Tarentaal and Gnu; introduction, farewell
Katie, Miss
Klrtz, Professor Emeritus
Lion, HRH of the Animal Kingdom
Mahlangu, Stella de Navio Fantasy
McCallum, Ian – medical doctor, psychiatrist, scientific
    nature tour guide, and classy rugby Springbok fullback
Mandela, President Nelson
Matlala, "Baby" Jake, world boxing champion and SA sports
    ambassador
Mitchell, Brian, exceptional world boxing champion
Nataniël, unique versatile artist and guru on royalty job description
Shuttleworth, Mark, remarkable entrepreneur and space traveler
Tarentaal, see Jimmy
Theron, Charlize, Oscar winner
Thobela, Dingaan, the Rose of Soweto
Thugwani, Josiah, Olympic marathon champion
Toweel, Viccie, boxing world champion
Tröll of Tröllandia, above Norway
Uncle (excluding Uncle Joe who is the author), farmer uncle
    (ch 5 & 11)
Uncle, second (ch 18)
Uncle, third (ch 20)

The Good Guys - Selected by Ms Tarentaal

Alexander, greatest general of all times
Aristotle, political philosopher
Beatrix, HM Queen of The Netherlands
Bonaparte, Napoleon, Emperor of France
Bongo, benevolent dictator and president of Gabon
Botha, General Louis, Prime Minister of the Union of
    South Africa
Churchill, Sir Winston
De Bono, Dr. Edward, thinking guru
Di, Wu, HRH Emperor of China
Diaz, air force General Rafael Del Pino, Cuban defector
Elizabeth II, HM Queen of the United Kingdom
Faustinus, Gaius Antonious, and Julia Marciana, civil
    administrators Britannia
Flanders and Swann, musicians and lyricists
Fraser, SA General C.A. Pop
Galileo, Galilee, scientist par excellence
Gandhi, Mohandas Karamachand, philosopher
Gates, Bill, IT wizard and philanthropist
He, Zeng, Chinese admiral of the high seas
Holomisa, General Bantu MP
Jolson, Al, the jazz singer
Kenny, Andrew
Kgosi Leruo Molotlegi – HM King of the Bafokeng
Kruger, Paul, President Zuid Afrikaansche Republik
Lekota, *Terror*, SA cabinet minister
Letsie II, HM King of Lesotho
Manuel, Trevor, politician and finance wizard
Maoui Auld Taya, President of Mauritania
Mobuto, Sese Seko, President of Zaire
Modjadji, HM The Rain Queen
Montgomery of Alamein, K.G., Field Marshal the Viscount
Mzimela, Mpiyezintombi, political leader
Nonkonyana, Chief Mwelo, political leader
Nongqawuse, prophetess
Ochoa Sanchez, General Arnaldo, Hero of the Republic of Cuba

291

Plato, Greek scholar and tutor par excellence
Schlemmer, Lawrence
Shaka, King of the Zulus
Sigcau, HM Queen of the Xhosas
Sihanouk, HM King of Cambodia
Slabbert, F. Van Zyl, versatile politician
Smuts, Field Marshal, General Jan C.
Socrates, another Greek
Suzman, Helen, parliamentarian and political activist
Symcox, Pat of Spinning Tales
Urquhart, Brian, intelligence officer and top international
    diplomat
Victoria, HRIH Queen of the British Empire
Zille, Helen
Zwelithini, HM King Goodwill of the Zulus

The Bad Guys - Selected by Mr. Gnu
Bokassa, Jean-Bédel, The Sun King
Castro, Fidel, dictator of Cuba (excluding Guantanamo) and
    comrade of SA president Mbeki
Drake, Sir Francis, pirating circumnavigator
Duvalier, Baby of Papa Doc of Haiti
Duvalier, Papa of Baby Doc
Gaddafi, Muhamar, president of Libya
Graham, Lieutenant-Colonel, British colonialist
Idi Amin, HM King of Scotland
Jaedicke, Robert of Enron fame
Menghistu, President of Ethiopia
Milner, Lord, colonialist in body and soul
Mugabe, Robert, megalomaniac, cricket lover and destroyer of
    Zimbabwe
Rhodes, Cecile John, arch-colonialist, builder of Zimbabwe
Smith, Sir Harry, colonialist
Soames, Lord, last African colonial governor
Soros, George, super red PC
Sports, miscellaneous ministers of
Taylor, Charles, President of Liberia

The Other Guys

Selected by Jimmy the Reed

Adam and Eve of Eden
Ahmadinejad, Mahmoud, President of Iran
Annan, Kofi
Blair, Tony, triple term British prime minister
Botha, Pik
Breytenbach, Breyten
Bush, George W. Snr.
Bush, George W. Jnr.
Goosen, Anton, composer and lyricist
Hacker, Rt. Hon. James
Holmes, Sherlock
Kennedy, JFK
Mallett, Nick, rugby guru
Matembe, Ms. Maria, Chairperson, Pan Afrikan Parliament
Moynihan, US Senator, Daniel Patrick
Mswati III, HM King of Swaziland
Museveni, President of Uganda
Nixon, US President Richard
Obasanjo, Olesugan, President of Nigeria
Pauritanians
Peters, Tom
Ponsonby, Lady with Mademoiselle Celine and Commissar
    Sternovsky
Ramaphosa, Cyril, business magnate
Sexwale, Tokyo, business magnate
Smith, Ian, Prime Minister of Rhodesia
Shipanga, Andreas, nice-guy, politician and stage manager
Terreblanche, Eugene, politician, dramatist, poet, equestrian
    and cleric
Zuma, Jacob, political leader and newsmaker

Selected by Tröll

ABBA
Ahtisaari, Martti, UN commissar and President of Finland

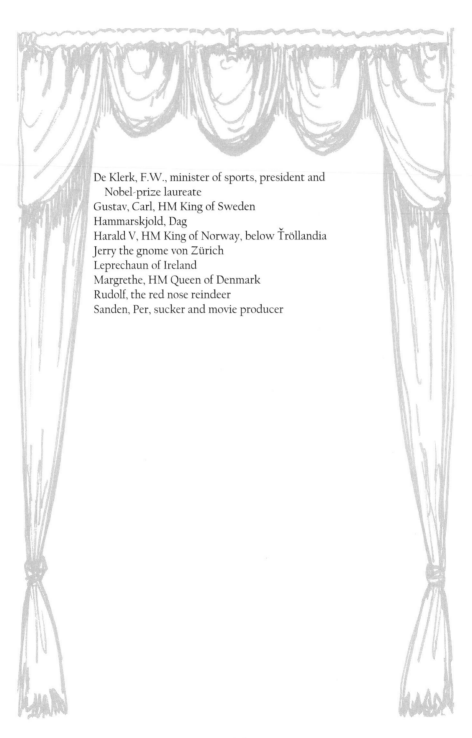

De Klerk, F.W., minister of sports, president and
   Nobel-prize laureate
Gustav, Carl, HM King of Sweden
Hammarskjold, Dag
Harald V, HM King of Norway, below Trôllandia
Jerry the gnome von Zürich
Leprechaun of Ireland
Margrethe, HM Queen of Denmark
Rudolf, the red nose reindeer
Sanden, Per, sucker and movie producer

Select Bibliography

Armstrong, S. 1989. *In Search of Freedom: The Andreas Shipanga Story as told to Sue Armstrong.* Gibraltar: Ashanti.

Best, G. 1982. *War and Society in Revolutionary Europe, 1770–1870.* Great Britain. Fontana Books.

Boshoff, S.P.E. & G.S Nienaber. 1967. *Afrikaanse Etimologieë.* Pretoria. Die Suid-Afrikaanse Akademie vir Wetenskap en Kuns.

Bridgland, F. 1993. *The War for Africa – Twelve Months that transformed a Continent.* Gibraltar: Ashanti

Burgess, O. 1988. *Suid-Afrika en die Demokrasie.* Pinetown. (Chapter 1 by G.A. Rauche – co author)

Crocker, C. A. 1992. *High Noon in Southern Africa – Making Peace in a Rough Neighborhood.* New York. W.W. Norton & Co.

Doyle, Sir A.C. *A Case of Identity.*

Erasmus, B.P.J. 2004. *On Route in South Africa.* Johannesburg: Jonathan Ball Publishers.

Ergang, R. 1967. *Europe from the Renaissance to Waterloo.* Lexington, MA: D.C. Heath & Co.

Exley, H. 1994. *Cricket Quotations – A Collection of Fine Paintings and the Best Cricket Quotes.* Watford, UK. Exley.

Geldenhuys, J. 1995. *A General's Story – From an Era of War and Peace.* Johannesburg: Jonathan Ball Publishers.

Gibran, K. 1992. *The Prophet.* London. Arkana Penguin Books.

Greene, R. & J. Elffers. 1999. *Power – The 48 Laws.* London. Concise Edition Profile Books.

Haskins, CP. The Ant and her World. *National Geographic*, June 1984.

Hawking, S. 1989. *A Brief History of Time – The Big Bang to Black Holes.* London. Bantam Books.

Heitman, H-R. 1990. *War in Angola: the Final South African Phase.* Gibraltar: Ashanti.

Huntingdon, S.P.1997 *The Clash of Civilizations and the Remaking of World Order.* London: Simon & Schuster.

Johnson R.W. 2004. *South Africa: The First Man, The Last Nation.* Johannesburg: Jonathan Ball Publishers.

Liberman, P. 1996. *Does Conquest Pay – The Exploitation of Occupied Industrial Societies.* Princeton, NJ: Princeton University Press.

Mackay, A.L. 1977. *Harvest of a Quiet Eye – A Selection of Scientific Quotations.* New York: Crane, Russak & Co. Inc.

Mason, D. 2003. *A Traveller's History of South Africa.* London. Orion Publishing Group Ltd.

McAleese, P & M. Bles. 1993. *No Mean Soldier.* London. Orion Publishing Group Ltd.

McCallum, I. 2005. *Ecological Intelligence – Rediscovering Ourselves in Nature.* Cape Town. Africa Geographic.

Montgomery, Field Marshal B.L. 1958. *The Memoirs of Field-Marshal, The Viscount Montgomery of Alamein, K.G.* London: Collins.

Negri, P. (ed) Jowett, B. (Translator). 2000. *Aristotle Politics unabridged.* New York. Dover Publications Inc.

O'Rourke, P.J. 2002. *Holidays in Hell.* London. Picador.

Oakes, D. (ed) 1989. *Illustrated History of South Africa – The Real Story.* Cape Town. The Reader's Digest Association South Africa (Pty) Ltd.

Parkinson, C Northcote. 1979. *Parkinson's Law.* New York: Ballantine books.

Peter L.J. & R. Hull. 1971. *The Peter Principle.* London: Pan Books Ltd.

Prochnow, H.V. & H.V. Prochnow (Jr.) 1979. *The Toastmaster's Treasure Chest.* Wellingborough, Northants. A. Thomas and Company.

Rees, N. 1980. "*Quote...Unquote*". London. Unwin Paperbacks.

Renwick, R. 1997. *Unconventional Diplomacy in Southern Africa.* London. Macmillan Press Ltd.

Ryan, C.1974. *A Bridge Too Far.* London: Hamish Hamilton Ltd.

Schulz, C.M. 1970. *Peanuts for Everybody.* New York. Fawcett World Library.

Stiff, P. 1989. *Nine Days of War.* Alberton, South Africa. Lemur Books.

Townsend, R. 1970. *Up The Organization.* London: Michael Joseph Ltd.

Tulloch, S. (ed). 1993. *Reader's Digest Oxford Complete Wordfinder.* London. The Reader's Digest Association Limited.

Urquhart, B. 1987. *A Life in Peace and War.* New York. Harper & Row, Publishers, Inc.

Van Aswegen, H.J. 1982. *Geskiedenis van Afrika, van die Vroegste Oorsprong tot Onafhanklikheid.* Pretoria. Academica.